Writings
in Time of War

PIERRE TEILHARD
DE CHARDIN

*Writings
in Time of War*

TRANSLATED BY RENÉ HAGUE

1817

HARPER & ROW, PUBLISHERS

NEW YORK AND EVANSTON

The essays in this book were first published in
ÉCRITS DU TEMPS DE LA GUERRE
by Éditions Bernard Grasset in 1965

Nihil obstat John M. T. Barton STD, LSS Censor
Imprimatur ‡ Patrick Casey Vic. Gen.
Auxiliary Bishop of Westminster
Westminster, 28 December 1967

*The Nihil obstat and Imprimatur are a declaration
that a book or pamphlet is considered to be free
from doctrinal or moral error. It is not implied
that those who have granted the Nihil obstat
and Imprimatur agree with the contents,
opinions or statements expressed.*

Contents

5

Editorial Note

The French edition (*Écrits du temps de la Guerre*), from which this translation has been made, follows the exact text of Père Teilhard's autograph manuscripts without any alteration except, for the convenience of the reader, in the typographic presentation. The editors' introductory notes to the essays are printed in italic. Père Teilhard's own footnotes have been included, and distinguished from those of the editors by the addition of his name. The date of composition is given at the end of each essay.

Preface

Père Teilhard de Chardin's war-time letters to his cousin Marguerite Teillard-Chambon[1] will have familiarized those who have read them with the early stages of his thought, and drawn their attention to the existence of a number of essays written at the front during the same period.

It is quite staggering to see a man working as a stretcher-bearer [2] in that ghastly fighting, living for the most part in the mud of the trenches, and at the same time taking advantage of his too brief rest periods to jot down on paper his notes and plans (cf. *Making of a Mind*, pp. 113-14, 241), to be worked up later into essays that dealt with the most profound problems.

As each was finished, it was sent off to his cousin (*ibid.* p. 189) or to his sister Guiguite (p. 135), or to one of his fellow-Jesuits, sometimes in the hope that it might be published (pp. 151, 209). At times he would ask his sister or his cousin to have some copies typed for his friends (pp. 204, 238, 266, 286). After a first draft, in which there were a considerable number of alterations and deletions, he would generally make a fair copy (pp. 238, 267). This explains how it is that we have two copies of some of the papers, with, of course, a number of variations. This is the case with *Mon Univers* 1918).

Shortly before her death Marguerite Teillard-Chambon bequeathed these manuscripts to her sister Alice, who agreed to their publication.

[1] *The Making of a Mind*, Collins, London, and Harper and Row, New York, 1965.
[2] On the title-page of some of these essays we find a note:
    Pierre Teilhard
    caporal brancardier
    4ᵉ Mixte T.Z.
    1ᵉʳᵉ compagnie (puis Compagnie H.R.) [i.e. H.Q. Coy.]

In *The Making of a Mind* (pp. 37–9) Marguerite wrote as follows:

'In the first essay, *Cosmic Life*, we find his initial awakening to an astonished awareness of the world, a pantheistic vision and its urgent temptation, already overcome by his demand for unity in a transcendence. In *The Struggle against the Multitude* he goes deep into the problem of the one and the many, a theme to which he returns in *Creative Union*. In *Mon Univers* he outlines a synthesis of the relations between God and the world, and a similar search for some "centration" of the universe is to be found in *The Soul of the World* and *La Grande Monade*.[3] The Christic theme had appeared as early as 1916, in *Christ in the World of Matter*.[4] It is rounded off and completed in *The Mystical Milieu* and *The Priest*, which herald *The Mass on the World* (1923), just as *The Mystical Milieu* does *Le Milieu Divin* of 1927.[5] In *Mastery of the World and the Kingdom of God*, Père Teilhard examines the meaning and conditions of the apostolate that the Church will have to adapt to the needs of the modern world.

'There is no need to add that there is no sign of haste in either the form or the substance of these first writings. The progress of the thought, like that of the writing, is deliberate and controlled. There is nothing of the dilettante in his work, for he had too much respect for the subjects he treated. Everything he wrote is really *written*. The very appearance of his manuscripts shows such a neatness of writing and arrangement that they might have been produced in a quiet study, even though his hand still shook from tiredness and nervous strain after a spell in the trenches.

'If the assured tone he writes in seems bold, tense with "prophetic impatience", with an undercurrent of youthful vivacity when he attacks various ways of thinking opposed to his own, it should be attributed to his anxiety to bring out some importa aspects of Christianity that were obscured for his contemporar s by other writers at that time. His "lucid and intrepid mind",

[3] *Cahiers* 2, Éditions du Seuil, Paris.

[4] *Hymn of the Universe*, Collins, London, and Harper and Row, New York, 1965.

[5] Collins, London and Harper and Row, New York (entitled *The Divine Milieu* in U.S.A.), 1960, Fontana (revised) edition 1964.

never shrank from the startling. It must be remembered, too, that he was writing primarily for himself. He was drawing up a testimony, almost, as we have seen, a te tament. He communicated his work to a restricted circle, with no hope of having it published. He had tried to do so with two articles on current problems; one was rejected, and the other was accepted after cutting.

'He asked himself whether he would ever be able to disclose all that he had seen and felt and thought during this amazing period of transformation. Just before his demobilization, he wondered anxiously, "Will they ever listen to me?"'

Later[6] Père Teilhard said of these 'war-papers' that 'they contain nothing that I have not said more clearly at a later date'. If, then, they are to be properly understood, it is important to relate them to later writings. It is to assist in this that two theologians, both friends of Père Teilhard, Mgr Bruno de Solages and Père Henri de Lubac, have together added introductory and other explanatory notes to this edition.[7] They will help to disclose in these essays an exactness of thought that a superficial reading might fail to appreciate beneath the flowing poetical style.[8]

A number of passages from some of these essays have already appeared among the *Pensées* in *Hymn of the Universe*, translated by Gerald Vann. Those versions (with some slight alteration at times) have been included in the present translation.

The following essays, which were included in *Écrits du temps de la Guerre*, have been omitted in this translation as having already been published or about to be published: 'Christ in the World of Matter' (*Hymn of the Universe*); La Nostalgie du Front'; 'La Grande Monade'; 'Mon Univers' (1918); 'Note pour servir à l'évangélisation des temps nouveaux 'Les Noms de la Matière' and 'The Spiritual Power of matter' (*Hymn of the Universe*).

[6] *Making of a Mind*, p. 37.
[7] Père Teilhard's own notes are indicated as such.
[8] Words or phrases enclosed in square brackets are Père Teilhard's (except in one or two instances when an obvious omission has been made good). He had a habit, when he re-read what he had written, of reinforcing a particular word or part of a sentence, by an addition written above the line (without any deletion) in order to bring out some exact shade of thought.

Cosmic Life

To *Terra Mater*, and through her to Christ Jesus, above all things.

'Cosmic Life' was finished on 24 April 1916, at Nieuport. It is the first of Teilhard's extant writings to be fully characteristic of its author. Knowing what risks he was exposed to at the front, Père Teilhard de Chardin wrote it as his 'intellectual testament', and it contains in embryo all that was later to be developed in his thought: in embryo, because what he has to say is less clearly focused, less accurately expressed and less completely proved than in later writings. (Some points, indeed, that he was later at pains to clarify, are presented in this essay simply as the evidence of Revelation.)

As in a number of other essays in this volume, the style in which the ideas are expressed is lyrical and elevated. In Père Teilhard's own words, it is the 'fire in his vision' that he is trying to communicate.

For a definitive presentation of his thought we must, accordingly, look to his later writings.

COSMIC LIFE

There is a communion with God, and a communion with
earth, and a communion with God through earth.
. . . And Jacob fought with the angel until day was come.

Introduction

What follows springs from an exuberance of life and a yearning
to live: it is written to express an impassioned vision of the earth,
and in an attempt to find a solution for the doubts that beset my
action—because I love the universe, its energies, its secrets, and its
hopes, and because at the same time I am dedicated to God, the
only Origin, the only Issue and the only Term. I want these
pages to be instinct with my love of matter and life, and to
reconcile it, if possible, with the unique adoration of the only
absolute and definitive Godhead.

My starting-point is the fundamental *initial fact* that each one of
us is perforce linked by all the material, organic and psychic
strands of his being to all that surrounds him. Not only is he
caught up in a network, he is carried along, too, by a stream. All
around us, in whatever direction we look, there are both links
and currents. Countless forces of determination hold us in their
grip, a vast heritage from the past weighs down upon our
present, the thousand and one affinities we are influenced by pull
us away from ourselves and drag us towards an end of which we
have no knowledge. Surrounded by all these forces that encroach on him, the individual shrinks to an imperceptible centre;
we might say that he is no more than *an observation post*, a sentient
focus-point of repulsions and attractions; he makes his choice
from among the countless energies that radiate through him; he
seeks, casting to and fro; he turns back upon himself and directs
himself so that he may breathe in more or less fully according to

the direction he takes, the energizing atmosphere that surrounds him, in which he is one single, conscious point. This is the *external condition* imposed on us: we are, we may say, more outside ourselves in time and space than we are inside ourselves, every second of our lives. The person, the *human monad, is*, like every monad, *essentially cosmic.*

Reflective thought, science, history and the social needs we experience, all combine to make us aware of the vast domain of the '*we that has no significance*' and the '*we that is in us in spite of ourselves*'; but long before that we hear a summons, rising from some hidden depth within ourselves, that calls on us to broaden our self-regard, and realize that in virtue of our immortal souls, we are *the countless centres of one and the same sphere*, made one [identical] by everything in them that is not part of their incommunicable psychism. We are all interconnected elements of one and the same curve that extends ahead of and reaches back behind us. By reason of some obscure innate affinity, some immanent need to put our hands on what is stable and absolute, we feel germinating in us, or suddenly bursting out, a yearning to exchange the isolation that concentrates us on ourselves for a wider existence and a unity of a higher order; these, we feel, will allow us to share in the totality of all that draws us along and all that we are in contact with. It is in the pantheist aspiration for fusion of all in all[1] that we see the *immanent side of our cosmic nature*, each proving the other, the one imposing itself on our will as irresistibly as the other imposes itself on our intelligence: but in each case only for those who can see and feel.

To make men see and make them feel—that is my first aim: to make an impassioned profession of my faith in the richness and value of the world and so vindicate myself against those who smile and shake their heads when they hear talk of an ill-defined nostalgia for something hidden within us which transcends and

---

[1] What follows (in section II) and a considerable number of later writings (in particular *Panthéisme et Christianisme*, 1923) express this more exactly, by distinguishing the two meanings of the word and the aspiration it stands for: the pantheism Teilhard rejects is that which is normally meant by the term, and the pantheism he accepts is that which he describes. In *The Universal Element* (below, pp. 292-3), in *Le Milieu Divin* (pp. 103-4, Fontana, p. 116) and elsewhere it is simply 'pantheism' that he rejects.

fulfils us—to win the day against them by showing them beyond all possible doubt that their self-sufficient individual personality is but a wisp of straw in the grip of forces they seek to shut their eyes to, forces that, when we speak of building up a temple to them, they dismiss as laughable. If man is to come up to his full measure, *he must become conscious of his infinite capacity for carrying himself still further*; he must realize the duties it involves, and he must feel its intoxicating wonder. He must abandon all the illusions of narrow individualism and extend himself, intellectually and emotionally, to the dimensions of the universe: and this even though, his mind reeling at the prospect of his new greatness, he should think that he is already in possession of the divine, is God himself, or is himself the artisan of Godhead.

I am not directly concerned with science, nor philosophy, nor apologetics. Primarily, I am concerned to express an impassioned vision. I shall limelight—though I shall not go out of my way to condemn—the *crisis* (*always the accompaniment of a new awakening*) that is now becoming acute in men's minds and hearts; simply as an observer in the first place. I shall watch the birth and development, in the depths of individual souls or in the turmoil of the masses, of the *cosmic temptation*; the homage paid to the golden calf, the incense rising up to the peak of human pride. Although, again, I shall offer hardly any proof, and shall rely simply on its coherence with and correspondence with the Rest, I shall allow another picture to emerge—at first in apparent opposition to the dreams of the Earth, but in reality to complete and correct them—that of the inexpressible Cosmos of matter and of the new life, the Body of Christ, real and mystical, unity and multiplicity, monad and pleiad. And, like a man who surrenders himself to a succession of different melodies, I shall let the song of my life drift now here, now there—sink down to the depths, rise to the heights above us, turn back to the ether from which all things came, reach out to the more-than-man, and culminate in the incarnate God-man.

Nevertheless, a man who is enamoured of truth and reality cannot allow himself *to drift indefinitely and confusedly* with every breeze that fills and swells his soul. However much he might wish to, it would still be impossible: by a logical necessity that is rooted in things and our view of them, the time comes sooner or later when we must at last introduce unity and organization **as** the fundamental basis of our own selves—we have to test and select and give an order of precedence to what we love and worship—we have to cast down our idols and allow only one altar to stand in the sanctuary. A choice has to be made, and for no man is it so fraught with indecision and anguish as for the Christian, for the man, that is to say, who kneels before a cross and hears a loved voice call on him to abandon all in order that he may possess all. Does it mean, then, that to be a Christian he must renounce being a man, a man in the full extent and depth of the word, avidly and passionately a man? If we are to follow Christ and share in his heavenly body, must we abandon the hope that every time our efforts succeed in mastering a little more determinism, every time a little more truth is won and a little more progress achieved, we make contact with and begin to make available some small portion of the absolute? If we are to be united with Christ, must we dissociate ourselves from *the forward drive inseparable from this* intoxicating, pitiless *cosmos* that carries us along and asserts itself in the mind of each one of us? And is there not the danger that such a dissociation will in some way mutilate those who try to effect it in themselves, cool their ardour and rob them of their strength? That is the problem implicit in life: in any Christian heart there is an inevitable conflict between the divine faith that sustains his hopes as an individual and the earthly passion that is the driving force behind all human effort.

Of all my convictions, none is dearer to me than the conviction that dissociation from everything that makes up the noblest charm and interest of our natural life cannot be the basis of our supernatural growth. If a Christian really understands the inexpressibly wonderful work that is being carried out around him, and by him, in *the whole of nature*, he cannot fail to see that the excitement and delight aroused in him by 'awakening to the cosmos' can be preserved by him not only in the form they take when transposed to a divine Ideal, but also in the substance of their most material and most earthly objects: to do so, he has only to learn to appreciate the value of *sacred evolution* as an instrument of beatification, and the eternal hopes it contains.

That, above all, is the message I wish to communicate: the reconciliation of God and the world [because it reconciles God and the world.] In what follows I have tried to express, with as clear a view of things as I can achieve, the loyal solution that has given balance and unity to my interior life; and I offer it to those who are chary of accepting Christ, because they suspect him of wishing to besmirch the fair face of the earth to which their love is irrevocably pledged; and I offer it to those, too, who, in order to love Christ, force themselves to turn their backs on what fills their souls to overflowing; and to those, finally, who have been unable to bring together as one the God of their faith and the God of their most ennobling labours, and who grow weary and impatient of a life that is dissipated in misdirected effort.

24 April 1916, Nieuport

I

Awakening to the Cosmos

A: THE VISION

1. *The Multitude.* The fundamental vision is that of plurality and the multitude, the multitude that surrounds us and the multitude that constitutes us, that is in restless motion around us, and that shelters within us.

For many, many years, in fact since all time, men have had before their eyes all these dust-like agglomerations, the stars in the heavens, the grains of sand in the dunes, the individuals in the crowd: and this was in addition to the necessity the mind cannot escape, when it seeks to define the continuous, of breaking it down into points (in its own image). It was this that made men feel that the universe must be atomic in its constitution. But it was only gradually and as a result of modern science's continually more subtle investigations, that this intellectual hypothesis was transformed, in a wide section of the world, both above and below us, into a concrete, and often direct, sensory intuition.

Today, it would certainly appear that, even if our perceptions are still irrevocably enclosed within certain limits of greatness and smallness, we can at least flatter ourselves that we have discovered and established experimentally the *law of recurrence* that governs *the structure of the cosmos*. The analysis of matter is making us see it as a limitless aggregation of centres taking over and mastering one another in such a way as to build up, by their combinations, more and more complex centres of a higher order.

In what we call the 'world of matter', the crystal or the colloidal particle can be broken down into molecules, the molecules into atoms, the atoms into electrons, and the electrons into some granular ether: while, advancing into a new order of magnitude, the planets represent the electrons of the solar system, which itself is an atom in some gigantic structure whose shape we cannot fathom. There, at each extreme, we meet Pascal's twin infinities.

Again, in the world of life, society and the polyp break down into individuals, the individual into parts, the parts into cells, the cells into ill-defined granulations, in which the laws of atomic motion and symmetry are involved in and confused with organic differentiation and spontaneity.

When the scientist examines the apparent continuity of material beings, or their disintegration into artificial and accidental fragments, he finds it replaced by a countless swarm of monads that are by nature distinct from one another. Nevertheless, these monads are not rents in the coat without seam which is the universe, since (and here we have the mystery of the cosmos and the secret of matter) both when at rest and when active, in their texture and their development, they are still one and the same thing: and that by reason of the forces that hold them together or arrange them in hierarchical order, and of the common currents that carry them along.

2. *Unity in the Ether.* The first aspect of this profound oneness of all the elements of the universe is their common 'rooting' in the

mysterious and pre-eminently cosmic entity that we call the *ether*.[2]

In spite of the strange properties that make it as physically real as a block of stone and at the same time as intangible as an abstract limit, physics is inexorably bound to accept the ether. It is the *medium* that must be posited for the transmission, or even perhaps the dispensing, of 'transient' energies,[3] to maintain or even to hold in tension the links that attract or repel the particles into which the world breaks down. Moreover, it is the *ultimate term* at which the cosmic particles are resolved, whether we regard them as eddies produced within a primitive homogeneous fluidity or simply as the countless centres around which one and the same fundamental substance radiates and folds itself. In either case, whether as the primordial stuff of things or as being the universal active medium (like *hyle* or *energeia*) it enters into our view of the world, by reason of being by nature the ultimate support of substance and activities, as a reality whose uniform plenitude can admit *neither hiatus nor break*: either of those *would open the door to non-being*. The ether is like some great reservoir of elastic fluid that could be twisted again and again without the least rift or break appearing, to isolate from the total mass the individual local realities produced by the twistings, however complex and independent of one another we may conceive them to be. At the same time it is a fluid whose nature is such that we can have no empirical knowledge of it: no natural constitutive part can be distinguished in it, nothing that resembles an atom or a molecule. Force cannot break the continuity of the ether, nor can it be broken down by analysis. We should think of it not as having the texture of a liquid into which the countless hordes of a thousand and one different particles are crowded together, but as the unimaginable state of *some centre that is*

---

[2] 'Ether' is a term that belongs to a stage of scientific thought now left behind. It is generally realized that since the famous Michelson experiment and Einstein's theories, scientists have abandoned the notion of the ether, useful though it was in the nineteenth and early twentieth centuries. This, however, is of only minor importance for that part of Teilhard's views on the cosmos (in this instance, the unity of the cosmos) that he develops here.

[3] Cf. *Creative Union*, E. 'Transience. True Matter', where Teilhard goes back on this view (p. 166).

*indefinitely extended in space, everywhere the same and yet everywhere
different from itself.*

Everything in the universe, we must realize, proceeds from the
ether, or in the ether.

I can put my hand at random on any element in the teeming
multitude and if I confront it with another one, also chosen at
random, I am obliged to admit that in both a real inner identity
lies hidden—that identity may, no doubt, be completed by an
individual and incommunicable immanence, but it is not
destroyed by it. It is identity in the ether, whose unique centre,
dispersed through all things, is the prime matter—indivisible in
spite of its immensity—of all that springs up within the vast
cosmos. Like knots spaced out along a cord, or like the folds into
which a single curtain falls, or the eddies forming on one and the
same surface, everything that moves and lives in the universe
represents, in one particular aspect, the modifications of one and
the same thing; and every monad, if it looks into itself, can find
that thing as the initial point at which all things make contact in
their inmost essence.

This *consanguinity* of the monads *in the ether*, which is their
common stock and the sap that feeds them all, might perhaps
serve to dispel, for philosophical thought, the disturbing illusion
of transience: the interaction of material beings takes place by
reason of, and at the level of, an identity. It is in any case the
physical reason why material beings, to whatever degree of
complexity they have risen, still exercise a reciprocal influence on
one another in proportion to their specific perfection. Sometimes with a richer, sometimes a poorer organic structure, sometimes more, sometimes less fully illuminated by consciousness or
governed by free choice, it is always, if we look deeply enough,
the ether that is being attracted or repelled deep within material
beings: it is the ether that confronts itself in this thing or that
thing, that presses on with them, we may say, towards some
hidden end. It is the ether that maintains the uniformity and
interaction of determinisms and that ensures the grip of one soul
upon another. The monad's unity of origin is necessarily continued in unity of behaviour, of affinities and growth. It becomes
definitively part and parcel of the total development of matter.

This is because the monads of our universe are not simply and solely the centres that emerged within a vast, immobile, homogeneous mass. As happens with the eddies in a river, their birth is accompanied by a more far-reaching movement which not only *carries them along* beyond themselves but is also, in some way, *the actual cause of their emergence.* How, exactly, are we to visualize the over-all movement that carries the world of matter along in space, or transforms its interior make-up? Is matter, first and foremost, as the dissipation of energy and the disintegration of atoms would suggest, 'what breaks down and sinks back'? Are the displacements that shift the stellar system carried out along trajectories that have no common meeting point? or are they rather the perception, on an extremely small element, of a gigantic eddy that is recommencing, on an enormous scale, the ether's endless task of folding-in upon itself? Only one thing matters for us here: it is that, in addition to an original identity of the centres and to a network of static (or at any rate permanent) links that holds them together, there are without any doubt large over-all currents that affect the multiplicity of atoms and stars, and through them *the common soul of an evolution* is infused into the common body of all that has its basis in ether.

And this step brings us to the confines of life.

3. *Unity through Life.* Nothing would appear to be more isolated, nothing more exclusive of all extra-individual existence, than the living monad.

Souls, immaterial or spiritual, are the type of the complete, of the self-contained, of the autonomous; in our experience and in our thought they represent *microcosms.* And yet, because of the extreme sensitiveness of their reactions and the deeply penetrative power of their introspection, nowhere can one distinguish more easily than in them the influences and functions and unity of the cosmos, nowhere do they appear more impressive and also more fruitful.

At the origin of the compulsions that subject souls to one another and to things outside them, we meet the inevitable ether. Even though it is still impossible, at our present stage of knowledge, to say exactly what are the relationships that produce the interdependence of these two great and still (so far as we know?) distinct realities, we can be certain that life stems from matter and cannot do without it. Life appeared, and develops, as a function of the whole universe; and therefore, through something in itself, it shares in the universe's original substantial unity, and in some hidden way is involved in the over-all movement, material in basis, which constitutes the total development of the cosmos. Moreover, in its manifestations and particularly in its lower forms it can hardly be distinguished from the inanimate structures produced by what we call physico-chemical forces. In its external shape, in its internal processes, in its powers of fermentation, and in its readiness to enter into aggregations of a higher order, the monocellular being behaves in many ways like a molecule. Life appears in phenomenal continuity with the network of material determinisms and constructions. When the individualization of organic and conscious monads produces folds in the basic fabric of the cosmos, it does not tear it, any more than does the separation of the atomic centres. *Already, through the matter that is common to them, all living beings are but one being.*

And it is primarily through their all possessing life that they are welded into one.

Life, we have just said, is in some way an extension of matter. With the elements, it retains some of the habits of matter. It can even, we shall see, copy it and mimic it by making itself mechanical. But it is even more distinct from matter in the particular way of involution by which the monads are born under its influence, and also in the general orientation of the current of increasing perfection along which it carries them. Through this matter that breaks up, and by means of it, life rises, combining the work of external organization that it carries out through individuals with a special internal involution through which there emerges in the heart of matter an increasingly more conscious side. Now, nothing contributes more to the unity of the centres than the common genesis that associates them in their structure and their destiny. We should look more closely at the pages of stone on which is written the history of the transformations of living organisms.

For anyone who can turn over those pages patiently, constantly, and religiously, there emerges from them a vast, luminous, picture. Even some of the most dedicated of those who have been able to read them have been powerless to describe it except in vague, dazzling terms of rays that melt into one another, of a glorious dawn, of an explosive surge; but they are all agreed in recognizing it as a *continuity*. If we look at it far enough back in the depths of time, the disordered anthill of living beings suddenly, for an informed observer, arranges itself in long files that make their way by various paths towards greater consciousness. Seen from a sufficient distance and in a particular light, individuals (principles, in appearance, of egocentrism and permanence) are recognized as no more than staging-posts in a movement, each individual's most essential function being to advance that movement a little further; and the very multiplicity of the attempts made to force matter to give way to spontaneity, and to organize it in centres that can be charged with cosmic energies, even that multiplicity is absorbed in the unity of one and the same general direction (of climbing up, we might say, one common gradient)—and that direction or gradient leads towards freedom and light. Many individual lives come to grief, or are trampled underfoot and sacrificed in this pell-mell rush towards the light of day; many false directions lead only to organisms that have no future, stifled in an excess of secondary trappings or paralysed by the mass. In this way whole groups are eliminated or survive only to provide a support for efforts that run parallel with them. These minor checks, however, are of no importance; it is the whole body of work done and success achieved that is paramount. The effort to climb upwards is maintained through and beyond partial checks, and the mysterious, unique, life-sap penetrates and makes its way, surrounded though it is by the inconceivable tangle of mechanical and organic activities. Infallibly, it rises up towards some more efficiently knit nervous system, and above all towards brain, where thought will be able to reflect upon itself instantly and unerringly. Bergson expressed this better, perhaps, than anyone; but all who are really close to life have felt, as he did and long before he did, their souls thrill to this confident belief.

First there is *the revelation of the unique matter*, and then, even more wonderful, *that of the unique soul*: first, what the laboratory shows us, and then what nature does; first the ether, and then life. How blind and 'unhuman', then, are those who look at the universe and refuse to recognize these things, or who claim to see them and yet remain unmoved by the impact of a vast super-abundance in which their whole being is swallowed up. It is not, you see, enough to hear what science has to tell us, and to observe from outside the cosmic currents taking shape, in their individual eddyings or their over-all drifts; it is those currents that make us what we are, it is through us that they run, and we must be able to feel them.

B: FEELING

... And I allowed my consciousness to sweep back to the farthest limit of my body, to ascertain whether I might not extend outside myself. I stepped down into the most hidden depths of my being, lamp in hand and ears alert, to discover whether, in the deepest recesses of the blackness within me, I might not see the glint of the waters of the current that flows on, whether I might not hear the murmur of their mysterious waters that rise from the uttermost depths and will burst forth no man knows where. With terror and intoxicating emotion, I realized that my own poor trifling existence was one with the immensity of all that is and all that is still in process of becoming.[4]

I can feel it: matter, which I thought was most my own, eludes and escapes me. Countless radiations run through me in every direction, and I am, in some way, no more than the place where they meet or conflict with one another. All sorts of hidden influences surround me and penetrate me—emanate, too, from me—bringing with them the echo and repercussion of all that vibrates and moves in the boundless ether. Moreover, all these impacts, all this penetration of the rest into me, are not *unjust intrusions* which I have the right, if not the power, to repel.

[4] Cf. *Le Milieu Divin*, pp. 54-5, Fontana, pp. 76-7, where Teilhard returns to this theme.

When they reach me, they are at home, for it is they that make me what I am.

I can feel, again—and this time much more distinctly—a multitude of the independent and spontaneous—atoms, molecules, cells—in turmoil beneath the unity of my own organic structure. Generally speaking and on the whole, their hierarchically ordered mass serves me faithfully. But each one of them retains its individual affinities with spheres of matter that are not my sphere; and, sooner or later, these sympathies are inevitably expressed in processes of disorganization whose end is 'the return to dust'.

The result of their activities, when they have been disciplined and completed by my soul, is without doubt a vital force—an aptitude for feeling and evolving—that I can claim as specifically my own: and yet although this force is indeed my own in the sense that it is I who concentrate it and experience it, I am quite unable to pin it down, whether I try to decipher any part either of its past or of its future. Behind the unity it assumes in my consciousness there lies hidden the dense multitude of all the succession of beings whose infinitely patient and lengthy labour has carried to its present stage of perfection the *phylum* of which I am for a moment the extreme bud. My life is not my own: I know this from the inexorable determinism contained in the development of overpowering emotions, in pain and in death. And I feel this, not only in my bodily members but in the very core of what is most spiritual in my being.

I am, obviously, free. But what does my freedom represent other than an imperceptible point buried in an indeterminate mass of laws and relationships that I cannot, by and large, control? All I can do is shrewdly to make what use I may of them, follow their slant, sail with their wind, appear to master them and bend them to my will—when all I am, in fact doing, is to set them off one against the other. Each one of us can distinguish in the depth of his being a whole system of deep-seated tendencies—a law of his own individual evolution—that nothing can suppress and that persists through every stage of greater perfection. This personal driving force is prior to and higher than free will; it is written into our character, into the rhythm of our thoughts, and into the

crude surge of our passions; and it is life's heritage to us, it is the
conscious evidence in us of the *vast vital current*, one trickle of which
forms us, it is our subjection to the great task of development of
which we, for one brief hour, are no more than the artisans.

If, as I said before, we step down into ourselves, we shall be
horrified to find there, *beneath the man of surface relationships and
reflection*, an unknown—a man as yet hardly emerged from unconsciousness, still, for lack of the appropriate stimulus, no more
than half-awake: one whose features, seen in the half-shadow,
seem to be merging into the countenance of the world.

No brutal shock, no, nor no gentle caress can compare with the
vehemence and possessive force of the contact between ourselves
as individuals and the universe, when suddenly, *beneath the
ordinariness of our most familiar experiences*, we realize, with
religious horror, that what *is emerging in us is the great cosmos*.

C: THE CALL

No man who has once experienced this vision can ever forget it.
Like the seaman who has known the intoxicating blue of the
South Seas—whatever he be whom the ray has touched upon,
whether scientist, philosopher, or humble worker—he lives for
ever with his nostalgia for what is greatest, most durable, for the
Absolute whose presence and activity around him he has felt for
one moment. The flash that opened his eyes remains as a light
imprinted deep within them; and he never ceases to thrill to the
awareness of contact with the universe. Others may smile at his
vain worries and his odd concern to extend man's consciousness
beyond the accepted limits of practical life. But the man with the
vision will follow his own road; he knows that many will understand his language and that they are waiting to hear him speak,
sorrowful and somehow stunted because hidden aspirations are
clamorous within them and they are unable to express them. This,
then, is *the word that gives freedom*: it is not enough for man to
throw off his self-love and *live as a social being*. *He needs to live*
with his whole heart, in union with the totality of the world
that carries him along, *cosmically*. Deeper than the soul of

individuals, vaster than the human group, there is a vital fluid or spirit of things, there is some absolute, that draws us and yet lies hidden. If we are to see its features, to answer its call and understand its meaning, and if we are to learn to live more, we must *plunge boldly* into the vast current of things and see whither its flow is carrying us.

II
Communion with Earth

A: THE TEMPTATION OF MATTER

When a man has emerged into consciousness of the cosmos, and has deliberately flung himself into it, his first impulse is *to allow himself to be rocked* like a child by the great mother in whose arms he has just woken. For some this attitude of surrender is a mere aesthetic emotion, for others it is a rule of practical life, a system of thought, or even a religion; but in it lies the common root of all non-Christian pantheisms.

The essential revelation of paganism is that everything in the universe is uniformly true and valuable: so much so that the fusion of the individual must be effected with all, *without distinction and without qualification.* Everything that is active, that moves or breathes, every physical, astral, or animate energy, every fragment of force, every spark of life, is equally sacred; for, in the humblest atom and the most brilliant star, in the lowest insect and the finest intelligence, there is the radiant smile and thrill of the *same Absolute.* It is to this Absolute alone that we have to cling, giving ourselves to it directly and with a penetration that can see through even the most substantial determinations of the real, and rejects them as superficial appearances. It is the eastern vision of the blue Lotus, instinct with passion because every tangible beauty is divinized by it, but weighted with matter whose hidden basis, stimulated by that same vision, strives to rise up, to enter into, and to absorb all spirituality.

What in fact, characterizes pantheist and non-Christian views is that the fundamental equivalence they introduce between everything that exists is produced, at the expense of conscious and personal life, for the benefit of the rudimentary and diffuse modes of being found in the lower monads. At first it would appear that in the eyes of the naturalist thinker or the Hindu *everything is animated; in reality, everything is materialized.* The luminous destiny of things, the paradise of souls they dream of, *become one with their dim source;* they are absorbed in the fundamental reservoir of homogeneous ether and latent life, from which everything has emerged and by returning to be lost in which it is destined to attain its beatitude. *Life is understood and experienced as a function of matter.*

. . . One day, I was looking out over the dreary expanse of the desert. As far as the eye could see, the purple steps of the uplands rose up in series, towards horizons of exotic wildness; again, as I watched the empty, bottomless ocean whose waves were ceaselessly moving in their 'unnumbered laughter'; or, buried in a forest whose life-laden shadows seemed to seek to absorb me in their deep, warm, folds—on such occasions, maybe,[5] I have been possessed by a great yearning to go and find, far from men and far from toil the place where dwell the vast forces that cradle us and possess us, where my over-tense activity might indefinitely become ever more relaxed . . . And then all my sensibility became alert, as though at the approach of a god of easy-won happiness and intoxication; for there lay matter, and matter was calling me. To me in my turn, as to all the sons of man, it was speaking as every generation hears it speak; it was begging me to surrender myself unreservedly to it, and to worship it.

And why, indeed, should I not worship it, the stable, the great, the rich, the mother, the divine? Is not matter, in its own way, eternal and immense? Is it not matter whose absence our imagina-

---

[5] The qualification of 'maybe', and later of 'I may have believed', should be noted. Père Teilhard is indicating that the personal tone of this analysis should not be taken literally, but is partly a literary device. Other instances of this will be found later.

tion refuses to conceive, whether in the furthest limit of space or
in the endless recesses of time? Is it not the one and only universal
substance, the ethereal fluidity that all things share without either
diminishing or fragmenting it? Is it not the absolutely fertile
generatrix, the *Terra Mater*, that carries within her the seeds of all
life and the sustenance of all joy? Is it not at once the common
origin of beings and the only end we could dream of, the primordial and indestructible essence from which all emerges and
into which all returns, the starting point of all growth and the
limit of all disintegration? All the attributes that a philosophy of
the spirit posits as lying outside the universe, do they not in fact
lie at the opposite pole? Are they not realized and are they not to
be attained in the depths of the world, in divine matter?

Lulled by the voice that charmed more than one wise man, it
was thus that my spell-bound heart and my reason, its willing
fellow-victim, would speak. It was heathendom's hour, the time
when the song of the Sirens rises up from the nether regions of
the universe. . . .

In the exhilaration, then, of these first delights and this first
encounter, I may well have believed in the glitter, the sweet
scents, the boundless expanses, the bottomless depths, and surrendered myself to matter. I wished to see whether, as the vast
hopes aroused in me by 'awakening to the cosmos' suggested, I
could arrive at the very heart of things; whether, by losing myself
in the world's embrace, I could find its soul. Ardently and with
no holding back, I made the experiment, unable to imagine that
the true could fail to coincide with the enchantment of the senses
and the alleviation of suffering. But I found that the more I
allowed myself to drift closer to the centre, ever more diffuse and
dilated, of primordial consciousness, the more the light of life was
dimmed in me.

In the first place, I felt that I was less a part of society; for matter
is jealous and will allow the initiate of its mysteries no witness.
Contact with other men is painful to the pantheist, or he tries to
see only their collective activities, like the inconsequent movements of a system deprived of freedom. *Persons* (except when love
intervenes) *are mutually exclusive through their centres*, and the
pantheist dreams of forming but one, of being synonymous, with

all around him. Thus he isolates himself, and he becomes intoxicated with his isolation. When I recognized that symptom I
already suspected that I was becoming less of a person. And yet
solitude has its own life-giving virtues. I was not, perhaps, in
spite of the lesson of the centuries, taking the wrong road when I
allowed myself to stray so far from mankind, depressing, be-
fogging and uninteresting as it is. And so I obediently yielded to
the thirst for being alone, and, to find a less irksome life, I made
my way into the desert.

What happened, however, was this: by the inexorable logic
that links the stages of our activity, a diminution of social contact
led, in me, to a diminution of personality. The man who finds his
neighbour too heavy a burden must inevitably be weary already
of bearing the burden of his own self. Thus I found myself seeking to cut down the work that every living being must produce
if he is to remain himself. I was glad to see my responsibilities
reduced; I could feel my cult of passivity being extended to
the very limit. Mighty nature is at work for us; she has made it
her business to look to the future, to be the guide, to make the
decisions, and all we have to do is to surrender ourselves to her
guidance: any interference on our part would be wasted labour
both for us and for nature. And thus it was that in one flash the
bewitching voice that was drawing me far from the cities into the
untrodden, silent spaces, came through to me. One day I
understood the meaning of the words it spoke to me; they
stirred the little-known depths of my being, holding out the
promise of some great bliss-giving repose; and I knew what it
meant when it whispered 'Take the easier road'.

Already, at the foot of the slope down which the sweet load
of matter was drawing me, I could see the swine of Epicurus
feeding.

It was then that faith in life saved me.

Life! When trouble lies heaviest upon us, whither shall we
turn, if not to the ultimate criterion, the supreme verdict, of life's
success and the roads that lead to it? When every certainty is
shaken and every utterance falters, when every principle appears
doubtful, then there is only one ultimate belief on which we can
base our rudderless interior life: the belief *that there is an absolute*

direction of growth, to which both our duty and our happiness demand that we should conform; and that *life advances in that direction*, taking the most direct road. I have contemplated nature for so long and have so loved her countenance, recognized unmistakably as hers, that I now have a deep conviction, dear to me, infinitely precious and unshakable, the humblest and yet the most fundamental in the whole structure of my convictions, that *life is never mistaken*, either about its road or its destination. No doubt, it does not define intellectually for us any God or any dogma; but it shows us by what road we may expect all that are neither delusions nor idols; it tells us towards what part of the horizon we must steer if we are to see the light dawn and grow more intense. I believe this in virtue of all my experience and of all my thirst for greater happiness: there is indeed an *absolute* fuller-being and an *absolute* better-being, and they are rightly to be described as a progress in consciousness, in freedom and in moral sense. Moreover, these higher degrees of being are to be attained by concentration, purification and maximum effort. I was, then, hopelessly mistaken in what I was just saying; I went completely astray when I yielded to the temptation of matter and relaxed the inner tension of my being in an attempt to enter limitlessly and unquestioningly into the universe. To grow greater in the truth, we must travel with our backs turned to matter and not try to return to it and be absorbed into it.

In the first exhilaration of my immersion in the universe I allowed myself to drift unresistingly towards effortless enjoyment and Nirvana . . . Now, like the diver who regains control and masters his inertia, I must make a vigorous effort, reverse my course and ascend again to the higher levels. The true summons of the cosmos is a call consciously to share in the great work that goes on within it; it is not by drifting down the current of things that we shall be united with their one, single, soul, but by fighting our way, with them, towards some term still to come.

B: TOWARDS SUPERMAN

1. *First stage: Mastery of the Universe.* If we refuse to allow ourselves to be the plaything of the universe's determinisms and blissfully to sink into the isolation they offer, it does not mean that we cease, in all circumstances, to put our faith in matter, or to believe that when we grasp it we hold the basic cosmic entity. If a man makes up his mind to place the happiness and value of his life in co-operating with the universe's essential task of producing some absolute, matter can still stand, and so remain until the end, in the foreground of his aspirations and hopes.

In this case, however, matter assumes a very different appearance from that ascribed to it by the philosophy of the lowest degree of consciousness and the least effort. It is no longer seen as the bewitching and voluptuous divinity in whose arms human activity is absorbed simply by a dream—to close one's eyes and surrender oneself. Now, it takes on a virile aspect, it toughens, and on its forehead there appears the mark of the Sphinx. Its beauty is still captivating, its breast fruitful; but the Mistress, ingratiating and yet dominating, has now been replaced by the disquieting Enigma, by the exciting Force. Matter is now the mysterious betrothed who is won, like the hunter's prey, in high combat . . . And to win her, it is not to the silence of sleep that we must turn, or to the wild empty spaces, but to the busy laboratories of nature or human skill.

As a man who has become alive to the primacy of work leans over his retorts or microscope, he sees, intensely illuminated, the potential significance and value of the particle of intelligence and activity he has at his disposal. It is his function to complete cosmic evolution by making the inexhaustible energies at the heart of which he is born 'work' as though with a leaven, until all the promise they hold is realized. Who could number the still dormant seeds, the rich potentialities, hidden in matter? The dullest, most inert object, once the appropriate stimulant has been applied to it, and it has been given the sort of complement or contact it needs and awaits, is capable of exploding into irresistible effects or of transforming itself into a nature that is prodigiously active.

As a result of natural contacts or of an instinctive, hidden, work, the Cosmos has already realized one part of its capabilities, giving us the world we know, with its individual substances and shades of life. But how many valuable properties are still to be discovered, that will perfect and transform the present picture of things? For too long, in seeking for health and growth, mankind has confined itself to docile empiricism and patient resignation. ... The time has now come to master nature, to make it unlock its secrets, to dominate it, to inaugurate a new phase; in that phase intelligence, which emerged from the universe, will turn back to it, to readjust and rejuvenate it, and make it provide its conscious portion with the full contribution it can make of growth in joy and activity.

We may ask what term is held out as the fruit of such efforts. The scientist's answer may still be vague, but he has behind him discoveries that have enabled him enormously to increase his power, to transform bodies and methodically to overcome disease. He can envisage a new era in which suffering is effectively alleviated, well-being is assured, and—who knows?—our organs are perhaps rejuvenated and even artificially developed. It is dangerous to challenge science and set a limit to its victories, for the hidden energies it summons from the depths are unfathomable. May it not even become possible to cultivate the brain itself, and intensify at will the power and keenness of thought?[6]

Borne up by this vast hope of indefinitely increasing his stature and of achieving his own beatification by using matter as a firm purchase-point, man devotes himself with new fervour to an impassioned study of the powers of the universe and becomes absorbed in the quest for the Great Secret. His austere task is enveloped in the mystical glow that lit up the anxious faces of the

[6] Although Père Teilhard had at this time already developed the idea that man has the duty of consciously and deliberately forwarding the progress of evolution, he had not yet, in considering that co-operation, arrived at his final concept of the centration of the noosphere. Cf. *The Phenomenon of Man*, Book Four, Collins, London, and Harper and Row, New York, 1959, Revised Edition, 1965.

alchemists, haloed the brow of the Magi, and divinized the bold theft of Prometheus; and, before each new property that is revealed to him, each a new window on the Promised Land, the scientist falls on his knees, almost as though to the revelation of an attribute of God.

2. *Second Stage: The Segregation of Mankind.* In and through the very effort man puts forth to master and exploit the world, he asserts his relative transcendence, his superiority to the rest of things. He stands out from the confused welter of monads. He learns to turn his attention more closely upon himself, to examine himself more carefully, to concentrate upon his own being and progress the love and concern he had allowed to extend too uniformly over the totality of the universe. First then, he recognizes in his attempts to live cosmically an initial error—an exaggerated cult of passivity amounting to an acceptance of the line of least resistance. He then suspects that his original pantheist attitude must undergo a further correction. The true way to be united with totality is not to squander oneself and spend oneself equally on all beings, but to make one's impact with all one's weight and all one's strength on that specially favoured point on which the universal effort converges and applies its mass. The essential law of cosmic development is not the egalitarian fusion of all beings, but the segregation that allows a chosen élite to emerge, to mature and to stand out alone. And, in this case, the coveted fruit that all things work to produce, in which all is summed up and fulfilled, in which all finds joy and pride, is mankind.

It matters little that, for the historian of human origins, man, when he first appears, does not seem worthy of so high a destiny. What though the roads by which he appeared and along which he advanced organically be humble and obscure—so humble and obscure, indeed, that he has much more the air of a common upstart than a predestined leader? What though he seem to have been carried by chance to the biological threshold at which many other phyla, more important than his, faded away or from which they fell back before crossing it? The cosmic importance of a being does not necessarily depend upon whether it is more close

or less close to the axis of the fascicle of natural growths.[7]
Scientists can, indeed, show us how large a part accident has
played in our destiny and how we occupy but a marginal position
within the group of living beings; but even so we men represent
that part of the world that has won through, that in which all the
life-sap of a recognizable evolution flows, in which all its efforts
are concentrated, towards the break-through that has finally been
effected. It is we, without any doubt, that constitute the active
part of the universe; we are the bud in which life is concentrated
and is at work, and in which the flower of every hope is enclosed.
If, then, a man who has heard the summons of the cosmos is to
remain faithful to it, he must overcome his repugnance for
contact with the mob, for the promiscuity and constraints of
cities and the smoke of factories, and, with all his soul, turn back
to mankind; for mankind is the object in which, rather than in his
own being, he must re-discover himself and to which his love
for his own self must be given.

Thanks to the mastery of matter that he has been working to
achieve, man of the laboratory and the factory has already, as we
have seen, been assisting most effectively the continued progress
and success of the development of the cosmos, as canalized by the
human stock. Other completely different factors, much more
directly appropriate to the special needs of new developments,
must also be distinguished and made use of: the factors that belong
to the social and moral order.

From the social point of view, the human monad presents
itself to an observer, whether he examines it from the outside or
from within, as a sort of molecule or cell essentially destined to be
integrated in a higher structure or organism. Not only is the
nourishment of numerous material perceptions and assimilations
indispensable to its make-up; if it is to attain its full development
it must also be complemented by other monads similar to itself.
It can be completely itself only by ceasing to be isolated. Like molecules whose coming together stimulates dormant properties, so

[7] Père Teilhard's later palaeontological studies brought him to a contrary
view: he believed in the axial position of man in the tree of life. See, for
example, *The Phenomenon of Man* (1930), Chapter XI of *The Vision of the Past*,
Collins, London, and Harper and Row, New York, 1966, pp. 165-6.

human beings fertilize and complete one another by making contact; and the association necessary to the multiplication of the human race is no more than a lower and extremely feeble proto-type of the rich developments produced by the intercourse of the souls. As particular positions and functions are assigned in the body to the cells, so, in society, the skills of individuals are defined and distributed, and provide one another with mutual support. Childish though it is to exaggerate the analogies with the organic presented by social groups, it is equally superficial to see in them only the arbitrary and contingent. *Although they never produce a network sufficiently close-knit and unified for us to be able to speak of a true collective soul,* yet the interrelations of men represent an essential, cosmic, work 'of nature'; they are an indispensable link in the series by which the universe moves towards its perfection. To co-operate in their establishment is much more than a super-ficial occupation, a pleasant or supererogatory pastime: it is truly to contribute one's effort to the fundamental work that has determined the movement of the universe ever since the be-ginning; it is to forward life's further developments.

So far as one can guess, the developments to be expected are primarily of the intellectual and moral order. The impression one gets is that *after having been completely occupied for a long time in the work of constructing organisms, life is only now beginning to see to its internal dispositions*; it is concentrating its attention and care on advances and refinements of a finally perfected consciousness. *At present, evolution is continuing* much more through *improvements of the psychological order* than through organic transformations. It is the same ontological effort still being pursued, but in a new phase and at a new level. What direct physical links exist in depth between souls, making them all share fully in the ontological advances realized by any one of them? By virtue of what reactions of spirit on matter does any progress in interior illumination and rightly ordered will make itself felt in all being and in the whole species, and so complete and perfect them organically? *What new state of existence* will eventually be produced by cultivation of the soul and harmonizing of social energies? It seems almost non-sensical to formulate these questions and the hypotheses they imply. As happens when we try to form some sort of picture of the very first origins of life or of mankind, so the mere attempt to give exact form to the aspirations that centre on the ultimate flowering of our race is sufficient to make them appear ridiculous. This, however, is very far from proving that the presentiments behind our aspirations are mistaken.

Those who hold firmly to their *belief in human progress* are, in fact, a numerous body. We may smile at their naïveté, and quote against them the disquieting evidence of men's conflicts and maliciousness, but they persist in their hope. They believe that to accept that mankind is simply drifting and coming to nothing, to deny that any promise is alive in it, is to despair of grasping any absolute in the universe, is to recognize that the cosmos is empty, its summons a falsehood, and life impotent and deceptive. Such a fraud, they say, cannot be reconciled with the most profound assurances life offers us. Under the combined efforts of science, morality and association in society, some super-mankind is emerging; and it is very probably in the direction of Spirit that we should look, if we wish to know what form it will take.

3. *Third Stage: The Liberation of Spirit.* As man advances in consciousness of his value as a person and of the real worth of the social groups in which he is integrated, so he ceases to find satisfaction in matter. When he first awoke to the cosmos, he had eyes and hands only for the immediate, solid, treasures that come to us, tangibly apprehended, with the earth. Now his attention is being drawn to, and his ambitions are concentrated upon, that specially favoured position to which he is introduced by a mysterious, laborious process of segregation (the combined work of nature and his own industry); he is beginning, therefore, to look down on the first object of his cosmic passion. Intellectually and emotionally the promises offered by matter have ceased to be paramount. He is tending to see in matter only an obstacle; it is becoming a dead-weight, a husk to be discarded as he journeys on. And the reason for this is that it is dim, heavy, passive, loaded with suffering, evil—while progress moves towards the light, to ease, and freedom, and blessedness, and purification of being . . . The significance and value of the world's work may well lie in spiritualizing matter, or, if matter is found to be impatient of

such transformation, in eliminating it. This is the new idea that is gradually warming to life in every high-minded, loyal, soul; it first attracts it, and finally wins it over.

A number of considerations, drawn from the order of experience, are at first introduced to support this brilliant hope. They allow one to believe that the reduction of Spirit to matter is not impossible, and is, indeed continually taking place; in consequence, transition from one to the other in the reverse direction is equally possible. Every activity, by reason of its very functioning, is encumbered with mechanisms which facilitate the execution of further acts but at the same time reduce and act as a brake on spontaneity. Even the most conscious act soon succumbs to the burden of habit; the habit passes from the psychic make-up into 'acquired' reflexes; and some acquired reflexes may well, perhaps, pass in turn into the general stock of hereditary characteristics transmitted from one generation to another. For example, the automatic instinct of insects, so astonishingly blind and exact, would seem to be simply the survival of former spontaneous processes; of old, these had been both exuberant and varied but for centuries now they have been channelled into the easiest and most satisfying directions. In this group of living creatures, their original 'freedom' has become so loaded with organic reflexes that it has almost disappeared and has been replaced by a group of 'tropisms'. Everything in matter that is passive and 'material'—its linkages, its determinisms, its inertia, its unconsciousness—may possibly be the result of a similar secondary transformation, a pseudomorphosis, by which primordial 'omni-spontaneity' was converted into mechanical obedience and routine. One is tempted to believe that this is so, if one notes that besides materialization by habit there can also be, exaggerating it, materialization by sheer numbers.

This also is a fact known by our daily intimate experience. Simply as a result of numerical magnitude, a particular inertia is developed in collective groups: certain constants and certain laws are produced in them, that can give a total sum of free options (provided it be sufficiently large) the overall appearance of a system of determinisms. There is nothing so difficult to transform, nothing that takes so long if you try to make it evolve, and nothing so troublesome to hold in check, as a multitude. Plurality throws a veil of lifelessness over the individuals it groups together. It forces the whole they form to take on the apparent characteristics of matter. The rigour and regularity of physical laws have no firmer support beneath us than the very multiplicity of the elementary effects that our perceptions synthesize. And above us, we feel, the large communities (racial, national, etc.) of which we are the atoms, absorb and dominate us; they do this through higher streams of influence which are, no doubt, born from the confluence of our own tendencies and passions, although, since they originate from a centre much more immense than ourselves, we cannot master them.

Matter, a deposit that is slowly formed in the tissues of our soul, or a solid block bound together by the cohesion of our individual personalities, constantly tends to catch up on us and to re-form above us. And this proves that by making an effort in the opposite direction we can force it to withdraw, and so win back ground from the unconscious and inevitable and even, maybe, re-animate all things.

Idealist thinkers offer us hope that this dream may indeed be realized. Matter, they tell us, in which a crude philosophy would see the support of all that exists and the stuff of which it is made, cannot subsist by itself; for matter is simply transience and multiplicity, while being, on the other hand, is essentially immanence and unity. The keystone of the universe, the centre of all interconnexions, without which the world collapses, disintegrates and vanishes, is the intellectual monad, the only monad that subsists in its perfect simplicity. History, no doubt, shows us an advance in the opposite direction: in the phenomenal development of time, the less conscious preceded the appearance of the more conscious ... That order, however, reflects only a subjective point of view; it represents an evolution, in relation to our own particular position, of the ontological conditions of our being. We reach back into the past, in phyletic series, just as in space the continuous disintegrates into atoms, and just as freedom is broken down into determinisms, or intuition into logical processes. We should not, however, be deceived by analytical illusions. The truth about the way in which things are constituted is this: *Everything that exists has a basis of thought, not a basis of ether.* Necessarily, then, consciousness has everywhere the power to re-emerge, because everywhere it is consciousness, dormant or ossified, *that persists.*

Thus, the verdict of philosophical thought confirms the hints suggested by experience, and enables us to envisage the increasing possibility of *the spiritualization of the universe.* Through a mental drive *sui generis* combined with a better organization of the forces that link monads together, the individual can co-operate in causing consciousness and flexibility to re-emerge in the multitude of atoms and the multitude of men, in both inorganic and living matter, and in social matter. This is his cosmic task: and it will lead mankind to freedom and happiness.

When final harmony at last reigns universally, resolving conflicts and cleavages, correcting baneful tendencies and un-lawful contacts, illuminating the depths of all things, then suffering and mischance and gloom will no longer disfigure the regenerated cosmos. Everything that was simply a hard, secondary, crust, every false or reprehensible relationship, all physical and moral evil, all the evil part of the world, will have disappeared: what remains will have flowered again, and Spirit will have absorbed matter.

4. *Fourth Stage: The Peace the World gives.* When man has reached this supreme point in the purification of his views and the widening of his desires, he halts and turns back upon himself. Weary of his own instability and insignificance, he has left his home to hasten in search of the absolute element in the universe, the element that calls for his worship. Now that he has found a direction in life, now that he has met the Divinity that his being was confusedly yearning to dedicate itself to, then, enriched by what he has found, he returns to the hidden shelter of his own heart and looks around. Has his aged, weary, heart at last found new youth? Is the hunger of his heart at last filled and satisfied? Is his anxious heart now at peace? What change is there in the man who has allowed the cares of, and consciousness of, the cosmos to form part of his interior life?

What such a man sees first of all is that his level of egoism has dropped. It is not that he no longer loves himself (which would be absurd), nor that he loves himself less (which would be pernicious) but that he loves himself in a different and better way. Ever since he saw the swarming of the multitudes and recognized the flow of the cosmic current, the petty well-being of his own person has ceased to appear to him the central concern of the universe, and is no longer of paramount importance to him. He no longer believes now that he is the only person in the world, there to enjoy himself and grow greater. Countless others, all around him, also have the right to be happy and successful. He sees them struggling on all sides; and he can discern, infinitely more important than any private undertakings, the development of a vast work that calls for all his good will and fills him with enthusiasm. He has, quite literally, shifted the axis of his life outside himself; he has, one might say, de-centred himself; in some way it is no longer himself that he cherishes in himself, but the great thing of which he is a constituent particle and an active element; it is the immanent Goddess of the World that rests her foot on him for a moment, to rise, with his support, a little higher still.

Indolence and lack of interest, then, have given way in him to a burning zeal to seek for the truth and a disciplined, eager, concern for progress. *Grandis labor instat.* No time must be lost, and no opportunity missed. However trifling it be, part of life's ultimate success depends upon the diligence with which I examine the world and make it more perfect in my own self. Awareness of this task spurs me on, and at the same time consoles me for my insignificance and obscurity.

Hitherto, the paltriness of my life and the contempt of my fellow-men used to be irksome to me. Until quite recently, not to be known or to be misunderstood, seemed an intolerable disappointment, and the fear of it paralysed my activity. But now that the true measure of things has been made clear to my soul, I am free. Why, before I act, should I be concerned to know whether my effort will be noticed or appreciated? Why should I feed my appetite for action with the empty hope of prestige or popularity? The only reward for my labour I now covet is to be able to think that it is being used for the essential and lasting progress of the universe. If I have faith in life, I believe that the world records everything good and useful that is done in it; it notes and assimilates to itself every movement and every impulse that is fitted to harmonize with its own becoming, of whose real goodness there can be no doubt. My life may be unknown, monotonous, commonplace, boring, hidden from all men's eyes . . . but I shall carry out its duties in the consciousness that I am effectively collaborating in the absolute evolution of Being. Lowly atom though I am, I shall fulfil an imperceptible function as such with a heart as all-embracing as the universe.

Even when I am confronted by suffering, my vision of the cosmos will justify me in remaining unmoved.

Observed in isolation, pain is inexplicable and hateful; but as soon as we attribute to it its proper place and role in the cosmos, we can read its features and distinguish its smile. It is pain that, by stimulating beings to react against conditions that are inimical to their full development, forces them to leave unprofitable roads; it stimulates them to undertake fruitful work and induces them to attain common harmony and to adapt themselves to one another in such a way as to avoid conflicts that injure and en- croachments that reduce them. It is pain again that, by detaching man from lower delights, forces him to seek joy in considerations and objects that 'worm and rust do not consume', that makes his soul return to the higher reaches of being, and keeps the vital pressure continually at work against the present limits of his development. It is pain, finally, that automatically punishes any transgressions of life's laws, and sees to it that they are expiated. Suffering stimulates, spiritualizes, and purifies. The converse, and at the same time the complement, of the appetite for happiness, it is the very life-blood of evolution; since, through suffering, it is the cosmos that wakens in us, I shall see suffering come without distress or fear.

Such, then, is the peace that the world gives. The responsibility for, and joy in, a great tangible value to be fostered, have trans- figured my life.

5. *Fifth Stage: The Soul's Lament*. At the very moment when I was flattering myself that I had at last found an unshakable

foundation of imperturbability, and an ultimate end that would soothe and polarize all my anxious aspirations, at that very moment I heard a long lament rising up from within me, the lament of my sacrificed soul, mourning the hopes it had for itself and that are now no more.

In the religion of divine evolution, the person counts for nothing. A passing eddy in the over-all current, no sooner formed than it vanishes, a graver first carefully sharpened and then thrown aside as soon as it is blunted, the individual has no importance and no future except in relation to the general progress. He can regard himself only as an ephemeral value; and the love he filches for his personal use and happiness is a sort of dissipation of the main energy. To find the Absolute on earth, the soul has had to renounce all that constituted the dignity and charm of its life. And this saying is so hard that, as we know, when the time comes for bearing the burden of a real sacrifice, no man can open his ears to it.

Nothing, then, it would appear, or practically nothing, will be left of the precious temple I have lovingly built and embellished in myself throughout a whole lifetime. Of all my concern to perfect and refine and adorn myself, of all the exquisite purity and delicacy that charmed and delighted me in those I love, nothing would remain for me, and nothing be preserved for them. Lost in the confused mass of our generation, one wave in a long series of waves thrown into the attack upon super-humanity, it would be our fate to succumb; we would have no consolation except that we had fallen that others might be more fortunate; we would see nothing of the victory, nor could we even be certain that a victory was infallibly being prepared. Could there, indeed, possibly be such an obliteration of what is supremely vibrant and moving in the human heart?

If, again, the *whole* of my labour were harvested, if the whole of my suffering were meaningful and fruitful, if all the betterment achieved by my work were made permanent and handed on, then I might perhaps be able to take comfort. All that was best of me would survive in the lasting evidence of my passage, for in it would be preserved and made eternal all the effective value of my life . . . Unhappily, whatever may be said, very little of what

a man thinks and knows and wills, very little of his own personal
value, succeeds in becoming exteriorized, and still less of such
good seed as is produced falls upon fertile ground. There are
mistakes, and waste, and breakdowns. Much effort is thrown
away, and much suffering is completely barren. If I rely only on
the cosmos to guard my treasure, I shall be profoundly dis-
illusioned; for its wastage is colossal, and its yield minute.

What, moreover, is that part of me that can be exteriorized?
Neither the scent nor the colour constitutes the flower; and it is
the flower, my feeling tells me, that is the treasure I carry within
me. Little by little, I have seen unfold in the depths of my being
this mysterious flower that I recognize as my own incommunicable personality; I have loved it with passion, because of all the
care I had given to protecting and embellishing it, and even more
because of all that I could discern in it that was greater than
myself and existed before myself. And now it is this so loved
monad that I see doomed to disintegration; to lose those inexpressible enchanting characteristics that determine its individuality; to disappear, practically without trace, sacrificed, even
to annihilation, to some hypothetical, faceless Divinity.

Could I but know for certain that some fragment of the
Absolute that momentarily circulates in my being, is held there,
is perpetuated there, and so preserves me for eternal life! . . .
Prophets of pantheism have risen up to promise me, in the name
of some astonishing metempsychosis, that my soul will persist
throughout different forms of association assumed by the
universe. But all they have offered me is the persistence and the
survival of a monad that cannot recognize itself from one stage
of its being to another; and it is the thread of my conscious
person, of my enriched memory, of my enlightened thought,
that I long to see prolonged, without break, and for ever.

If, then, the word is not to be heard on earth, may it come
down from heaven: the word that, integrating into one synthesis
the yearnings of the soul and the demands of the universe, will
reveal to us by what mysterious organic union of the extreme
terms, individual aspirations can be fulfilled in the realization of
the whole!

III

Communion with God

A: THE WORLD OF SOULS

The sovereign charm of Christianity is that it is above all a religion of persons, the religion of souls. Whereas the worshippers of earth, in their search for a stable and permanent Godhead, can look only towards a Becoming, or a collectivity, or some extremely simple lower term of matter, the Christian believes that he holds within himself an immortal substance, an incorruptible fruit which is the object of every process and every proliferation in the universe. The term he awaits for the world is not some distant hypothetical superhumanity: in each one of the souls that is born from it, and then takes flight, the cosmos is incessantly fulfilling its finest hopes. The cosmos is no more than an impermanent stem that can wither away: all that it can contain of Absolute is to be found in the souls that gather it up, give it stability and then, when death harvests them like ripe fruit, carry it with them; souls, for whom nothing in heaven or upon earth is too beautiful and precious; souls, the quintessence of the perfections developed by natural life, and the seat of the inexpressible amplification effected by sanctification.

So speaks the voice of Christianity, and it would seem that to hear it an intensely pure joy should invade and possess my heart. And yet the very first thing I find is that the sense of peace that comes with the promise of immortality is mixed with a deep distrust. I have tasted too deeply the joy of expanding my being to the dimensions of all that lives to be able henceforth to confine myself to the limits of my own self; I have been too conscious of the thrill of universality in my soul, to accept a bliss that leaves me in isolation. Do not the promises of Christianity mean the end of cosmic hopes? Does not the primacy of the monad tarnish and destroy the mysterious charms of the Pleiad? If we are to have the happiness of knowing that we are Some Thing, must we not give up the heady euphoria of feeling that we are enveloped by, traversed by, drawn along by Another Thing, vaster and more important than ourselves?

We may take heart, for such fears are vain. Here as elsewhere, all the highest and most legitimate ambitions entertained by the heart of man are respected and satisfied a hundredfold by Revelation. For the believer whose eyes have seen the light, souls are not formed in the world as discontinuous and autonomous centres, nor do they so leave it. Even more fully and more blissfully than in any human pantheist dream, sanctified monads are atoms immersed in, nourished by, and carried along by one and the same unfathomable primitive substance; they are elements that are combined and given a special character by a network of intimate interconnexions, in order so to constitute a higher unity. *While Christianity is a supremely individualist religion, it is at the same time essentially a cosmic religion,* since, when the Creation and the preaching of the Gospel have completed their work, Christianity discloses to us not simply a harvest of souls but a *world of souls.*

If we look at this world, we see that the fundamental substance within which souls are formed, the higher environment in which they evolve—what one might call their own particular Ether— is the Godhead, at once transcendent and immanent, *in qua vivimus et movemur et sumus*—in whom we live and move and have our being. God cannot in any way be intermixed with or lost in the participated being which he sustains and animates and holds together, but he is at the birth, and the growth and the final term of all things. Everything lives, and everything is raised up—everything in consequence is one—in Him and through Him.

Worthily to describe the rapture of this union and this unification, the pantheists' most impassioned language is justified, whether unspoken in the heart or given expression by the tongue: and to that rapture is added the ecstatic realization that the universal Thing from which everything emerges and to which everything returns, is not the Impersonal, the Unknowable and the Unconscious, in which the individual disintegrates and is lost by being absorbed: it is a living, loving, Being, in which the individual consciousness, when it is lost, attains an accentuation and an illumination that extends to the furthest limit of what is contained in its own personality. God, who is as immense and all-embracing as matter, and at the same time as warm and intimate as a soul, is the Centre who spreads through all things; his immensity is produced by an extreme of concentration, and his rich simplicity synthesizes a culminating paroxysm of accumulated virtues. No words can express the bliss of feeling oneself possessed, absorbed,[8] without end or limit, by an Infinite that is not rarefied and colourless, but living and luminous, an Infinite that knows and attracts and loves.

Souls are irresistibly drawn by the demands of their innate powers, and still more by the call of grace, towards a common centre of beatitude, and it is in this convergence that they find a first bond that combines them in a natural Whole. The paths they follow inevitably meet at the term of the movement that carries them along. Moreover, grace, which introduces them into the field of divine attraction, forces them all to exert an influence, as they proceed, upon one another; and it is in this relation of dependence, which is just the same kind as that which links together material systems, that there lies the so astonishingly 'cosmic' mystery (we might almost say the phenomenon) of the *Communion of Saints*.

Like particles immersed in one and the same spiritual fluid, souls cannot think or pray or act or move, without waves being produced, even by the most insignificant among them, which set the others in motion; inevitably, behind each soul a wake is formed which draws other souls either towards good or towards evil.

There is an even more striking similarity with the organisms that life on earth forms and drives, in mutual interdependence, along the road of consciousness, in that souls know that the evolution of their personal holiness reaches its full value in the

[8] The ms. reads *absorber* (absorb): when altering the latter part of the sentence, Père Teilhard forgot to substitute the past participle *absorbé* for the active verb.

success of a global task that goes beyond and is infinitely more important than the success of individual men.

There is this difference, however: under the influence of natural evolution, community of work produces only a Whole whose texture is divergent, so that its parts can pull away and disintegrate at the whim of all sorts of accidents or impulses; again, the group of living beings that are the most united in their destiny, that is to say the human group, has not (or not yet?) advanced beyond the stage, in its unification, of an organized collectivity. On the other hand, souls that have attained holiness can envisage at the term of their development and confluence a solidarity of a very different nature.

Grace, in fact, is more than the common environment or over-all current by which the multitude is bound together into the coherence of one solid whole or one single impulse. For the believer, it represents, quite literally, the common soul that brings them under the infinitely benign domination of a conscious mind. The Communion of Saints is held together in the hallowed unity of a physically organized Whole; and this Whole—more absolute than the individuals over which it has dominion, in as much as the elements penetrate into and subsist in God as a *function* of Him and *not as isolated particles*—this Whole is the Body of Christ.

B: THE BODY OF CHRIST

Minds that are afraid of a bold concept or are governed by individualistic prejudices, and always try to interpret the relationships between beings in moral or logical terms, are apt to conceive the Body of Christ by analogy with human associations; it then becomes much more akin to a social aggregation than to a natural organism. Such minds dangerously weaken the thought of Scripture and make it unintelligible or platitudinous to thinking men who are eager to trace out physical connexions and relations that are specifically cosmic. They unjustifiably diminish Christ and the profoundly real mystery of his Flesh. The Body of Christ is not, as some unenterprising thinkers would have us believe, the extrinsic or juridical asso-

ciation of men who are embraced by one and the same bene-
volence and are destined to the same reward. It must be understood with boldness, as St John and St Paul and the Fathers saw it
and loved it. It constitutes a world that is natural and new, an
organism that is animate and in motion, one in which we are all
united, physically and *biologically*.

The exclusive task of the world is the physical incorporation of
the faithful in the Christ who is of God. This cardinal task is
being carried out *with the rigour and harmony of a natural evolution.*

At the source of its developments an operation was called for,
transcendent in order, to graft the Person of a God onto the
human cosmos, under conditions that are mysterious but physically governed. This would give immanence to, or 'immanentize',
in our universe the principle around which a predestined body of
the chosen is to achieve its segregation. *Et Verbum caro factum est.*
This was the Incarnation. From this first and fundamental contact
between God and the human race—which means in virtue of the
penetration of the Divine into our nature—a new life was born:
an unlooked for magnification and 'obediential' extension of our
natural capabilities—grace. Grace is not simply the analogous
form found in a number of different immanencies, the life,
uniform and at the same time multiple, shared by living creatures.
It is the unique sap that starts from the same trunk and rises up
into the branches, it is the blood that courses through the veins
under the impulse of one and the same Heart, the nervous current
that is transmitted through the limbs at the dictate of one and the
same Head: and that radiant Head, that mighty Heart, that
fruitful Stock, must inevitably be Christ. Through grace,
through that single and identical life, we become much more than
kinsmen, much more, even, than brothers: we become identified
with one and the same higher Reality, which is Jesus Christ.

Christ could, no doubt, be content, exercising no more than a
collective spiritual influence, thus to give life to the human cells
that prolong him, mystically, through the universe: but he does
more. By means of sacramental communion he consummates the
union of the faithful in Himself through an individual and
integral contact of soul with soul, flesh with flesh; he instils even

into the matter of their being, side by side with the imperative need to adhere to the mystical Body, a seed of resurrection. Christ, as does all life, anticipates our desires and efforts: in the first place through the Incarnation, and then through the Eucharist, he organizes us for himself and implants himself in us. But, again as all life does, he demands the co-operation of our good will and our actions.

We give him this essential collaboration by exerting an effort actively to become assimilated, by lovingly submitting our own autonomy to His: this assimilation lies in loving-kindness and humility, in community of suffering, by which the Passion of Calvary is continued and completed, but above all in charity, that wonderful virtue which makes us see and cherish Christ in every man and so enables us to forward, in the 'immediacy' of a single act, the unification of all in One.

We may be tempted to believe, and may perhaps be told, that in the course of this painfully acquired communion, all we are doing is simply to bring about moral beauties in our souls and a superficial resemblance to God, similar to those improvements through which, in social life, men who attach importance to their personal cultural development, are accustomed to better their natural personality. Nothing could be more mistaken. Our efforts have an impact that is far more permanent and profound. When our activity is animated by grace it is as effective and 'creative' as life, the Mother of Organisms, and it builds up a Body in the true sense of the word. This is the Body of Christ, which seeks to be realized in each one of us.

The mystical Body of Christ should, in fact, be conceived as a physical Reality, *in the strongest sense the words can bear.* Only so can the great mysteries and the great virtues of religion, only so can Christ's role as mediator, the importance of Communion, and the immense value of charity, *assume their full significance*; only so can the Person of the Saviour retain its full hold on our minds and continue to provide the driving force our destinies demand.

To this faith, Jesus, I hold, and this I would proclaim from the house-tops and in all places where men meet together: that You do more than simply stand apart from things as their Master, you are more than the incommunicable splendour of the universe;

you are, too, the dominating influence that penetrates us, holds us, and draws us, through the inmost core of our most imperative and most deep-rooted desires; you are the cosmic Being who envelops us and fulfils us in the perfection of his Unity. It is, in all truth, in this way, and for this that I love you above all things.

Caught in the flames of a seemingly self-contradictory desire, I thirsted, Lord, to become more my own self by emerging from myself; and it is you who, faithful to your promise, quench my thirst with the *living Water* of your precious Essence, in which he who loses himself finds his soul and the soul of all other men made one with his own.

Already, when I contemplated your Godhead, I had the rapture of finding a personal and loving Infinite; and the association of those words held such sweetness for me that to repeat them seemed a bliss to which there would be no end; it was like the single note produced by the Angel's viol, of which St Francis never wearied. And now I know more: the very multitude of my race comes to life in your humanity; the breath that gives solidity and harmony to its scattered elements is not a Spirit whose higher nature is disconcerting to us, it is a human soul that feels and vibrates as I do; it is your very soul, Jesus. I know, too, that, in a supreme condescension to my yearning for activity and change, you offer me this higher, definitive, world which you concentrate and shelter in Yourself, but you offer it *unfinished*, so that my life may draw sustenance from the intense satisfaction of, in some small way, giving You to Yourself. Here, then, is the one thing that matters, absolute and tangible, that I dreamed of assigning as an objective and ideal to all my human efforts: it is the Kingdom of God, whose realization we have to work for, and which we have to win. Your Body, Jesus, is not only the Centre of all final repose; it is also the bond that holds together all fruitful effort. In you, side by side with *Him who is*, I can passionately love *Him who is becoming*. What more do I need for final peace to spread through my soul, in a way for which I could never have hoped, satisfying even its most apparently impossible aspirations for cosmic life?

There is one thing more, Lord: just one thing, but it is the most difficult of all, and, what is worse, it is a thing that you, perhaps, have condemned. It is this: if I am to have a share in your kingdom, I must on no account reject this radiant world in the ecstatic delight of which I opened my eyes.

C: THE STUMBLING-BLOCK OF THE KINGDOM OF HEAVEN

Like snowy peaks floating, almost unreal, over the mist, their bases gradually disclosed by a gentle breeze, so the heavenly Jerusalem was first seen in the clouds of heaven and then established its foundations on earth. Through the mediation of Christ, the supernatural cosmos exposed its roots, closely woven into our universe. It was in our world that the Saviour germinated: and he grows again and reaches his full stature through the continuation of our humble labours and our patience. That providence should so often condescend to our immanent concern for perfection and happiness should, one would imagine, satisfy to the full and disarm all our demands. Unhappily, that is far from being so; for, however terrestrial and human the Body of Christ may be, however deeply it may have been implanted in our cosmos and our life, it still appears at first alien to the world: it develops in the world but as though, one might say, it were not there.

If we are to prepare for ourselves the joy of breaking its treacherous spell, we must not be afraid of testing, in all sincerity, the effect upon our minds of this prospect (or should we say illusion?).

God has made good will the basis upon which our supernatural growth is founded. The pure heart, the right intention, are the organs of the higher life towards which, it would appear, all the soul's hopes are directed: the fundamental principle in the building up of the Body of Christ is *making use of the subjective moral value* of human acts. In the domain of morality the Divine and the Terrestrial meet and are fused into one.

There can be no doubt but that this is a most heartening concept. Since man is always the master of his intention, nothing can rob the least of his actions of the supreme and vital value of merit. In all circumstances, and through all our activity, we can dedicate ourselves to the work of universal salvation. Nothing could be a greater solace. Unhappily, as we all realize, there is another, and a more awkward, side to this ordered arrangement, in that it almost entirely neglects the matter of the act, its natural value and effectiveness. It is, no doubt, immensely consoling that the 'success' factor should become of secondary importance, but at the same time it contains a great danger and a great weakness. Once we accept that principle, what will give fire to our struggle, whence will come the fruitful anguish of the quest for truth? Only the *moral content of things* matters: and there is *no fixed relation* between that content and their cosmic quality—or rather there is often an inverse ratio.[9]

Such in fact, is the Christian estimate, paradoxical though it be, of suffering: not only is evident, tangible, failure classed as accidental mishap, but it can even be regarded as preferable to actual success, on the ground that failure offers a wider basis for sanctification than success. No doctrine is more eminently in harmony with the teaching of the Gospels than the primacy of humility and suffering. There can be no possible doubt but that Christ took the road of abnegation, detachment and renunciation, and that his disciples must follow him. The road along which his Kingdom makes progress is the way of relinquishment, of blood and tears—the way of the Cross. It is thus, as though through a painful metamorphosis—a whole life being born from a whole death—that the divine cosmos germinates from the ruins of the old earth.

This can mean only one thing, that Revelation satisfies the *form* of our cosmic aspirations by offering them an unhoped-for entry into a world that is endowed with entirely new and ideal properties, but at the same time it does, in fact, bitterly disappoint our thirst for the Absolute, by affirming that the initial *object* of its ardent desire is secondary, useless and even damnable. The supernatural organism—and the divine Kingdom—develop *through* human progress, and at the same time independently of it or, what is much more disconcerting, *in rupture* with it. In

---

[9] The problem treated here, of the Christian value of temporal action, was later to be one of the basic themes of *Le Milieu Divin*. It is, one might say, the transposition into an evolving universe of the classic notion of the 'duty of state'.

consequence, they tarnish the flower of progress, or kill it completely. Whether the terrestrial world *achieves its success, or whether it ends in failure*, I shall *equally well* attain the term of my own development—even more certainly, maybe, if failure is the answer. This is how things appear to be ordered: shocking to the unbeliever, and disconcerting for the Christian, too, since the latter is unwilling to abandon his hope of contributing through the work he does as a man and through his material conquests to the building up of some κτῆμα ἐς ἀεί.

If only such a Christian could believe that it was only his sensibility that was affected, if only he could say to himself that his distress was simply a nostalgia for the terrestrial horizons to which his soul is attached, as one is attached to the walls and familiar sounds of the old home one first knew—in that case he would cheerfully make the sacrifice asked of him. Obedient to the stern laws that govern all Becoming, he would have the strength, in order to rise higher, to say goodbye to lower and more easily tapped sources of pleasure. Unhappily, however, his anguish lies deeper. It is not simply the heart that suffers and protests, it is the mind that cannot understand.

The mind cannot see that there can be a grave conflict in the eminently harmonious and comprehensive work of sanctification, that a deep rift can open up between heaven's design and the earth's most noble ambitions. Christ, it is true, cursed the world . . . but his curse fell on the self-sufficing world, the indolent pleasure-seeking world, and not on the world that works and raises itself to greater perfection—on the world of selfish enjoyment, and not on the world of disinterested effort. The latter carries further the Creator's impulse and so cannot merit God's hatred; it lives and progresses, without any doubt, in faith in a future that is immanent in it. Of the two or three natural dogmas that mankind, after long centuries of debate and after ceaseless critical examination, is now definitely establishing, the most categorical and the dearest to us is certainly that of the infinite value of the universe and its inexhaustible store of richness. 'Our world contains within itself a mysterious promise of the future, implicit in its natural evolution.' When the newborn mind surveys the grandeurs of the cosmos, those are the first words it falters; and that is the final assertion of the scientist as he closes his eyes, heavy and weary from having seen so much that he could not express.

Supposing, then, that I, in the name, I claim, of my religion, am so bold as to snap my fingers at this great hope which is the idol of my generation, what words shall I use if I am to be understood by nine-tenths of my fellow-men? What a pitiful figure shall I cut besides those men who fight so fiercely for life, whose bold persistence, again and again *condemned a priori* though it be by a certain school of knowledge or of prayer that unenterprisingly refuses to be committed, *invariably ends* in bringing about the triumph of *human* science and of *human* power? With men all around me, I shall be an isolated individual, an eccentric, a deserter, rapidly diverging from the only truly active and living branch of mankind. I shall be degraded, less than a man, working without conviction, or ardour or love.

I still, it is true, have this resource (and it is a duty, too), to co-operate in the world's temporal progress 'in order to do the Will of God', 'to exalt the Church', 'to confound the unbelievers'. But these various motives are terribly uninspiring, distant, and indirect compared with the sharp spur so urgently applied by the necessity '*to succeed*' in order '*to be*'. It is all very well to point out to me that there is a divine precept to make the earth bear fruit, but if you then go on immediately to add that the fruits my labours should produce are *in themselves* worthless and perishable, that the world has been given to me, as the wheel to the caged squirrel, in order to keep me busy *in vacuo*, what fire can you expect to animate my good will? If I am to devote myself ardently and sincerely to the work of the cosmos, if I am to be able to compete on equal terms with the children of the earth, I must be convinced not only of the merit of what I do but of its value. I must believe in what I am doing.

And in fact, whether I want to or not, I do so believe. When I am working in a laboratory, I believe in science. When I am fired by enthusiasm for a war between two cultures, I believe in a superman, and I am grateful to God for making it possible for me to expose myself to a ghastly death in order to win the day for an ideal of civilization. And in so believing, I do not feel that

I am denying my faith in Christ or in any way detracting from the absolute love I have sworn to him. On the contrary, I feel that the more I devote myself in some way to the interests of the earth in its highest form, the more I belong to God.

That I should feel this so strongly can only mean that, in spite of any misinterpretation of words or principles, there can be a reconciliation between cosmic love of the world and heavenly love of God. In my own action and in that of all Christians, through the harmonious collaboration of nature and grace, the cult of progress and the passion for the glory of God are *in actual fact* reconciled. There must, then, be a formula for expressing this rationally. Somewhere *there must be a standpoint* from which Christ and the earth can be so situated in relation to one another that it is impossible for me to possess the one without embracing the other, to be in communion with the one without being absorbed into the other, to be absolutely Christian without being desperately human.

Such a standpoint may be found in the domain of the great unexplored Mystery, wherein the life of Christ mingles with the life-blood of evolution.

IV

Communion with God through Earth

A: THE COSMIC CHRIST

By grace, Jesus Christ is united to all sanctified souls, and since the bonds that link souls to him in one single hallowed mass end in Him and meet in Him, and hold together by Him, it is He who reigns and He who lives; the whole body is His in its entirety. Souls, however, are not a group of isolated monads. As the 'cosmic view' specifically shows us, they make up one single whole with the universe, consolidated by life and matter. Christ, therefore, cannot confine his body to some periphery drawn within things; though he came primarily, and in fact exclusively, for souls, he could bring them together and give them life only by assuming and animating, with them, all the rest of the world; through his Incarnation he entered not only into mankind but also into the universe that bears mankind—and this he did, not simply in the capacity of an element associated with it, but with the dignity and function of directive principle, of centre upon which every form of love and every affinity converge. Mysterious and vast though the mystical Body already be, it does not, accordingly, exhaust the immense and bountiful integrity of the Word made Flesh. Christ has a *cosmic Body* that extends throughout the whole universe: such is the final proposition to be borne in mind. '*Qui potest capere, capiat*'.

For all its apparent modernity, this Gospel of the cosmic Christ, in which the salvation of our own times may very well lie, is indeed the word handed down from heaven to our forefathers, it is the new treasure stored, with foresight, side by side with the ancient riches. If we read Scripture with openness and breadth of mind, if we reject the timid interpretations of the narrow common-sense that is ready to take the words of Consecration literally (because faith obliges us to do so) but in all other contexts looks for the meaning with the least impact, we shall find that it speaks in categorical terms. The Incarnation is a making new, a restoration, of *all* the universe's forces and powers; Christ is the Instrument, the Centre, the End, of the *whole* of animate and material creation; through Him, *everything* is created, sanctified, and vivified. This is the constant and general teaching of St John and St Paul (that most 'cosmic' of sacred writers), and it has passed into the most solemn formulas of the Liturgy: and yet we repeat it, and generations to come will go on repeating it, without ever being able to grasp or appreciate its profound and mysterious significance, bound up as it is with understanding of the universe.

With the origin of all things, there began an advent of recollection and work in the course of which the forces of determinism, obediently and lovingly, lent themselves and directed themselves in the preparation of a Fruit that exceeded all hope and yet was awaited. The world's energies and substances—so harmoniously adapted and controlled that the supreme Transcendent would seem to germinate entirely from their immanence —concentrated and were purified in the stock of Jesse; from their accumulated and distilled treasures they produced the glittering gem of matter, the Pearl of the Cosmos, and the link with the incarnate personal Absolute—the Blessed Virgin Mary, Queen and Mother of all things, the true Demeter . . . and when the day of the Virgin came to pass, then the final purpose of the universe, deep-rooted and gratuitous, was suddenly made clear: since the days when the first breath of individualization passed over the expanse of the *Supreme Centre here below* so that in it could be seen the ripple of the smile of the original monads, all things were moving towards the Child born of Woman.

And since Christ was born, and ceased to grow, and died, *everything has continued in motion because he has not yet attained the fullness of his form.* He has not gathered about Him the last folds of the garment of flesh and love woven for him by his faithful. *The mystical Christ has not reached the peak of his growth—nor, therefore, has the cosmic Christ.* Of both we may say that *they are* and at the same time *are becoming*: and it is in the continuation of this engendering that there lies the ultimate driving force behind all created activity. By the Incarnation, which redeemed man, the very Becoming of the Universe, too, has been transformed. Christ is the term *of even the natural* evolution of living beings;[10] evolution is holy. There we have *the truth that makes free*, the divinely prepared cure for faithful but ardently moved minds that suffer because they cannot reconcile in themselves two almost equally imperative and vital impulses, faith in the world and faith in God.

[10] Once the universe (nature) is an evolution, we may say with regard to evolution what St Thomas, speaking of the supernatural, said with regard to nature: *Non est aliquid naturae, sed naturae finis*—it is not something that belongs to nature, but nature's (final) end.

B: THE HOLINESS OF EVOLUTION

1. *The Hand of God upon Us.* 'The world is still being created, and it is Christ who is reaching his fulfilment in it'. When I had heard and understood that saying, I looked around and I saw, as though in an ecstasy, that *through all nature I was immersed in God*. The whole inextricably tangled and compressive network of material interconnexions, the whole *plexus* of fundamental currents once again confronted me, just as it did when first my eyes were opened; but now they were animated and transfigured, for their dominance, their charm and their appeal, all beyond number or measure, appeared to me in a glow of illumination and I saw them hallowed and divinized in both their operation and their future. 'God is everywhere', St Angela of Foligno said, 'God is everywhere'.

During the godless crisis into which I was flung by my initiation into the cosmos, after the first revelation of my involvement in the world and of my being carried along by it, I relaxed in a sort of sensual abandonment, the instinctive reaction of an autonomy that is exhausted by its own limitations and impotence. Unhappily, the Divinity that I had then thought to discern, was a temptress, bringing dissolution in her train; her alluring face masked a lack of thought and an empty heart.

Now, I am coming again to see the possibility of allowing myself to follow my first impulse without any danger of diminishing my personality or of finding that what I am grasping is a phantom. Every exhalation that passes through me, envelops me or captivates me, emanates, without any doubt, from the heart of God; like a subtle and essential energy, it transmits the pulsations of God's will. Every encounter that brings me a caress, that spurs me on, that comes as a shock to me, that bruises or breaks me, is a contact with the hand of God, which assumes countless forms and yet always commands our worship. Every element of which I am made up is an overflow from God. When I surrender myself to the embrace of the visible and tangible universe, I am able to be in communion with the invisible that purifies, and to incorporate myself in the Spirit without blemish.

God is vibrant in the ether; and through the ether he makes his way into the very marrow of my material substance. Through Him, all bodies come together, exert influence upon one another and sustain one another in the unity of the all-embracing sphere, the confines of whose surface outrun our imagination.

God is at work within life. He helps it, raises it up, gives it the impulse that drives it along, the appetite that attracts it, the growth that transforms it. I can feel God, touch Him, 'live' Him in the deep biological current that runs through my soul and carries it with it.

God shines through and is personified in mankind. It is He to whom I lend a hand in the person of my fellow-man; it is His voice I hear when orders come to me from those who have authority over me—and again, as though in a further zone of matter, I meet and am subject to the dominating and penetrating contact of His hand at the higher level of collective and social energies.

The deeper I descend into myself, the more I find God at the heart of my being; the more I multiply the links that attach me to things, the more closely does He hold me—the God who pursues in me the task, as endless as the whole sum of centuries, of the Incarnation of his Son.

Blessed passivities that intertwine me through every fibre of my body and my soul; hallowed life, hallowed matter, through whom, at the same time as through grace, I am in communion with the genesis of Christ since, when I obediently lose myself in your vast folds, I am immersed in God's creative action, whose Hand has never ceased, from the beginning of time, to mould the human clay that is destined to constitute the Body of his Son— to your sovereign power I swear allegiance; I surrender myself to you, I take you to myself, I give you my love. I am happy that Another should lead me and make me go whither my own will would not take me. I bless the vicissitudes, the good fortune, the misadventures of my career. I bless my own character, my virtues, my faults . . . my blemishes. I love my own self, in the form in which it was given to me and in the form in which my destiny moulds me. What is more, I strive to guess and anticipate the lightest breezes that call to me, so that I may spread my sails more widely to them. I would have my soul become a monad, flexible and obedient, transparent to the Will of God with which nature is charged and impregnated through and through.

. . . And in this first basic vision we begin to see how the Kingdom of God and cosmic love may be reconciled: the bosom of Mother Earth is in some way the bosom of God.

2. *The Wrestling with the Angel.* We are not, however, simply nurslings rocked and suckled by Γαῖα μητήρ, Mother Earth. Like children who have grown up, we must learn to walk by ourselves and give active help to the mother who bore us. If, then, we make up our minds to accept wholeheartedly the manifestations of the divine will registered in the laws of nature, our obedience must make us throw ourselves into positive effort, our cult of passivities must ultimately be transformed into a passion for work. What, we now see, we have to do is not simply to forward a human task but, in some way, to bring Christ to completion; we must, therefore, devote ourselves with still more ardour, even in the natural domain, to the cultivation of the world.

The Revelation of the cosmic Christ had made our hearts more vividly conscious of how much we are bound up with our contact with things. Now, it is with added urgency that there echoes in our ears the Voice that summons us to master the secrets and energies of the universe and to dominate it. *If the Kingdom of God is to come about, man must win the sovereignty of the earth.*

To establish the truth of this statement it would not, strictly speaking, be essential to define in what way the world's progress towards perfection, whether natural or achieved through human skill, can truly contribute to the plenitude of Christ. Since immanent progress is the natural Soul of the cosmos, and since the cosmos is centred on Christ, it must be accepted as proved that, in one way or another, collaboration with the development of the cosmos holds an essential and prime position among the duties of the Christian. It is in one single movement that nature grows in beauty and the Body of Christ reaches its full development.

It is, nevertheless, essential to the precision of our work and the delight we take in it, that we should try to define more exactly some of the factors responsible for this coincidence and some of the lines along which it runs. We must find out what can be the absolute residual elements in the cosmos which are destined to be incorporated in the celestial edifice; in what way the segregation of the elect into a hallowed mass may be influenced by the discoveries of pure science, of physics or history; and how, apart from the growth of supernatural merits, Christ is realized in Evolution.

A first answer, very modest and yet, if fully understood, one of urgent importance, is as follows: more than any other man, the Christian is attached to the work of the cosmos, in as much as that work is necessary *if the world is to endure*. Let us, for a moment, put it at the lowest. Let us admit that in itself the material, biological and social stock on which individuals mature, is liable to wither away entirely. Let us admit, too, that its fruits must continue indefinitely to be produced in a similar form common to all, no profound transformation having henceforth the power to introduce any variation into the human species. In that case the cosmos has no value other than that of a seed-bed or training ground in which, through scientific examination and contemplation of created beings, the soul, 'in a practice run' improves and sharpens its faculties, and uses lower objects to learn how to choose and love. But even so, this stock, this centre of culture, must endure and remain fresh and green as long as Heaven continues to call for saints; and this it cannot do without great heat and great tension. Like every moving body, the world holds together only through its driving force and momentum. Were the multitude of monads it contains to check the ferment of their activities, their industry and their natural exploration, the world would crash like an aircraft whose engines fail. We Christians sometimes ask ourselves anxiously what good purpose is served by our long spells of laboratory work, our endless digging into everything that conceals a mystery. We should take comfort. We are exhausting ourselves in *at least keeping the earth going* until the Body of Christ is consummated.

In truth, however, it would not be enough to ensure the harmony of creation and to encourage us to continue our efforts, if the useful purpose served by the natural products of our labours were no more than this work of maintenance. Let us admit, again, that, in its stock, the cosmos can perish, leaving no residue. Who can prove to us that the immortal persons, detached from it in the course of centuries, are not subject to some absolute natural development, that the original small, tart, berries will not be succeeded by plumper and more delightful fruit? Man, through his spiritual soul, steps up into a new ontological and biological level. Who can assure us that no slope rises up from that level, giving access to modes of life we have never dreamt of? Natural evolution, we were saying, seems now to be fully occupied with what concerns the soul. From being organic and predominantly determined it has become predominantly psychological and conscious; but it is not dead, nor has its reach even been shortened. There are some particularly ancient psychic elements, such as the mutual love of man and woman, in which we can already appreciate the width and richness, the complexity and purity, which the work of time has succeeded in giving to the primitive kernel of a feeling that was instinct with brutish sensation . . . Who knows *what astonishing species and natural gradations* of soul are even now being produced by the persevering effort of science, of moral and social systems—without which the beauty and perfection of the mystical Body would never be realized?

Supposing we carry our human ambitions to their furthest limit: hitherto we have refused to admit that anything absolute in the cosmic stock, from which mature souls are detached, will endure. What pusillanimity of concept made us do so, what right had we to? In its dogmas and sacraments, the whole economy of the Church teaches us respect for matter and insists on its value. Christ wished to assume, and had to assume, a real flesh. He sanctifies human flesh by a specific contact. He makes ready, physically, its Resurrection. In the Christian concept, then, *matter retains its cosmic role as the basis, lower in order but primordial and essential, of union*; and, by assimilation to the Body of Christ, some part of matter is destined to pass into the foundations and walls of the heavenly Jerusalem. Whence, then, will be drawn this privileged and chosen matter which is to serve the new earth? Are we to see in it no more than a by-product of sanctification, developed by a reflux of grace upon the perishable envelope of souls? Maybe. But why, *which is more natural,* should not the purified substance of risen organisms owe some part of its perfections to the accumulated co-operative efforts of progress and evolution? The cosmic mind, although it cannot prove it to itself, is deeply attached to this hope, which gives it the joy of feeling that there is an incorruptible element in even the terrestrial side of its works. By thus allowing nature to take a further step forward it at least achieves a result that is worth the work put into it. The same result could no doubt have been achieved by a godless man, but what does that matter? The unconscious does indeed collaborate with life. From another point of view, philanthropy, which is an entirely natural and secular virtue, can readily be transformed in its entirety, both acts and object, into divine charity. In the same way, if *concern for progress* and the *cult of the earth,* are given as their final end the fulfilment of Christ, why should not they be transformed into a *great virtue,* as yet unnamed, which would be *the widest form of the love of God, found and served in creation?*

In virtue, therefore, of his faith, the Christian is justified in claiming a place among those who work for the greatest advancement of the earth; and the soul he brings to that work will be ablaze with the fire that inspires the conqueror. To the Christian, too, for all his renunciation and detachment and humility, it is of vital importance, *it is a matter of life or death,* that the world should succeed in its enterprise, even in its temporal enterprise. Only a moment ago the believer saw in Nature above all the enveloping arms of God, his creative Hands that mould . . . Now he combines the spirit of abandonment with the spirit of domination, and in order to obey he strips for the fight; although in his heart he secretly bows down before matter, he engages it in a duel that will continue until the consummation of all time—*Jacob's wholehearted struggle against a grip that he worships.*

3. *The Meaning of the Cross.* A price has to be paid for the struggle. The earth groans in travail with Christ. *Omnis creatura*

ingemiscit et parturit—like a wagon that creaks and grinds, progress advances painfully, bruised and tearful.

One might at first be deceived by the mistaken views of pagan pantheism and believe that to adhere to the cosmic doctrine is simply to pass from a narrow and commonplace self-love to a wider and more subtle egotism—a neat way of encompassing more enjoyment with less risk. Nothing could be less true.

If he is to act in conformity with his new ideal, the man who has determined to admit love of the world and its cares into his interior life finds that he has to accept *a supreme renunciation*. He has sworn to seek for himself outside himself, in other words to love the world better than himself. He will now have to realize what this noble ambition will cost him.

In the first place he must, in any case, work to drive things, and his own being, up the steep slope of liberation and purification, he must discipline or conquer the hostile forces of matter, of the forest and of the heart—he must bring about the victory of duty over attraction, of the spiritual over the senses, of good over evil . . . The multitude of the dead cry out to him not to weaken, and from the depths of the future those who are waiting for their turn to be born stretch out their arms to him and beg him to build for them a loftier nest, warmer and brighter.

He may perhaps have to accept the role of the imperceptible atom which loyally, but without honour, carries out the obscure function for which it exists, to serve the well-being and balance of the Whole. He must agree to be, some day, the fragment of steel on the surface of the blade that flies off as soon as a blow is struck, the soldier in the first wave of the attack, *the outer surface, made use of and sacrificed, of the cosmos in activity*.

He must often, unhappily, resign himself to *not being made use of*, to disappearing without having been able to contribute his effort, or say what *he* has to say—to quitting life with a soul tense with all that adverse circumstances have not allowed him to exteriorize.

He must even (and this is harder to bear than any stifling repression or obscurity) have to admit to himself that he is *unusable* and *ineffectual*.

In an organism as vast as the universe any amount of goodwill
and countless resources remain unused, and a host of failures is
the price that has to be paid for a few successes. The obscure, the
useless, the failures, should take joy in the superiority of the
others whose triumph they lend support to or pay for. All
this is indeed hard. The world, and subjection to the world, and
the duty of serving the world, are hard to bear, like a cross; and
it was *to force us to believe this* that Christ wished, overlooking all
the highways of the earth, to rise up in the form of the Crucifix,
the symbol in which every man could recognize his own true
image.

We should like to be able to doubt this, to hope that suffering
and wickedness are transitory conditions of Life, to be eliminated
some day by science and civilization; but we must be more
realistic and have the courage to look existence in the face. The
more subtle and complex mankind becomes, the more numerous
the chances of disorder and the greater their gravity; for one
cannot build up a mountain without digging a great pit, and
every energy has equal power for good and for evil. Everything
that *becomes* suffers or sins. The truth about our position in this
world is that *in it we are on a Cross*.

Now, Christ did not wish his distressful figure to be no more
than a warning permanently dominating the world. On Calvary
He is still, and primarily, *the centre* on which all earthly sufferings
converge and in which they are *all assuaged*. We have very little
evidence about the way Our Lord *tests* His mystical Body, in
order to take delight in it, but we can get some idea of how he
can gather to himself its sufferings; and the only way, even, we
can appreciate the immensity of his Agony is to see in it an
anguish that reflects every anguish ever experienced, a 'cosmic'
suffering. During his Passion, Christ felt that he bore upon his
soul, alone and battered, the weight of all human sorrows—in a
fantastic synthesis no words can express. All these he took to
himself, and all these he suffered.

Further, by admitting them into the domain of his consciousness, he transfigured them. Without Christ, suffering and sin
would be the earth's 'slag-heap'. The waste-products of the
world's activities would pile up into a mountain of laborious

effort, efforts that failed, efforts that had been 'suppressed'. Through the virtue of the Cross this great mass of débris has become a store of treasure: man has understood that the most effective means of progress is to make use of suffering, ghastly and revolting though it be.[11]

The Christian experiences suffering just as other men do. As others, so must he do his best to lessen and alleviate it, not only by humble prayer but also through the efforts of an industrious and self-confident Science; but when the time comes when suffering is inevitable, then he puts it to good use. There is a wonderful compensation by which physical evil, if humbly accepted, conquers moral evil. In accordance with definable psychological laws, it purifies the soul, spurs it on and detaches it. Finally, acting as a sacrament acts, it effects a mysterious union between the faithful soul and the suffering Christ.

If it is undertaken first in a disposition of pliant surrender, and continued in a spirit of conquest, the pursuit of Christ in the world culminates logically in an impassioned enfolding, heavy with sorrow, in the arms of the Cross. Eagerly and wholeheartedly, the soul has offered and surrendered itself to all the great currents of nature. When it reaches the term of all that it has gone through and when at long last it can see things with a mature eye, it realizes that no work is more effective or brings greater peace than to gather together, in order to soothe it and offer it to God, the suffering of the world; no attitude allows the soul to expand more freely, than to open itself, generously and tenderly—with and in Christ—to *sympathy with all suffering*, to '*cosmic compassion*'.

4. *The Place of Hell.* By involving himself in evolution, Christ

[11] This new approach would seem to derive, in the first place, from the discovery that the universe is an evolution. So long as it was thought to be invariable ('What has been will be', 'There is nothing new under the sun') the duty of state appeared to be static, and, since it is often unpleasant, it could be regarded as primarily an expiation. As soon, however, as we become aware of an evolution, a development that tends to depend more and more upon ourselves, then an aspect of effort, of conquest and construction enters into the duty of state. It can become an inspiration, the Christian seeing it as realizing a necessary condition for the Kingdom of God.

has brought its resources and mechanism to their acme of perfection and fruitfulness. Everything, everything without exception, even suffering and misfortune, can, in the order of salvation, be of service to the monad of good will. *Omnia cooperantur in bonum*—'all things work together for good'.

Following the laws that govern every process of becoming, and in particular every form of segregation, the Genesis of the mystical and cosmic Body, though theoretically possible without any loss, is yet accompanied, in fact, by *a dissipation of energy and life* for which countless *mortal and venial faults* are responsible. Why must this be so?

What is more, the sinister and frightening *loss of the damned*—a permanent loss, mark you—recurs—freely, on our side, and yet with all *the marks of an organic inevitability*. Why, again, must this be so?

The man who has strengthened and trained his powers of insight in his intuition of the cosmos, of its global harmony and its demands, may not be able, it is true, to answer those questions; but it will be no shock to him to find that here, as elsewhere, a hell is the natural corollary of heaven, and he will learn to dread it.

Let us pray:
Lord Jesus Christ, you truly contain within your gentleness, within your humanity, all the unyielding immensity and grandeur of the world. And it is because of this, it is because there exists in you this ineffable synthesis of what our human thought and experience would never have dared join together in order to adore them—element and totality, the one and the many, mind and matter, the infinite and the personal; it is because of the indefinable contours which this complexity gives to your appearance and to your activity, that my heart, enamoured of cosmic reality, gives itself passionately to you.

I love you, Lord Jesus, because of the multitude who shelter within you and whom, if one clings closely to you, one can hear with all the other beings murmuring, praying, weeping. . . .

I love you because of the transcendent and inexorable fixity of your purposes, which causes your sweet friendship to be coloured by an intransigent determinism and to gather us all ruthlessly into the folds of its will.

I love you as the source, the activating and life-giving ambience, the term and consummation, of the world, even of the natural world, and of its process of becoming.

You the Centre at which all things meet and which stretches out over all things so as to draw them back into itself: I love you for the extensions of your body and soul to the farthest corners of creation through grace, through life, and through matter.

Lord Jesus, you who are as gentle as the human heart, as fiery as the forces of nature, as intimate as life itself, you in whom I can melt away and with whom I must have mastery and freedom: I love you as a world, as *this* world which has captivated my heart; and it is you, I now realize, that my brother-men, even those who do not believe, sense and seek throughout the magic immensities of the cosmos.

Lord Jesus, you are the centre towards which all things are moving: if it be possible, make a place for us all in the company of those elect and holy ones whom your loving care has liberated one by one from the chaos of our present existence and who now are being slowly incorporated into you in the unity of the new earth.

To live the cosmic life is to live dominated by the consciousness that one is an atom in the body of the mystical and cosmic Christ. The man who so lives dismisses as irrelevant a host of preoccupations that absorb the interest of other men: his life is projected further, and his heart more widely receptive.

There you have my intellectual testament.

24 April 1916. Easter Week.
Fort-Mardik (Dunkirk).

The following passage is written on a loose sheet attached to the manuscript notebook:

Nota. Cosmic Life describes the aspirations and formulates the practical activities of a *concrete life*. If one tries to bring out the presuppositions and principles it is based on, one finds that it introduces a completely new orientation into Christian ascetical teaching.

In 'classical' interpretations, suffering is *first and foremost a punishment, an expiation*; its effectiveness is that of a sacrifice: it is born of a *sin*, and makes reparation for the sin. It is good to suffer, in order to master oneself, conquer and free oneself.

In contrast with this view, suffering, according to the general line followed by *Cosmic Life* and the ideas it puts forward, is primarily the consequence of a *work of development* and the price that has to be paid for it. Its effectiveness is that of *an effort*. Physical and moral evil *are produced by the process of Becoming*: everything that evolves has its own sufferings and commits its own faults. The Cross is the symbol of *the arduous labour of Evolution*—rather than the symbol of *expiation*.

These two points of view can obviously be reconciled, if, for example, we admit that the natural consequence of the Fall of Man was to return Mankind to its connatural setting of progress and work 'by the sweat of its brow'. (And, in that case, it is noteworthy that, as far as appearances go, the Fall leaves no mark at all, since its visible penalty is contained in Evolution, with *Expiation* coinciding with Work.)

. . . Even so, there is a great difference of emphasis between *expiatory ascesis* and the *ascesis underlying 'cosmic life'*.

. . . And I would have been dishonest not to point this out.

17 May 1916

Mastery of the World and the Kingdom of God

The first distinct reference to the subject-matter of this essay occurs in a letter from Père Teilhard to his cousin, Mlle Marguerite Teillard-Chambon, dated 4 August 1916:

'*It seemed to me, in support of my theories of Christian co-operation with progress, that there was a real law or natural duty of pursuing research to the very end. Don't you agree that it's a matter of loyalty and "conscience" to strive to extract from the world all that this world can hold of truth and energy?* There must be nothing *in the direction of more-being that remains* unattempted. *Heaven would have us help ourselves (help it). It seems to me impossible to concede that revelation should have come to release us from the duty of* pursuit; *and in the grave defect (or rather temptation) of "extrinsicism" from which churchmen suffer (in wanting to make theological and* a priori *judgments about all reality) I see as much laziness as complacency. It's not only from cosmic enthusiasm but also as a* strict natural moral duty *that we must strive to see* more clearly, *and thus act more effectively. Under pain of sin, we must try every road . . .* (plumb all things, even since the coming of our Lord).'

Some days later, he was distressed and upset by the death of his friend Pierre Boussac, who had been hit in the back by a shell splinter. He wrote, again to his cousin, on 8 September:

'*At first I thought that my reaction would be an embittered rejection of all that I had "worshipped". Instead of working to improve things in the world and extend its conquests (in the spirit you know) would it not be better to abandon to its own sort of suicide this ridiculous world that destroys its finest products, and then, devoting one's mind entirely to supernatural things, sing a dirge over the ruins of all that here below seems beautiful and precious? . . . But then I pulled myself together. I reflected that God constantly, even when it's a matter of what are manifestly most saintly undertakings, allows the premature disappearance of the instruments best fitted to achieve his glory. I told myself that man's labour, whatever form it may take, must be essentially tenacious, patient, gentle, . . . and I told myself that I would carry on.'*

In the same letter he says that he has 'not yet got down to writing a draft':

'*There'll be a first chapter which I'll probably do separately, on "the duty of research". I think that man has a fundamental obligation to extract from himself and from the earth all that it can give; and this obligation is all the more imperative in that we are absolutely ignorant of what limits—they may still be very distant—God has imposed on our natural understanding and power.*'[1]

Père Teilhard's regiment was billeted at that time in Nant-le-Grand, a little village in the Meuse, south of Verdun, in a 'very damp, wooded, valley'. It was there that he wrote 'Mastery of the World and the Kingdom of God', which he finished on September 20th.

---

[1] 'Making of a Mind', pp. 116, 123–124, 126.

MASTERY OF THE WORLD
AND THE KINGDOM OF GOD

Man lives both by bread and by the Word of God

Introduction

I have already tried, in writing *Cosmic Life*, to point out that a legitimate reconciliation can be effected between Christianity and the world, on the basis of an honest pursuit of progress, founded on conviction, and a wholehearted sharing in a certain faith in life and the value of evolution.

In that essay I pictured the soul, aroused to a passion for extra-individual and cosmic realities, flinging itself upon the universe in the whole of which it hears the summons of a Godhead; and I described how, when the soul grasps it, the Absolute is seen to be and assumes the form of a movement of ascent and segregation, made up of bold conquest, intensive socialization, and constant detachment. This movement goes on until the truth come down from heaven meets the truth developed on earth and synthesizes all the world's hopes in the blessed reality of Christ, whose Body is the centre of elect life.

What I wrote was, to be exact, the story of a conversion.

What I now wish to do is to return to that idea of a legitimate and indispensable reconciliation of mankind's natural and super-natural evolution, and treat it more objectively, more coolly and more systematically. Every man who is anxious to introduce unity into his life must squarely face, and openly proclaim, these two facts: first, that a too 'detached' Christianity or an exclusively secular cult of the world, is incapable of giving the heart of man all the nourishment it requires, or of existing in isolation; and secondly, that both, on the other hand, are manifestly well fitted to complete one another, and so enable our action to put out its full effort in carrying out its logical purpose.

I wish to prove that the proper balance of man's development is not to be found exclusively either in obedience to terrestrial laws and impulses, or in adhering to dogmas and a spirit revealed to us by our Heavenly Father, but in an effort towards God that forces the blood through every single vein in the universe without exception. It is in order to prove this that I am undertaking this study, for the glory of God,[2] for peace, unity, and the freedom of minds of good will.

(Feast of the Seven Sorrows of Our Lady)
Nant-le-Grand (Meuse)
15 September 1916

I

The Two Halves of Truth

1. *The Service of the Earth.* No one can observe, over a sufficient length of time, the activity of the mass of mankind—expressed in its appetites, in the things it takes pleasure in, in the things it worships, in its conquests—without being astounded by the extraordinary depth and power of the changes he notices. From time to time a great common aspiration comes to the surface from roots that lie deep down in mankind. At a given moment, the whole mass of souls thrills as it opens its eyes to a new light. Their multitude, for all its diversity, forms one whole in the unanimous and undisputed acceptance of a truth that is spontaneously taken as established; and, in one body, they set out together as though to find a new Holy Grail.

Thus we find the humanists and scientists of the Renaissance

---

[2] 'For the glory of God'. It was again 'the greater glory of God' he was to invoke in March 1955, some days before his death, in his *Recherche, Travail, et Adoration*.

possessed by an irresistible passion for nature, new-found and loved to distraction. Later, an almost frenzied sense of exaltation brings tears to the eyes of our forefathers at the mere mention of the words, taken to heart once and for ever more, liberty and fraternity. Later again, only yesterday, a reasoned conviction of man's power, combined with a keen intuition of the universal process of becoming, inflexibly determined the advance of progress in the direction of mastery of the world. And now today, we see new currents of thought and new desires multiplying in every domain. In education, as in religious activities, there is a tendency to make progressively more allowance for the freedom of the individual, and this because there is a general awareness of the respect to which the unique and incommunicable development of every soul is entitled. In political and social affairs, the ideas of democracy and association are irresistibly making their way into the consciousness of the humblest worker. Class comes into conflict with class, in the search for a greater measure of justice. Nationalities seek to emerge, and are establishing themselves, cutting across the secondary accidents of political combinations; and at the same time, transcending existing frontiers, a start is being made in forging new links that nothing will henceforth be able to break. Meanwhile feminism has asserted itself among the claims both of masses and of an élite; and sooner or later woman will have to be given a generous place in the sun.

Minds that are exclusively accustomed to looking in everything for the rational explanation and the consciously appreciated causes, are at a loss when they are presented with these turbulent awakenings and obscure tendencies. At first, their curiosity is aroused, but they soon turn away, shocked or with a smile. They feel that such phenomena are too erratic to detain the historian, too wayward to merit the attention of the serious thinker; they should be classed among the unpredictable whims of chance or the superficial ups and downs of fashion. Such people understand nothing of the mystery of life.

On the other hand, let a man whom long acquaintance has made familiar with the sources of matter and energies and with their underlying currents, let him come along and observe these same phenomena: he no sooner looks at them than he is seized and held captive by an absorbing, almost religious, interest. The symptoms are so marked that he cannot be mistaken. This spontaneous and independent behaviour, this inexhaustible fertility, this iron hand that yet takes hold of living beings and cherishes them so gently, he has met these too often before to have any further doubt. It is, indeed, the mysterious Divinity that 'possesses' and stirs up nations at the turning-points of history; *it is* once again *that same Divinity, it is Evolution.*[3]

Since the time when, through the perfecting of the human brain, Spirit emerged within matter as its own master, it appeared as though Life's transforming effort had come to a halt or slowed down. Once the break-through had been made, there had been a drop in the pressure that kept organisms at boiling point, waiting and seeking for full consciousness. It could, indeed, be a fact that the world of living bodies, like that of the stars, is in process of becoming stabilized, but it does not follow that evolution is therefore dead. It still retains and continues its drive, under the perhaps solidified shell of our individual organs, animating and directing the subtle, fluid, substance of souls. In a process that is infinitely more varied and exciting to watch than that which earlier developed bones and tissue and nerves, *it is Spirit that is now evolving.*[4]

Carrying on from the transforming thrust that produced the successive series of animal forms, psychological evolution, as revealed to us by history's fresh starts and crises, still retains the features and habits that characterized the action of that force upon growing organisms.

The paths it follows are *unpredictable* and *instinctive*. No one can say whence its spirit will come, nor whither its breath will

[3] Cf. *Le Coeur de la Matière* (1950), first part, 3 (La découverte de l'Évolution): 'It was during my theology years, at Hastings, that there gradually grew in me—much less as an abstract notion than as a presence—to such a degree as to fill my whole spiritual horizon—the consciousness of a deep, ontological drift that embraced the whole of the Universe I lived in.'

[4] This idea is constantly found in later writings. See, in particular, 'The Formation of the Noosphere' (*Revue des Questions scientifiques*, Louvain, Jan. 1947, pp. 7–35), and 'The human rebound of evolution and its consequences' (*ibid*, 20 April 1948), in *The Future of Man*, pp. 155–84, and 196–213.

carry; and the most certain way of running athwart it is to try to anticipate or force it.

When it *emerges* it is still *incompletely formed*, driving before it a confusing mixture of good and evil. Its waters, working their way in secret underground, or lashing themselves into a storm, seem to be continually loaded with impurities and débris; sometimes, again, they overflow before they find their final bed, and wash away part of the established order. We cannot, therefore, judge this flood until it has settled down and is running clear. Only then can one see, and have to admit, that it is *infallible* in its advance. After each new crisis, mankind has to yield to the evidence that it has changed for the better and has made progress; for life, and life alone, knows what is best for its children, and, what is more, reality always follows the most favourable line of development.

Man's evolution, again, is *irreversible* in its conquests.[5] Once Spirit has opened its eyes to the light, it never loses sight of it. It holds on to what it has won, irrevocably incorporated into its own substance. Nothing, henceforth, can make it return to the illusions and dreams of its childhood, nor can anything divert it from the goal it has sensed.

And why? Because the current that carries souls along with it, like that which carries nature, is *irresistible*. No temporary embankment or dyke can hold it in check. It wears them down, makes its way around them, shatters them. Inevitably, in the end, it runs free. Make way for the growing earth!

If a man is faithfully seeking for truth and for a rule to govern his activity, what will he do when he finds his whole being held in the mighty grip of this higher force? He will surrender himself, abandon himself, actively, to the process of Becoming that is forced upon him through every fibre of his body and soul. *He will pledge himself to the service of the earth.*

[5] 'Irreversible' is a favourite word with Teilhard. *On the law of irreversibility in evolution* (1923), in *Vision of the Past*, p. 49. 'As soon as evolution reflects, it can neither accept nor carry itself farther, without recognizing that it is *irreversible*, that is to say immortal'. 'An irreversible ascent into the *Personal*' (*The human rebound of evolution*, 1947) in *The Future of Man*, Collins, London, and Harper and Row, New York, 1964, pp. 206-7. 'The irreversibility of Reflection' (*La Réflexion de l'Énergie*, 1952), etc.

Here, indeed, we have the great mystery, the great sense of inadequacy conveyed by the natural current of things. We feel that we are bound, by the most fundamental passivities of our being, to the duty of forwarding the evolution of institutions and ideas; and yet when our reason tries to justify to itself the command to work that it sees psychologically written into our nature, it finds itself at a loss, *presented*, to its astonishment, *with a void*.

If I am to take up, with faith and passion, the task of scientific conquest of the world, I must have a guarantee that *no sphere of foreseeable radius* limits the results I can expect from my efforts; for if such a limit exists, I imagine that I have already reached it, and my enthusiasm for the sacred task of research dries up at its source.

If, forgetful of self, I am to lend my freedom to the work that moral perfection and social improvement call for, I feel that I must, similarly, be able to anticipate with assurance a term to and a boundless recompense for my renunciation. A moral system (cf. Boutroux)[6] ceases to exist as soon as you remove from it its characteristic of pursuing an ideal, and reduce it to being a formula for 'living happily and peacefully in society'.

In other words, the immanent evolution of the world *can answer the demands and questions of reason—can be safe from the revolts of freedom*—can stand on its own feet, one might say, only if it offers the Spirit that is engendered by it an absolute and assured term to its further developments and to its servitude.

While evolution may tentatively imply the existence of this ideal term, and even hint at the road by which it is to come, it can put no name to it; it cannot give any exact definition of it.

Like an unfinished pyramid, rising step by step from its base, it lies open to infinity.

[6] Teilhard had just been reading, in a copy of the *Revue hebdomadaire* sent by his cousin, an article by Boutroux on freedom of conscience. It has, he writes, 'once again made me deeply aware of the necessity to reconcile, on the basis of a sincere love of natural progress, the claims and absolutes of believers and unbelievers'. He adds, criticizing a comment Boutroux made about religion, 'One can recognize, under this grossly erroneous expression, the fundamental mistrust of a faith that, in his view, deflowers the world by denying its evolution any absolute value'. (*Making of a Mind*, p. 121.)

Does this mean that there is some fault inherent in the construction of the universe and that the world, by having produced the Spirit that can sit in judgment of it, will die from an internal contradiction?

2. *Life in Heaven.* Far above terrestrial differences, far removed from the interminable conflicts of thought and the ephemeral combinations of the flesh, floats the World of Revelation. In that world, everything is stability, everything is clarity, in the sublime regions, closed to science, of final ends and real substance. God has spoken. His Word has come down upon the Spirit of Man; and forthwith all the countless multitudes of beings have taken on, in depth, their true and finally determined perspective, and their exact value.

God, the personal and loving Infinite, is the Source, the motive Force and the End of the Universe. The world emerged from the heart of his creative power, laden with rich seed. The world grew in stature, and sinned, and, even more wonderfully, was made new again. And now the souls of the just, the world's harvest ripened in the course of so many centuries, are being released from it to pile up, grain by grain, in the granaries of heaven, there to be incorporated, cell by cell, in the total Body of Christ. That is the plain truth. The world came from God, to return enriched and purified to God. Such is the design of the universe. To open wide our hearts to the love of the Being who animates every creature as he draws it to himself; jealously to shut out from our affections the transient passions of here below; to die that we may rise again—there we have the secret of life, simple and yet difficult, that our good will has to decipher.

The human soul, deeply moved by the harmony of this divine world, is vibrant with a *mystical ambition.* In the blessed intoxication of suddenly finding the universe it lives in transfigured, and carrying, perhaps, too far its interpretation of the mystery of Renunciation and the Cross, it has dreamed of losing no time in separating its course from that of nature. We must, the soul tells itself, forget the material universe and its painful advance towards an uncertain progress. We must break with its petty and lowly ideal. We must reject the vain figure of a superficial science; and then, when the fetters of matter have finally been broken, we must rise up to Heaven, borne on the wings of contempt of the world and contemplation of God. Before leaving this perishable world, Man sought to pitch his tent on the mountain of heavenly realities. He took refuge deep in the caves of the desert, or high on the pillar of the Stylites.

But, as time went by, *he grew hungry*, . . . he had forgotten that he still needed the nourishment of earthly bread . . . And when, that he might not succumb to starvation, he sought to put his hand again to the plough he had abandoned, he found that *his hand had lost its skill*, and *his heart its enthusiasm*.

No longer, alas, do we live in the days—if there ever were such days—when man's daily bread seemed to call for no more care than to gather the forest fruits or to toss the seed into a barely-scratched furrow! As the centuries roll on, the business of maintaining life becomes increasingly laborious and absorbing. The material economy of the human race already calls for immense effort. What, then, can we say if we reckon up the endless research and calculation required for the organization of social classes and their welfare? What of the perpetual effort demanded by the necessity—a vital necessity, moreover—to answer the questions that human reason is asking ever more insistently?

To nourish mankind, to enable it to survive and continue on its road in spite of the increasing complexity of its organization and needs, to ensure the maintenance of its physical welfare, to fuel the devouring furnace of its intellectual preoccupations, this is indeed a labour so vast that only those who have put some part of their faith and of their hope into it, only those who have sworn to love it with an unswerving love and to put all their fervour into it, will have the strength and drive to carry it through.

Now, can that man sincerely profess this faith, and hope, and love, who over-hastily dismisses nature, and claims to be so indifferent to the earth and so contemptuous of it that he lives among men as a stranger? Revelation, on which he seeks to base the substance of all his behaviour, throws light only on the further developments within things. Its commandments and counsels solve problems of a general order. It provides a basis and a goal for speculation, and breathes a Spirit into Action; but it *has nothing to say* about the nature of cosmic energies and the promises they hold, about details of politics and the social state, or about the definitive *forms* of thought and human organization. The man who looks for no more than Revelation remains lost in vagueness and uncertainty: and, what is an even more serious evil than such hesitations, he has *extinguished* in himself *the sacred fire of Research*. Small wonder, then, that the portion of field entrusted to him remains uncultivated, or barely scratched by the ploughshare, just enough to meet the requirements of a meagre crop.

This, moreover, is not all. In seeking to rise too rapidly and too high, man has perhaps found that there was a weakening in the very energies that he hoped to concentrate, too exclusively, on heaven. God has not seen fit to create in us a new and distinct centre of affection, through which we might love him. In accordance with the particular ordering of our world, in which *everything is made by the transformation of a pre-existing analogue*,[7] it seems evident that, initially, divine Charity exists in us simply as the flame, supernaturalized and purified, that is kindled at the prospect of the Earth's promises. It could never possibly persist in a heart that had ceased to be fired by the quickening contact of tangible realities. Great love of God normally presupposes the maintenance of a strong natural passion. If the tree that is deprived of the soil that nourishes it withers and dies, are we justified in hoping that grace will make it grow green again in order to graft itself onto it?

Theoretically—biologically, one might go so far as to say—

[7] Cf. *Le Phénomène Humain* (1928, unpublished): he speaks of 'an essential correction which must be applied to all our views whenever we are trying to follow any line of reality through a new circle of the universe. The world is transformed from one circle to the next. It experiences an internal enrichment and recasting. Each time, in consequence, it presents itself to us in a new state, in which the sum of its earlier properties is partly retained and partly converted into a new form.' Speaking of anthropocentrism, he writes in a letter of 29 April 1934, 'The whole difficulty lies in making "corrections by analogy". It's the old scholastic truth, given new youth in the perspective of Duration'. Cf. letter of 29 Oct. 1949: 'I believe that you can push the theory of Analogy further in an evolutionary universe than in an immobile world-structure' (To Père de Lubac).

there would be nothing surprising in the idea of a rupture—of a blessed divorce—between Christianity and the world. Since life is a perpetual wrenching of itself out of its state of rest, nothing would be more 'natural' than to meet a sacrifice, a supreme immolation, on the threshold of the new and definitive life. Unhappily, the facts will not allow it. Man cannot yet so abandon himself to God, so live in heaven, as to relieve himself of his connatural task; *nevertheless*, since the heavens have lain open, that task *may well seem to him irreparably tainted.*

Like an unfinished pyramid that remains hanging in emptiness from its apex, so life, if accepted in accordance with a certain absolute way of understanding Revelation, seems to lack any real base.

Does this mean—if we can conceive such an impossibility—that by making man have no stomach for a task that is essential to him, the divine illumination has introduced a contradiction into the heart of the masterpiece its power has created?

II

The Clash

Historically, through seeking each in isolation to govern the behavour of men, the two halves of truth have come into conflict. But it was some time before this happened.

For many centuries after the apostolic age—practically until the Renaissance—the duality of the two currents of life, the current that runs within the earth and that which comes down from heaven, remained blurred. *To all appearances, they ran in one stream*; for at that time man's evolution was going through a religious phase, and the Christian religion, for its part, had, as it happened, monopolized thought, the sciences and the arts, so completely that one might have said that they had become immobilized in its light.

Nevertheless, the time came when the autonomous pressure of natural aspirations made itself felt, and threatened to shatter the containing walls in which it was thought to be imprisoned. Heaven and earth had been blended together, human growth and religious perfection had been identified. The two specific movements could not be made to form one: an internal discord became apparent. This was *the break*.

Reacting against what it held to be an enslavement, the earth reviled the Church, and claimed the right to develop without any need of heaven, of its counsels or its help. This took the form first of naturalism and later of secularism. The Church, in turn, anathematized the world, and appeared to regard the work of Progress as diabolical.

And in consequence each of these two powers suffers cruelly from its isolation.[8]

For a moment, *the earth* believed that it could *forget* or *deny* the essential need for the infinite presupposed by the quest for truth or its practice. It was so absorbed by and took such delight in its earliest conquests, that at first it could only relax in amazement and feel that it lacked nothing more. When, however, its first enthusiasm for these new joys and for its own independence had worn off, the earth turned a critical eye on its works and sought to assess its hopes. It was then that the yawning void, deep within it, that calls out for the Absolute, seemed blacker than ever, and that it tried to *forge for itself some Divinity*, born or still to be born, whose glory would crown and illuminate the endless slope of evolution: omnipotent science, mankind, the superman. Idols all—and who, even among their most ardent devotees, would be so bold as to draw the exact features of any of them or wholeheartedly worship them?

In the domain of practical action and moral conduct, the disappointment and confusion are even more extreme. Not only does *reason find it impossible to choose* between the kindly doctrine of *charity*, that has compassion for the portionless, and the stern school of *might* that picks out the victors, not only can it not impress on men *the eminent value of virginity*, nor convince them of

[8] This is, of course, only an extremely simplified version of the historical picture.

the *duty of fecundity*—but, what is more, it realizes that it is incapable of finding a *natural basis for morality* itself. The imperative pronounced by its exponents is always an absolutely unqualified statement, or an expression of economic necessity. Man's autonomy then revolts against a duty that cannot justify itself rationally, and abandons itself to enjoyment and the line of least effort, or, perhaps, to violence and anarchy. The whole work of human development, the object of such wide adulation, seems as if it must disintegrate in a corruption for which there is no remedy.

At the same time religion, too, is bitterly aware of its impotence and defencelessness. Since it appeared to reject nature, it feels an alien body in mankind: it no longer enjoys the confidence of that lower, but so persuasive, life that continues to dominate the bodies and souls of its baptized children. Religion seeks to sanctify them and guard them jealously for itself alone, but they hear *another voice*, a winning voice that casts its spell over them, the voice of their first mother, the earth that suckled them. Religion is dimly conscious of this voice, and can even hear it; but because it *cannot understand* its language and its appeal, it mistrusts it and condemns it. Since it cannot silence the enchantress[9] it would like, at least, to take her place and *speak for her*. But what can it say with any truth or insight about a world that does not belong to it? The Church (since she did not need it) was not given a special sense of terrestrial life: and that is why, when her rulers have sought to monopolize the *whole* control of mankind and the *whole* of human knowledge, they have been obliged, deeply humiliating and mortifying though it be, to remain silent, or make mistakes, or drag unwillingly behind.

Too often, Christians have seemed to behave as though the universe around them were immobile.

'*E si muove*'.

Think of all the infantile maledictions pronounced by Churchmen against new ideas!

Think of all the avenues of enquiry that have at first been forbidden and later found to be rich in results!

[9] Cf. *Le Milieu Divin* (1927), p. 155: 'The Earth's enchantments can no longer do me harm'.

Think of all the futile subterfuges designed to make people believe that the Church was directing a movement by which it was, in fact, being forcibly dragged along!

In the field of evolution the Church certainly gives the impression of lagging behind, of allowing herself to be towed. And, in order to live the life of their own times, her bewildered children seem almost to be begging in the streets for crumbs of truth and practical knowledge.

When Christ's ardent disciples see this, they are overcome by a woeful amazement. And even when they are not spiritually impoverished and attenuated by an over-scrupulous isolation, their hearts suffer mortal agony at seeing their loved and admirable Mother so unjustly belittled and misunderstood.

III

Harmony

The time has come, as we can all see, at last to put together the broken pieces, to re-unite the complementary properties, to weld the apex of the pyramid to the base. Religion and evolution should neither be confused nor divorced. They are destined to form one single continuous organism, in which their respective lives prolong, are dependent on, and complete one another, without being identified or lost: the one offering an infinite ideal and immutable laws, and the other providing a focus of activity and a stuff that is essential to the transformation of beings in process of growth, Since it is in our age that the duality has become so markedly apparent, it is for us to effect the synthesis.

There can be no doubt about it: human progress cannot (on the ground of its autonomy, indisputable and legitimate though it is) be suspected of being a dangerous force—what force, indeed, is without its danger?—nor can it properly be condemned as a manifestation of evil and an incitement to it. It holds its essential place in the designs of providence. Does it not come to us winged and haloed like an angel, the humble brother of Revelation and, with Revelation, the messenger sent to guide us as we advance along the road of life?

The Church, then, must do more than tolerate it, and accept it, as an inevitable compulsion or a necessary stimulus. She must, as we anxiously wait for her to do, recognize it officially; she must adopt it in its principle (if not in all its methods); she must unreservedly encourage bold experiments and attempts made to open new roads. So long as she neglects to include, among the Christian's essential obligations, *the sacred duty of research*,[10] in other words his being bound, under pain of sin, to assist in the specific and temporal betterment of the earth—it will be a waste of time for her apologists to put forward the illustrious names of scientists who have also been men of prayer. She will still have to prove that if science flourishes in her wake, too, it is *by right* that this is so, and *under her influence* and not in spite of her or through a happy chance.

Who then, at last, will be the *ideal Christian*, the Christian, at once new and old, who WILL SOLVE IN HIS SOUL THE PROBLEM OF THIS VITAL BALANCE, BY ALLOWING ALL THE LIFE-SAP OF THE WORLD to pass into HIS EFFORT TOWARDS THE DIVINE TRINITY?[11]

That Christian will be the man who has understood that if he is to be supremely the child of God, if he is to fulfil his holy Will in its entirety, he must show himself more assiduous in working for the earth than any servant of Mammon. For some of the faithful, no doubt, this work will consist in spiritualizing the hearts and minds of men by the example of a life that is perfectly

[10] On the basis of this duty and the *vital importance* the Christian can see in research, see *Cosmic Life*. (Note by Père Teilhard, who was often to return to this subject, even at the end of *Le Milieu Divin*, pp. 151–3; Fontana pp. 152–4). For other references see Henri de Lubac, *The Religion of Teilhard de Chardin*, Collins, London, and Desclée Co. Inc., New York, 1967, pp. 26–7.

[11] Cf. the heading to *Note pour servir à l'évangélisation des temps nonveaux* (Epiphany, 1919): 'The great converters (or perverters) of men have always been those in whom the soul of their time burned *most intensely*'. There is always a personal tone in Teilhard's apologetics. Even when, later, he wrote an essay in apologetics 'to order', he described it as 'an attempt to bring out my own reasons for believing'. One should also, of course, when Teilhard uses the first person, make allowances for the literary form of expression.

chaste and 'unmovingly' contemplative. These, we might say, will represent *the Christian component in the pure state*: but, quite apart from their being *separated from* the world through their *social* and *cosmic aim*, their vocation will still be exceptional. Even if the others, who will be the great majority, have devoted their lives to the practice of the evangelical counsels, their sacred task of sustaining natural life will rank among the most direct and effective factors in their sanctification.

For these latter, *not to seek*, not to plumb to its depths the domain of energies and of thought, not to strive to exhaust the Real, will be a grievous *triple fault*, a fault of *infidelity* to the Master who has placed man at the heart of things in order that he may see him, consciously and freely, prolong their immanent evolution and God's creative work.

A fault of presumption, that would make them *tempt God*, by hoping to obtain from indolent prayer, from Revelation or Miracle, what only natural toil can supply.

A fault, thirdly, *of intellectual intransigence*. They are invincibly convinced that if their adherence to their creed is to be beyond reproach, their assault upon the Real must be so constant and insistent that a Divinity other than Jehovah must make himself manifest, if, impossible though this be, he still lies hidden.

Nihil intentatum—nothing left untried—is their motto (the very motto, indeed, of evolution), which, in the fulfilment of nature's lofty destiny, *brings them into line with* the noblest spirit of Revelation.

The sincere and convinced artisan of progress is, in fact, *a man of great and endless renunciation*. He works; he is oblivious of self; he is even detached, because he loves causes better than himself, and he seeks for life's success much more than for his own selfish personal achievement. Even if, from his point of view, suffering is not seen directly as a punishment that expiates, nor exclusively as a factor or symptom of rupture with the earth, but rather as the condition of progress and the price that has to be paid for it— even so, he can at least still claim to be an authentic servant of the Cross.

In a very real sense, too, he can flatter himself that *he serves but one master*—the master of heaven and earth—in that he believes that his work of disclosing a new truth to men is of no less ultimate value and no less sacred than fighting for his country or administering a sacrament.

In so doing, he does not believe that he is transgressing the gospel precept that we must *contemn and hate the world*. He does, indeed, despise the world and trample it under foot—but the world that is cultivated for its own sake, the world closed in on itself, the world of pleasure, the damned portion of the world that falls back and worships itself.

Moreover, he is not so concerned with the immediate and visible success of his work as to be deprived of joy and peace. *Victory* will come from God, in the form his providence decides, *gratuitously* in his own good time; for the worker whose trust is in God knows that no attempt, no aspiration, conceived in grace, is lost: they attain their end by passing through the living Centre of all useful activity.

There is no question, obviously, of the Church's *magisterium* indiscriminately extending its faith, or even its approval, to include the particular detail of every adventure undertaken by mankind. To do that would be precisely to confuse once again the qualities proper to each current of life, and to reintroduce disorder; but the Church, for the sake of the faith and pride of her children, must finally decide to bless and encourage their undertakings, however turbulent and impetuous they may be at first. They must feel her look of approval and tender regard directed upon them, as well as the control of her vigilant hand, when they seek—both in virtue of their citizenship of the world and in the name of God's service—to head the movement that makes the universe follow a curve of progress that is governed by an incommunicable law. Never again, please God, may we be able to say of religion that its influence has made men more indolent, more unenterprising, *less human*; never again may its attitude lie open to the damning suspicion that it seeks to replace science by theology, effort by prayer, battle by resignation, and that its dogmas may well debase the value of the world by limiting in advance the scope of enquiry and the sphere of energy. Never again, I pray, may anyone dare to complain of Rome that it is afraid of anything that moves and thinks.

Even when it has become clear to all that religious faith is not hostile to progress but represents, rather, an additional force to be used by Christians, in the name of what they hold most sacred, to forward the common task of evolution, even then, I fear, we shall not have complete harmony between the children of Heaven and the sons of the earth. Too many will still prefer to turn away from the Gospel and worship the Golden Calf or look in the sky for some star other than Christ. The Parousia, we know, is promised as a dawn that will rise over a supreme onslaught of error . . .[12] Life, at any rate, will neither openly approve nor find excuses for the lack of faith that will mark those last days: and this is because while the Church will be fighting in a continually more acute moral crisis and in a continually more stifling naturalist atmosphere, yet, wise with the experience of centuries, she will be able proudly to point out to life her finest children busy in *forwarding, side by side, mastery of the world and the Kingdom of God.*[13]

20 September 1916

[12] In later years, Père Teilhard sometimes took a more optimistic view. He still, none the less, maintained the dramatic possibility of evil being the final choice. Cf. Henri de Lubac, *The Religion of Teilhard de Chardin*, Collins, London, and Desclée Co. Inc., New York, 1967, Chapter 10, *Evolution and Freedom*.

[13] This passage is already very close to the conclusion of *Le Christique*, written in 1955: 'Everywhere on earth, at this moment, the two essential components of the ultra-human, love of God and faith in the world, each in a state of extreme sensitivity to the other, pervade the new spiritual atmosphere created by the emergence of the idea of evolution. These two components are everywhere in the air, but they are not generally strong enough, *both at the same time*, to combine with one another in *one and the same subject*. In me, by pure chance . . . their relative proportions happen to be correct, and the fusion has been effected spontaneously—not powerful enough, yet, to propagate itself explosively—but nevertheless sufficiently so to establish that the process is possible and that, *sooner or later, there will be a chain-reaction.*

The Struggle against the Multitude

A possible interpretation of the form of the world

(The original contains a dedication to Marguerite Teillard-Chambon: 'An affectionate token of union in thought and Christ, Pierre, 25 March 1917'.)

In a letter dated 24 March 1917, to his cousin Marguerite Teillard-Chambon ('Making of a Mind', p. 189), Père Teilhard writes:
'At the same time as this short note I'm sending you a notebook with my essay on the Multitude. Let me know whether you've received it. Its philosophical significance is obviously very roughly worked out, and may even seem Manichean. I've left it just as it is partly because I find it impossible to express myself better, and partly because it seems to me that under phraseology that may be somewhat erroneous or contradictory there lies a "pointer to truth" that might be impoverished by language more strictly logical or superficially orthodox. All the same, I'd rather have had something more personal and more completely finished to dedicate to you than this is'.

In reading this essay, accordingly, we should make allowances for Père Teilhard's reservations, and remember that it was certainly not intended for publication. He is trying here to bring out a particular point of view but realizes that he has not succeeded in getting it properly into focus. (This applies particularly to the first part.) Later, on 17 April 1923 ('Letters from a Traveller', Collins, London, and Harper and Row, New York, 1962, pp. 66–7), he wrote, 'I find that the single great problem, of the One and the Manifold, is rapidly beginning to emerge from the over-metaphysical context in which I used to state it and look for its solution. I can now see more clearly that its urgency and its difficulties must be in terms of real men and women'.

At that time, Père Teilhard was in the rear area of the front, at Pavant (Aisne).

THE STRUGGLE
AGAINST THE MULTITUDE

A possible interpretation of the form of the world

Ut unum sint, sicut unum sumus.
Si quis vult animam suam salvam facere, perdet eam.

A: THE NON-BEING OF THE MULTITUDE

Of every being we know it is true to say that the more it is divided, the less existence it has. To relax the tension of our spirit is to make it sink back towards matter. Disintegration of animal life reduces our bodies to crude substance. All the elements of the earth, without exception, lose their characteristic properties and cease to exist for us, as their mass is progressively reduced. By dispersing, a being is annihilated. It vanishes in plurality. If, along the line of its essential capacities and natural 'planes of cleavage', the stuff of things were to become infinitely loose-textured, infinitely dissociated, it would be as though it had ceased to exist. Dissolved in non-activity and non-reaction, it would be indistinguishable from nothingness; it would be tantamount to, and so identical with nothingness.[1] So true is this, that only the eye of the Creator could follow it in this tenuousness, in what we might call the blackness of its night, where it exists as an infinitely diffuse capacity to concentrate, condense, associate . . . *Physically speaking, to annihilate the world would be to reduce it to dust.*[2]

[1] See (pp. 151-2) the note to *Creative Union*, which shows that Père Teilhard realized the inadequacy of this metaphysic and was trying to remedy it.

[2] Père Teilhard who, as a natural scientist, always tries to form a picture of what he is describing, is here making it clear that this view is not, properly speaking, metaphysical.

Thus, while true growth is effected in a progress towards unity, less-being increases with fragmentation.[3]

At their vanishing point, things present themselves to us in a state of division, that is to say in a state of supreme multiplicity. They then disappear in the direction of pure number. They founder in multitude. No-being coincides, and is one, with completely realized plurality. Pure nothingness is an empty concept, a pseudo-idea.[4]

True nothingness, physical nothingness,[5] the nothingness found on the threshold of being, that on which, at their lowest levels, all possible worlds converge, *is pure Multiple, is Multitude.*

Initially, then, there were two poles of being, God and Multitude. Nevertheless, God stood alone, since supremely dissociated Multitude had no existence. From all eternity God saw beneath his feet the scattered shadow of his Unity, and, while that shadow was an absolute capacity for producing something, it was not another God, since it did not exist of its own accord, had never existed, and would never have been able to exist—its essence being to be infinitely divided in itself, in other words to lie on the very verge of non-being. Infinitely vast and infinitely rarefied, the Multiple, made nothing by its very essence, slept at the opposite pole from Being, which was one and concentrated.

It was then that the superabundant unity of life engaged, through the creation, in battle with the non-existing Multiple that was opposed to it as a contrast and a challenge. *So far as we can see, to create is to condense,* concentrate, organize—*to unify.*

When, accordingly, the substantially subsisting breath of God had produced a tremor in the zones of the impalpable, being emerged new-born from the depths of plurality, still drenched in Multitude. The centres that constituted it were so packed together that their agglomeration formed a *continuum.* At first there was only a sort of distended centre, *whose unique character lay in its excess of unreduced plurality*: this was to be the medium in

---

[3] A position that St Thomas would have endorsed: *Unum et ens convertuntur,* 'The one and being are interchangeable'.

[4] This questionable proposition is to be found in Bergson, too.

[5] The comment made in note 2 applies also to this phrase.

which all the rest was to exist and the web from which it would be woven. So the ether came into being.

Now, as a result of an unremitting work of condensation that was going on in this, countless nuclei gradually detached themselves on the underlying substratum of indiscernible Multitude and infinitesimal being which it presented. As time passed, an infinite number of distinct points appeared, puncturing the being that was still confused and dissociated; and, seized with creative restlessness, these points made their way towards one another, sought one another out, and united with one another. They grouped themselves in continually more complicated and more uncommon systems, and each advance in the reduction of the centres—in other words each new victory over the Multitude— was marked by the appearance of new properties.[6]

It was thus that the world of matter became embodied—as a sum total of Multitudes each one of which floats within another more tenuous than itself; a slowly constructed pyramid, whose sides become apparent only when its shoulders reach a certain degree of contraction, while its infinitely widespread base is lost in nothingness.

It was thus that the finely distilled essence of the universe, consciousness and thought, was produced, deep in the heart of the monads, by the addition and mutual fertilization of accumulated qualities that assembled from the four corners of nothingness.[7]

It is because we have not understood this genesis of spirit that we are shocked to find that the immaterial force behind living beings is so impermanent, and that *it is so easy to make souls die*.[8] Psychic. simplicity, as we know it, is born of the Multitude. It flowers on organic complexification, supreme in numerical total,

[6] Here we have the first adumbration of what was later to become Teilhard's scientific theory of complexification: a being is the more complex, the greater the number of differentiated elements it includes, with more interconnexions, and forming a more fully centred organization. The complexity in the world increases, and consciousness increases with complexity.

[7] When Père Teilhard expresses his view of the relationship between matter and spirit more precisely, he does not say that matter becomes spirit but that spirit is *born upon* the complexity of matter.

[8] Soul is used here in the scholastic meaning of the word, which includes the vegetative soul (in plants) and the sensitive soul (in animals).

and supremely overcome. *Existing in proportion to the Multitude it has conquered* and shelters within itself, it inevitably entails in the being a maximum tendency to decompose. The soul is created through the grouping and co-ordination of materiality. It is intimately linked with the dissolution and domination of a complexity that has been carried to its peak. That is why, in animals, it becomes excessively fragile as it becomes more refined, until suddenly, when we reach man, the countless factors that generate spirit melt into so perfect a point that nothing can dissolve their fusion; in consequence, the human soul can detach itself and subsist in immortality, even when the lower fascicle of the body falls apart and disintegrates.

The human soul, then is eminently spiritual because it is eminently rich in conquered multiplicity.

Nevertheless, in spite of this, or rather because of this, it does not represent the simplest term we can assign to creation.

Man, who in his genesis resembles all the other monads, is flung into the Real with a prodigal hand. Initially, no doubt, he was only a small group; but reproduction saw to it that the handful of seed should multiply. And we should realize that this multiplication was no mere windfall, no happy accident. *The human soul is made for not existing alone.* The world of man, as are all the lower spheres of created being, is essentially pluralist. The rational soul *is by nature legion.*

This can mean only one thing, that it is made for the union that simplifies beings while appearing to make them more complex.

If it is true, then, that *all Multitude* (all Multitude that is capable of accepting harmony) *is the non-being of something* more simple than itself and higher than itself which can be and seeks to be born of its coherence—since there still subsists around us a complexity (the complexity of souls) which is richer than that from which our thought was born—if that be true, then we have proof that a more fully realized spirituality than our own is possible. Above the refinement and condensation of every material virtue in the substance that reflects and abstracts, there lies the *anticipated concentration of all thoughts* in a single Mind and a single Heart.

Thus mankind, in its teeming mass of souls, each one of which concentrates a world, is the starting point of a higher Spirit: the

Spirit that will shine forth at the point on which purified souls will concentrate, the Spirit that will represent, in its supreme simplicity, the Multitude of multitudes that have been tamed and unified. It will be the most simple because the most comprehensive, the needle-sharp peak on which the whole Multitude will have converged, there to remain suspended. It will be Unity triumphing over Non-being: it will be α and ω.[9]

It is buoyed up by this ill-defined hope that the world gets on with its work and creation continues, through our labour, our suffering, and our sins.

B: THE EVIL OF THE MULTITUDE

1. *Pain.* Pain is the lively perception of our diminution of being, when the latter is aggravated or when it simply persists. *Logically*, then, it is closely connected with the insufficiently reduced Multitude we carry within us. If complete dissociation could be felt, it would, by annihilating us, produce absolute suffering.

Within the extremely restricted field of our experience, we can, *in actual fact*, constantly see for ourselves, to our distress, how painful it is to live through the stages that separate plurality from unity, and how deeply is driven the divine spur that goads us on towards the degree of simplification that is to effect our beatification.

The Multitude, all the more painful in that it exists in the most intimate depths of our lives, *is at the root of all our evils*.

The Multitude attacks us *from without* and corrupts us. Through the purchase we offer to external impacts, through the countless roots we trail in the cosmic maelstrom, the fundamental fragmentation of the world is ceaselessly working to dissolve us, either by violence or by contagion.

The Multitude, again, reigns *within us*, in the badly disciplined lives that congregate in our organism, always ready for inter-

---

[9] The letters of the Greek alphabet applied by the Apocalypse to Christ, the beginning and end of the universe. It is Christ who is the head of the mystical body, in which he unites souls. This concept is the inspiration behind the preceding paragraphs.

necine warfare, or to desert us and return to the common mass.

It rages *at the border-line of body and soul*, in that region of slow release in which spirit emerges from flesh, the latter completely absorbed in the demands and cares of phyletic life, the former trembling with anxiety to find its home in the Absolute it can glimpse.

It makes its way, finally, *even into the texture, apparently so one of our spirituality*. We flatter ourselves that, through something in ourselves, we are a substance of extreme purity: and yet how imperfect and covered in blemishes is that transparency, how rudimentary, how furrowed by mysterious cracks, that simplicity still remains.

We are only too conscious that the plurality of our loves awakens in the new-found cohesion of our spirit an echo of humiliating and wearisome materiality: for all our hopes of them, the fragmentary goods that attract us, drag us in every direction, and on each occasion their lack or their loss leaves us with a painful scar.

Moreover, it is not only alien plurality that rises to the surface in us without warning, or can be seen mirrored in our unity. It is in the depths of our most authentic, most self-contained, nature that we feel the restless movement, *at the heart of what is most spiritual in us*, of a veritable organic multiplicity. Sometimes immanent antagonisms, intra-spiritual discords, come to the surface in us; they tear and torment us, as though parts of our soul were cutting themselves off and dissociating themselves, or were brutally hacking their way across one another. There are conflicts of growth between our faculties—sicknesses and *agonizing deaths of our passions* and our beliefs, which kill one another and supplant one another, and inexorably pass out of our control.

There is the multiplicity of the flesh, the dualism of human nature, the very complexity of the soul in which, at its highest peak, the dust of a world that has as yet hardly taken on solidity, shivers and shakes: the misery of our own personal Multitude within us.

And the misery, too, of the universal Multitude around us.

The suffering of being a wandering fragment of an unfinished whole calls for greater subtlety of perception, if it is to be recognized, than does the evil of sheltering discord within oneself. We think that we feel the pain of a world struggling towards unity much less acutely than the torture that comes from our own ill-simplified individual person, each part still striving to assert itself at the expense of the others.

And yet that first pain attacks us on all sides.[10] Day after day it obtrudes itself on us. The forms it takes, however, are so familiar, so commonplace, that we never look in them for the dominating origin that is common to them. We fail to recognize them.

When our soul is bitterly conscious of the impenetrability that makes it a closed and mysterious world to all others, powerless to communicate its ideas or express its affliction, or to have its love appreciated —

When it experiences the icy fear of feeling lost, all alone, surrounded by the horde of living beings—a nameless throng, heartless, faceless, whose limitless number, could our soul look out over its whole vast surge, would terrify it like some ghastly monster —

When, worn out with exhaustion, we sink back under the deadweight of inertia that must be heaved up if we are to guide men towards a little greater wisdom, a little more goodness —

When the voice is choked in the throat, hoarse with proclaiming the truth, without ever succeeding in making itself heard above the clamour of the cities or without even causing their busy or indifferent inhabitants to turn their heads —

When our heads reel at finding ourselves, utterly alone, lashed to the prow of the advancing world, with no one correctly to measure our worth, no one to have any sincere concern for us, no one to take over from us the task and responsibility of building our destiny —

On all these occasions we imagine that what we still hear is the lament of our own little self-centred being, begging some extra portion of happiness.

[10] Here Père Teilhard is describing what he first called 'the pain of isolation' letter of 6 Jan. 1917, in *Making of a Mind*, p. 163).

In reality, *the groan within us is the groan of something greater than us.* The voice we then hear is the voice of the single soul of the ages to come, weeping in us for its Multitude. And it is the breath, again, of this nascent Soul that passes into us, in the *fundamental*, obstinate, incurable *yearning* for *total union, the union which gives life* to all poetry, all pantheism, all holiness.

Entranced by those great homogeneous systems—ocean, air, desert—man, poised over emptiness and silence, locked up within himself, envies the intimate fusion of the drops of water in the sea, of the molecules in the atmosphere; and he glimpses the bliss there would be in becoming continually more intermingled with Another, in sinking deeper and deeper into it, like smoke that vanishes, like the sound that dies away in space, like the stone that slips gently down to the bottom of the sea.

When sweet harmonies bring a thrill of pleasure even to his very spirit, man dreams of his whole being becoming caught up in the essential music of the world, which would awaken and incorporate in its rhythm the resonance that lies muted in the depth of every human monad.

He adorns with the most hidden virtues, and projects into the most mysterious distance, the intoxication of the unions that Nature effects for him. He idealizes them, magnifies them, sees a divine significance in them, hears in them an echo as vast as the universe. With his loves he mingles the concept of a nuptials with the world.[11]

Weary, at last, of irretrievably exhausting his impetus against the walls of an opaque body—and of never finding in sensible experience (always superficial) *the clue to anything* and of being unable to discover anywhere, in the dark places of his soul, the way through that leads from one soul to another—man begins to

[11] We would love as dearly as we love ourselves, The Earth, Nature,
instinct,the sea, the infinite . . .
Oh, to live so!
Our whole being permeated by those deep-lying energies,
That so, one day, our two fused spirits
May hear within them the song of all the world's voices!
(Emile Verhaeren, *Les forces tumultueuses*, L'Amante: Note by Père Teilhard).
He had just been reading this: Letter of 12 March 1917, in *Making of a Mind*, p. 188.

sigh for death; for death, maybe, will give back to his soul its initial mobility and community.

We carry within us the dull, gnawing *pain of individuation*, by which the separation of souls is maintained and permanence given to their plurality: it is a ceaseless vibration, deep within us, of which our individual agonies and raptures are passing harmonics.

In us men heart-rending suffering and exasperating longing have been implanted as a summons that incessantly calls us to a more perfect unity: why should we persist in aggravating by our own fault, and doubling by sin, the pain of Multitude?

2. *Sin.* Sin, in the will that commits it, is at first simply a misguided and particularist attempt to attain the pre-eminently desirable synthesis of being. All forms of concupiscence lure us by offering the *bait of unity*.

Its first and most unsophisticated form, concupiscence of the flesh, projects below us the tempting picture of an easy return to total matter. Taking advantage of a distorted perspective that creates *a point of universal confluence* at an infinite distance behind us, it persuades us that the nexus of things must be realized below, in the depths of the undifferentiated and unconscious. 'Spirit', it whispers, 'has taken the wrong road. Concentration of the soul widens the cracks that make the world suffer. We must stop climbing' . The man who listens to this voice is lost to life. He goes to swell the herd who reckon to conquer the Multitude by flinging themselves upon it and making it their bride.

In a more subtle, and diametrically contrary, process of unification, the man who is intoxicated by concupiscence of the mind flatters himself that he can overcome the painful fragmentation of beings by reducing them to his own individual unity. Attributing an absolute value to this second perspective, which makes us see the *world as radiating out from us—spreading out, we might say, prostrate at our feet*—the being that is consumed with pride sets itself up as the centre of the universe. Everything must group itself around it and obediently look for its natural order.

Whether sensual or proud, each sinner in his own way hopes to bring about the reign of happiness by suppressing plurality. In each case, however, the final result is equally unfortunate: all they do is to *re-establish the Multitude* in forms it has long left behind, or cause it to be reborn in a new form, proper to spirit, and more dangerous and pernicious than ever before.

Impurity, for its part, brings about a physical dissolution and materialization of beings in their individual structure. When we embrace the Multitude in order to be lost in it, in some mysterious but real way we break the fragile links of our own spirituality. Just where spirit was beginning to glow in its beautiful transparency, this lower form of sin re-introduces every disintegration and exposes every essential joint. When the soul redescends the road of life and creation it becomes corrupt. It surrenders the tender flower of its innermost integrity. This is a thing we all know and for which we have all blushed.

When we sin through arrogance we are more proud of our impiety. There is a semblance of grandeur in imitating the self-aggrandizement of Lucifer: we feel that there is something fine and noble in setting ourselves on an equality with God. If only we could see how shamefully, through our fault, the robe of cosmic unity is torn when we try, in our selfishness, to gather it around ourselves. It is not simply the internal structure of every monad that is then imperilled, it is the very Hope of the World, it is the Spirit whose birth is awaited from the mutual fertilizing of all spirits that is threatened. With every monad folding back jealously upon itself and claiming the right to bring all the others into subjection, the whole throng of monads is dissociated and scattered. Pride and selfishness are the supreme solvents of the unity, and hence of the spirituality, that is to come. Whether they attack individuals or corrupt nations, they act—and it is in this that their palpable malignity consists—like an impurity, cosmic in order, that degrades the world and keeps it chained to materiality.

Non-being, pain, sin—ontological evil, sensibly experienced evil, moral evil—these are *three aspects of the same evil principle*, whose reduction calls for an infinity of time, a principle that is ever being reborn—the Multitude.

3. *The World in Peril.* Until man appeared upon earth, the fountain of life rose up before the Creator, smooth and straight, in the transparence of a single coherent effort. Obediently applying themselves to the task of reproducing and improving themselves, the lower animal forms were unswerving in their pursuit of the synthesis, within them, of spirit.

The time came when the spirituality that was developing in the lower shoots of life attained the degree of consistence that enabled it to isolate itself, in the middle of the world-current, as a thing that was now mature. Hitherto, the centre of gravity of instinct had always, in living creatures, been contained in the phyletic region of the soul, in which a concern to maintain and preserve the species was dominant. It now suddenly crossed over into the individualist zone towards which, from the very beginning, it had slowly been deploying. The human soul appeared, more palpably as something drawn towards its own centre than as something demanded by the hopes of the race.

Instantly, there was a change in the apparent texture of life.

There had just been a sudden fall in the cohesive force that held together the human monads which folded back upon their own interior being and ignored their common future. Creation was going through a dangerous but inevitable phase, in which the surface tension of souls and their collective impetus was reaching a minimum; the exuberant thrust of life, in consequence, was tending to slacken and be dispersed. (Individual activity, we can understand, had to take possession of its own inner domain before it could be employed in a loftier task.) What had been no more than a *delicate stage* in the synthesis of spirit *suddenly became an acute* and almost fatal *crisis*: and for this the rash or vicious use of *our liberties was to blame*.

In the first place, because our minds were *critical*, and became more and more markedly so, we began to suspect our most natural aspirations, and were anxious to know, immediately and distinctly, where we were going and with what end in view. We undertook to rationalize, by our own powers, the mystery of our destiny: and what happened was that, since *our knowledge was not yet up to the level of the sure and secret instinct that we mistrusted in ourselves*, each one of us believed that he could find the right road that all should follow. So, each pulling in his own direction, the fine impetus that was carrying the compact, close-knit mass of living beings towards one and the same vaguely sensed goal, suddenly hesitated, undermined by an inner discord.

Then, *pride of strength* intervened, to complete the work of disorganization that nature had laid us open to and ignorance was aggravating. In their isolation, the monads began to hate one another, to fight for the leading place, to become intoxicated with independence and equality. Absorbed in their quarrels, they did not see that the whole swarm of them was falling headlong, and that at the heart of each one the fragmentation their jealousies were forcing on the world was inevitably being continued in the form of a deep-seated corruption.

Like a limpid stream that has reached the end of its course, so the fountain of life lost its fine transparency; since that time it has been scattering in drops, soon to be dust, which inevitably fall to the ground.

The appearance of the immortal soul produced a formidable crisis of individuation in the world, in other words *a counter-attack by the* shrinking, suffering, guilty, *Multitude*. We have only to use our eyes to see it: a dance of particles that the Brownian movement causes to zig-zag feverishly under the microscope. In that we have an exact image—perhaps, indeed, the reality—of our restless human activity. There is no unity, no foresight, in our proceedings—nothing but an orderless short-range fussing to and fro.

Are we to believe that the world, like a rocket shot into the night, disintegrates and dies in this shower of sparks?

No: the work is not yet finished, nor is it doomed. This temporary disintegration of life is not ordered towards death but towards the more perfect realization and, if need be, the resurrection, of spirit. One thing, however, is needed to re-unite and gather together the unnumbered, scattering flock—*a most mighty Shepherd*.

C: VICTORY OVER THE MULTITUDE

The principle of unity which saves our guilty world, wherein all is in process of returning to dust, is Christ. Through the force of his magnetism, the light of his ethical teaching, the unitive power of his very being, Jesus establishes again at the heart of the world the harmony of all endeavours and the convergence of all beings. Let us read the gospel boldly and we shall see that no idea can better convey to our minds the *redemptive function of the Word* than that of a unification of all flesh in one and the same Spirit.[12]

1. *The Divine Magnetism.* Christ's primordial role is to draw to himself all that, before him, moved at random. For lack of an influence powerful enough to guide their wayward paths into a uniform direction, intelligent creatures, we have seen, hesitated and parted company. For the universe to subsist, *even in its natural evolution*, it was necessary above all that the dynamic soul of one and the same vigorous impetus should again be instilled into men. God chose the love of his incarnate Son as the *prime mover of the restored universe.*

Christ, then, clothed his person in the most sensible and most intimate charms of human individuality. He adorned that humanity with the most entrancing and most masterful splendours of the universe. And he came among us as the synthesis, surpassing all hope, of all perfection, such that every man was necessarily obliged to see and feel his presence, either to hate him or to love him.

As soon as he had appeared, a thrill passed through the seething mass of mankind that made it tremble in every fibre. It vibrated as one whole—since a Multitude of the elect was already isolating itself in the midst of the Multitude that still persisted, in spite of everything, in wandering aimlessly. In serried ranks, those who had freely chosen fidelity gathered around the Shepherd whose

[12] Any reader who may be surprised by this forthright statement should remember what St John says in his Gospel (11:51-2): 'He [Caiaphas] did not say this of his own accord, but being high priest that year he prophesied that Jesus should die for the nation, and not for the nation only, but to gather into one the children of God who are scattered abroad'.

voice, like an assurance of life, echoed deep in their hearts. And they answered him, 'Wheresoever you go, we shall follow in your footsteps'.

On that day *ignorance was conquered* by the Incarnation, and the universe was given back its eagerness for its unparalleled development: on the day when Christ, to save the world that was withering away even in its natural roots, took his place at the head of Creation.

Moreover, the road our Saviour followed and man was called on to follow with him, was *that very road* that being had always taken in order to leave non-being far behind. The reflective, heavenly, task to which Christ summoned and drew us, united in a common urge, was an exact continuation of the unconscious, terrestrial work of former ages: for, under an outward appearance of kindly and humble moral teaching, *the law of purity and Christian charity* hides an operation that is pure fire, in which the original plurality of being is recast and fused until its unity is consummated.

2. *The Christian Virtues.* Nobody here below can fully understand the message of virginity. Even those who practise it, it would seem, repeat it after Christ without getting to the bottom of its mystery. Like a sweet sound, or a scent that moves us without our knowing why, purity, by its very name and still more, much more, when it shows its face, awakens our soul to an appeal that comes to it with complete assurance and yet cannot be defined. Purity, we vaguely feel, touches the secret places of our most personal make-up. It engages the most subtle hopes of our substantial being. Purity is written into our lives, but what standpoint are we to adopt if we are to try to understand a little the creative function that, by the grace of God, it fulfils in us?

Supposing we look at it from the standpoint of the Multitude.

The pure heart is the heart that not only loves God above all things but sees him present throughout all things. Whether the just man rises up above all creatures to an almost direct apprehension of Godhead, or whether, as it is every man's duty to do, he throws himself upon the world that has to be made more perfect and conquered by him, in either case his eyes are turned upon

God alone. For such a man, *things have lost their surface multiplicity*. In every one of them, conformably with their individual qualities and charms, God offers himself to man, for man truly to make him his own. The pure soul, and this is its *natural* privilege, moves within a vast and higher unity. In contact with this, it must inevitably itself become unified to its very core, and, in consequence, it is impossible not to see what an invaluable ally the progress of life will find in virtue.

While the sinner, who surrenders to his passions, disperses and dissociates his spirit, the saint, whose procedure is the exact reverse, escapes from the complexity of affections that keeps alive in created beings the memory and symptoms of their original plurality. By that very fact, *he loses his materiality*. Everything is God for him, God is everything for him, and for him Christ is at once God and everything. Upon such an object, which in its simplicity—as the eyes can see, the heart feel, and the mind apprehend—exhausts the truth and beauties of heaven and earth, the faculties of the soul converge; there they meet one another, are fused together in the flame of a single act in which perception and love are lost in one another. The *specific act of purity* (what the scholastics would call its formal effect) is thus *to unite the inner powers of the soul* in the act of a single passion of extraordinary richness and intensity. Ultimately, the pure soul is the soul that overcomes the multiple, disorganizing, attraction of things and tempers its unity (in other words matures its spirituality) in the red-hot fires of God's simplicity.

What purity effects within the individual being, charity brings about within the collectivity of souls. It is surprising (if we think of it with a mind that has not been dulled by habit) to note what very great pains Christ took to insist on the duty men have to love one another. Mutual love is the Master's new precept, the characteristic that distinguishes his disciples, the sure mark of our predestination, the principal task of every human life. It is on the basis of charity that we shall be judged, and it is by charity that we shall be either condemned or justified. Why was Christ so insistent? If all he meant was that we should be concerned with philanthropy, with lessening of suffering here below, with a greater measure of earthly well-being, how are we to explain the gravity of our Saviour's tone, of his promises and threats?

Here again, without any doubt, a great mystery lies hidden beneath this undemanding Christian teaching. Once more we meet the mystery of the Spirit that has to be built up on the ruins of the Multitude. Christian brotherly love seeks to do much more than to make good the harm done by selfishness, and ease the injuries inflicted by human malice. It is much more than a soothing lotion poured by the Good Samaritan into the wounds of society. There is an organic and 'cosmic' *opus operatum* of charity. By bringing souls together in love, charity gives them the fertility that enables a higher nature to be born from their union. It ensures their coherence. It gradually dissolves their multiplicity. *It spiritualizes the world.*

Purity, charity—we might be inclined to believe that the Christian virtues are *static* virtues, and that by their exercise man hypnotically concentrates on his own consciousness, to no useful purpose, or becomes bogged down in sentimental and sterile compassion. Christ's moral teaching seems timid and uninspired to those who fight for the vigorous and aggressive conquest of the peaks to which life is climbing. In real fact, *no terrestrial effort* is more constructive, *more progressive*, than Christ's. It is not arrogant strength, but the holiness of the gospels, that maintains and continues the authentic effort of evolution.[13]

Where human holiness offers itself as a means to his ends, God is not content to send forth in greater intensity his creative influence, the child of his power: *he himself* comes down into his work to consolidate its unification. He told us this, he and no other. The more the soul's desires are concentrated on him, the more he will flood into them, penetrate their depths and draw them into his own irresistible simplicity. Between those who love one another with true charity he appears—he is, as it were, *born*— as a substantial bond of their love.

Thus, as the multiplicity within us and around us disappears, so something more than a certain higher spirituality emerges:

[13] A month earlier, on Feb. 17th, Père Teilhard had written: 'If I really want to be a link between Our Lord and the regiment, I have to be the one who is most ready to accept the will of God, the most patient, the most mortified (without, of course, being clumsily passive), (*Making of a Mind*, p. 185.)

it is God himself who rises up at the heart of this simplified world. And the organic form of the universe thus divinized is Christ Jesus in his own personal, mystical and cosmic body, who, through the magnetism of his love and the effective power of his Eucharist, gradually gathers into himself all the unitive energy scattered through his creation.

3. *New Joy and New Suffering.* As Christ becomes incarnate in the universe and expels the guilty plurality of the world, so, step by step, the other evil effect of the Multitude—suffering—retreats and decreases. In its most external and sensible forms, no doubt, pain has not yet ceased to threaten us and disorganize us. The earth is still a place of blood and tears. Already, however, the blood flows less freely and the tears are not so bitter. Above the torn flesh and the agonized hearts, into that deep zone in which the soul is moulded for eternal life, *peace has entered*, a peace such as the evil world has no knowledge of and cannot give— mastering peace, which conquers, and flows back to cover even the outermost layers of sensibility—*the peace that is the awareness of Unity*.

The human heart finds first in Jesus Christ the answer to its prayers, so manifold and so impatient that it seemed as though nothing could ever satisfy them all at one and the same time. The insoluble problem of our desires is solved without difficulty by the adorable divino-human reality who comes effortlessly, as it were, *to fill exactly to the brim their deep and complex void.* Passions cease to trample on one another and tear one another apart; the flesh bows meekly before spirit and is tamed. The riddle of our growth is explained in one word. Since Christ has been at hand, *our whole being* is expanding and is *delectably made one*.

At the same time, since Christ has been at hand, *communication has been established between the souls* that, before his coming, knew the misery of feeling isolated, shut in, impenetrable to one another. At last, crossing the fallen barrier of their temporary envelope, they are meeting and making contact in the unity of Christ.

Christ consumes with his glance my entire being. And with that same glance, that same presence, he enters into those who are around me and whom I love. Thanks to him therefore I am united with them, as in a divine *milieu*, through their inmost selves, and I can act upon them with all the resources of my being.

Christ *binds* us and *reveals* us to one another.

What my lips fail to convey to my brother or my sister he will tell them better than I. What my heart desires for them with anxious, helpless ardour he will grant them if it be good. What men cannot hear because of the feebleness of my voice, what they shut their ears against so as not to hear it, this I can confide to Christ who will one day tell it again, to their hearts. And if all this is so I can indeed die with my ideal, I can be buried with the vision I wanted to share with others. Christ gathers up for the life of tomorrow our stifled ambitions, our inadequate understandings, our uncompleted or clumsy but sincere endeavours. *Nunc dimittis, Domine, servum tuum in pace. . . .*

It happens sometimes that a man who is pure of heart will discern in himself, besides the happiness which brings peace to his own individual desires and affections, a quite *special joy, springing from a source outside himself*, which enfolds him in an *immeasurable sense of well-being*. This is the flowing back into his own diminutive personality of the new glow of health which Christ through his Incarnation has infused into humanity as a whole: in him, souls are gladdened with a feeling of warmth, for now they can live in communion with one another.

They see with amazement that the monstrous multitude of human kind forms but one heart and one soul, indistinguishable from the Heart and Soul of Christ.

But if they are to share in this joy and this vision they must first of all have had the courage *to break through the narrow confines of their individuality, depersonalize themselves, so to speak*, in order to become centred in Christ. For this is Christ's law, and it is categorical: *Si quis vult post me venire, abneget semetipsum.*

Since happiness consists in becoming unified, it may seem a contradiction to say that the simplification of being must be effected through suffering. Nothing, nevertheless, is more true, nor more confirmed by centuries of religious experience, nor more in accordance with the explanation of the world as emerging from the Multitude: *that same pain which kills and decomposes* is essential to being if it is to live and become spirit—of this Christ warned us, of this every day brings us a new proof, and this the mechanism of creation demands.

In order first to concentrate upon itself, and assert itself, the soul cannot confine itself to a gentle effort of recollection. The substance of its affections is laden with all sorts of outworn alien elements. Countless parasite branches, offshoots of its activity, seek in the universe for useless or evil pleasures. Between the soul and the creatures it lives among too many interconnexions and 'symbioses' have been established, for the sake of immediate and easily won satisfaction. In this at once crude and complex form, man is not yet ready for union with God. There is much that he must first expel, prune and cut away. Thus a whole initial *unification—pleasurable* and *tempting*—that he had developed for his happiness here and now, *will be broken down* before the true simplicity that he awaits and has been promised is realized. And this means that in order to be one, incorruptible, beatified, the soul must first be divided; it must suffer a sort of decomposition, and carry within itself the pain of the Multitude.

Purity is a basic condition of this self-renouncement and mortification.

And charity much more so.

Once a man has resolved to live generously in love with God and his fellow-men, he realizes that so far he has achieved nothing by the generous renunciation he has made in order to perfect his own inner unity. This unity in its turn must, if it is to be born anew in Christ, suffer an eclipse which will seem to annihilate it. For in truth those will be saved who *dare to set* the centre of their being *outside themselves*, who dare to love Another *more than themselves*, and in some sense become this Other: which is to say, who dare to pass through death to find life. *Si quis vult animam suam salvam facere, perdet eam.*

Clearly, the believer knows that at the price of this sacrifice he is gaining a unity greatly superior to that which he has abandoned. But who can tell the anguish of this metamorphosis? Between the moment when he consents to dissolve his inferior unity and that other, rapturous moment when he arrives at the threshold of his new existence, the *real* Christian feels himself to be hovering over an abyss of disintegration and annihilation. It seems to him as though his substance were falling asunder and reverting to the Multitude. The salvation of the soul must be bought at the price of a great risk incurred and accepted. We have, without reservation, to stake earth against heaven; we have to give up the secure and tangible unity of the egocentric life and risk everything on God. 'If the grain of wheat does not fall into the ground and die, it remains just a grain'.

Therefore when a man is burdened with sorrow, when he falls ill, when he dies, none of those around him can say with certainty whether his being is thereby diminished or increased. For under exactly *the same appearances* the two opposite principles draw to themselves their faithful, leading them either *to simplicity or to the Multitude*: the two principles which are *God* and *Nothingness*.

4. *Consummation*. Through earthly combinations that knit together and fall apart, the work of creation proceeds irresistibly, as determined by Christ, who sustains it by his influence, his Person, and his prayer: *Ut unum sint, sicut unum sumus*. That is the definitive formula which gives us the key to the Gospel and to the world. In the light of that saying, what can we discern at the ultimate term?

When the plenitude of time has been realized, we may anticipate a supreme synthesis of all created perfections. Dominated by the Spirit of Christ, who will test their totality as a Soul of souls, the chosen monads will be grouped and fused, on the last day, in a simplicity which, *being born from the greatest possible complexity of beings*, will be *the highest spirituality attainable* in the present order of things.

In this amazing simplicity, which will be realized in each soul according to its merit, souls will attain supreme mastery of their personality. Moreover, in each of them, the intermediate degrees of the simplified Multiple spaced out between Christ and nothingness, will subsist in some form: they will remain distinct within the glorious Unity they contribute to form. The Multitude, in fact, will have been, not destroyed, but mastered. *The flesh will have risen again.*

We cannot readily conceive the acme of a quality except in the form of a perpetual growth, nor the synthesis of two extremes except in the image of a continual alternation to and fro, from one to the other. Because of this, we can picture to ourselves this final unification of beings as a process of continual, delectable, progression, and at the same time of perpetual oscillation of the elements towards the Whole: in this, the parts are constantly becoming more completely one in their conformity with one another and their union—or, to put it another way, they are becoming acutely conscious of themselves and then losing themselves in the all-encompassing embrace.

That may give us just a hint of heaven—and its bliss.

Nevertheless, in contrast with this *spiritualized Multitude*, there will be some part of being abandoned, *in full life*, to disorganization; there will be spirit that *falls prey to the Multitude*. Those creatures who have been false and have persisted in cutting themselves off from God, will undergo the terrifying assault of a resurgent multitude seething in the heart of their immortal substance. Suffering, in full consciousness, the punishment of nothingness, they will struggle in a hopeless effort to dissolve into dust.

And in them, too, unity will triumph.

26 February 1917
22 March 1917

The Mystical Milieu

On 10 June 1917, Père Teilhard was at Paissy, to the rear of the notorious Chemin des Dames. For some time he had been thinking of writing a spiritual essay, which he had discussed with his cousin Marguerite in letters that have since been lost. He writes to her (on June 10):
'I'm continuing to improve and gradually give precision to the ideas and the scheme I spoke of in my earlier letters. I'm tending to give still more prominence to the realism by which mysticism lives, and also to analyse more clearly the alternating movement that carries the soul away from (and in turn drives it back to) the Divine Milieu, homogeneous and essential, the vehicle being the particular determined forms of the real that we have to know and love and fulfil'.

(*Making of a Mind*, p. 195)

Two months later, he was at Beaulieu-les-Fontaines in the Oise. There he had the use of a quiet room, which enabled him to work regularly. On 5 August, 'The Mystical Milieu' was nearly finished. 'Inspiration is coming more readily as the work progresses. I shall perhaps have finished my draft by the 15th. It's disappointing to realize how impoverished and reduced your ideas become when you try to fit them into a common plan. Each one becomes a small stone, cut down and shaped, when it might be the nucleus of a whole building . . . Just one reference, one paragraph, for what calls for a complete study . . . In the end, I'll have put into 30 or 40 pages what I could spend my whole life talking about'.

(*Ibid.* p. 199)

'The Mystical Milieu' contains, in fact, 43 large pages. It was finished at Beaulieu-les-Fontaines on 13 August 1917 and sent off immediately:

'14 August. Yesterday, I sent Guiguite 'The Mystical Milieu' so that she can send it on to you when she's read it. I'd have liked you to have been the first to see it—the more so that you're certainly the person who will understand me best. I thought I rather owed it to Guiguite to start with her—apart from the fact that as you're going to keep the manuscript you might as well have it last. You'll see that there's nothing very new in these pages. They're primarily a clarification of points that you're already familiar with; and in the end I can't help wondering whether they're really very intelligible to anyone who hasn't read the 'Cosmic Life' and 'The Multitude'. You'll probably find that once again I've compressed it too much. But if only you knew how difficult I find it to write at greater length without losing the general thread of my theme. And in essays such as this, it's the general thread that counts for most'. (Ibid. p. 200.)

We should note that last sentence. It is perhaps more applicable to this than to any other of Père Teilhard's essays. The thought expressed in 'The Mystical Milieu' develops, in fact, in a sort of dialectic, each stage of which becomes meaningful and can be judged only in the light of the whole. A series of 'circles' is successively described, which gradually make up the 'Milieu' in which the soul lives. This method of composition has been compared with that of St Teresa's 'Interior Castle'. Even more than when reading St Teresa, it is important not to stop short at, and so consider in isolation, any one of the layers that analysis can distinguish in the experience the writer is describing. St Teresa was indicating the stages of a journey: in this essay, a similar basic experience is given unity through the conjunction of the five circles: the circles of presence, consistence, energy, spirit and person.

THE MYSTICAL MILIEU

'In eo vivimus, et movemur, et sumus.'

A: THE CIRCLE OF PRESENCE

A limpid sound rises amidst the silence; a trail of pure colour drifts through the glass; a light glows for a moment in the depths of the eyes I love . . .

Three things, tiny, fugitive: a song, a sunbeam, a glance . . .

So, at first, I thought they had entered into me in order to remain and be lost in me.

On the contrary: they took possession of me, and bore me away.

For if this plaint of the air, this tinting of the light, this communication of a soul were so tenuous and so fleeting it was only that they might penetrate the more deeply into my being, might pierce through to that final depth where all the faculties of man are so closely bound together as to become a single point. Through the sharp tips of the three arrows which had pierced me the world itself had invaded my being and had drawn me back into itself.

The vibration aroused a resonance in all my affections. It drew me out of myself, into a wider harmony than that which delights the senses, into an ever richer and more spiritual rhythm that was imperceptibly and endlessly becoming the measure of all growth and all beauty.[1]

---

[1] 'In this passage . . . we can see the impact of a sensitive emotion; but, instead of folding back upon itself in enjoyment, it becomes the source of an infinitely extended process of amplification: the waves it has produced are not lost in a peripheral zone, but cause the being to reverberate even in what is at once its most intimate and most resonant centre, "where all the faculties of man are so closely bound together as to become a single point". Just as it is the whole of this man that suffers the impact of the three sensibly apprehended arrows, so it is the whole world that has made its way into him'. M. Barthélemy-Madaule, *Bergson et Teilhard de Chardin* (1963), p. 80.

I felt my body, my soul, and even my spirit[2] pass into the
ethereal tint, unreal in its freshness, that caressed my eyes. Serene
and iridescent, its colour bathed more than my senses; it in some
way impregnated my affections and thoughts. I melted away in
it, lost in a strange yearning to attain some individuality vaster
and simpler than mine—as though I had become pure light.

And, under the glance that fell upon me, the shell in which my
heart slumbered, burst open. With pure and generous love, a
new energy penetrated into me—or emerged from me, which, I
cannot say—that made me feel that I was as vast and as loaded
with richness as the universe.[3]

Thus, while the pursuit of an essential fulfilment of our
nature gathers us in upon ourselves, and forces us into the limitations and isolation of individuation, each one of our emotions,
the more it is aesthetic, the more it tends to break up our autonomy.
The Real incessantly reawakens us to an impassioned awareness
of a wider expansion and an all-embracing unity. It is in the
arousing of this restless yearning that the hallowed function of
sense-perception finds its consummation.

We imagine that in our sense-perceptions external reality
humbly presents itself to us in order to serve us, to help in the
building up of our integrity. But this is merely the surface of the
mystery of knowledge; the deeper truth is that when the world
reveals itself to us it draws us into itself: it causes us to flow out-
wards into something belonging to it, everywhere present in it,
and more perfect than it.

The man who is wholly taken up with the demands of every-
day living or whose *sole* interest is in the outward appearance of

---

[2] Note the threefold division (body, soul, spirit), traditional in Christian
thought since St Paul, I Thess. 5:23, and spontaneously re-adopted by the
majority of mystical writers.

[3] We may reasonably see in this a personal allusion by Père Teilhard to what
he called 'the discovery of the feminine'. Cf. André-A. Devaux, *Teilhard et
la vocation de la femme* (1964): a discovery that was neither to 'divert' nor 'dis-
sipate' his energies. Cf. *Le Coeur de la Matière* (1950), Conclusion. *Le Féminin
ou l'Unitif*; and below, pp. 192–202, *The Eternal Feminine*.

things seldom gains more than a glimpse, at best, of this second phase in our perceptions, that in which the world, having entered into us, then withdraws from us and bears us away with it: he can have only a very dim awareness of that aureole, thrilling and inundating our being, through which is disclosed to us at *every* point of contact the unique essence of the universe.

The mystic is *the man who is born to* give first place in his experience to that aureole.[4]

The mystic only gradually becomes aware of the faculty he has been given of perceiving the indefinite fringe of reality surrounding the totality of all created things, with more intensity than the precise, individual core of their being.

For a long time, thinking he is the same as other men, he will try to see as they do, to speak their language, to find contentment in the joys with which they are satisfied.[5]

For a long time seeking to appease his mysterious but obsessive need for plenitude of being, he will try to divert it onto some particularly stable or precious object to which, among all the accessory pleasures of life, he will look for the substance and overflowing richness of his joy.

For a long time he will look to the marvels of art to provide him with that exaltation which will give him access to the sphere —his own sphere—of the extrapersonal and the suprasensible; and in the vast unknown of nature he will strive to hear the heartbeats of the higher reality which calls him by name.

Happy the man who fails to stifle his vision, rejecting the pretext that it is absurd to take interest in the world once one has reached the circle in which it ceases to be perceptible to the majority of human beings.

Happy the man who will not shrink from a passionate questioning of the Muses and of Cybele concerning his God.

But happy above all he to whom, rising beyond aesthetic dilettantism and the materialism of the lower layers of life, it is given to hear the reply of all beings, singly and all together:

---

[4] Cf. The conclusion. The born mystic is the man in whom the mystical experience has particularly strong 'natural roots'.

[5] 'Who would say this of anybody but himself?' rightly asks M. Barthélemy-Madaule, *op. cit.* p. 486.

'What you saw gliding past, like a world, behind the song and behind the colour and behind the eyes' glance does not exist just here or there but is a presence existing equally everywhere: a presence which, though it now seems vague to your feeble sight and your crude being, will grow in clarity and depth. In this presence all diversities and all impurities yearn to be melted away'.

When he has pursued to the end the vocation contained in all sense-perception—when his eyes have once become accustomed to the Light invisible in which both the periphery of beings and their centre are bathed—then the seer[6] perceives that he is immersed in a *universal Milieu*,[7] higher than that which contains the restlessness of ordinary, sensibly apprehended, life: a Milieu *that knows no change*, immune to the surge of superficial vicissitudes— a *homogeneous* Milieu in which contrasts and differences are toned down. As yet, he can say nothing of this diffuse Reality except that it exists, that it is enveloping and that in a mysterious way it is beatifying. It is enough for him, however, to have glimpsed its serene and luminous folds. Nothing henceforth can shake his determination to move for ever into its embrace and to find his happiness in there becoming ever more lost.

Lord, it is you who, through the imperceptible goadings of sense-beauty, penetrated my heart in order to make its life flow out into yourself. You came down into me by means of a tiny scrap of created reality; and then, suddenly, you unfurled your immensity before my eyes and displayed yourself to me as Universal Being. Lord, in this first image, so close at hand and so concrete, let me savour you at length, in all that quickens and all that fills to overflowing, in all that penetrates and all that envelops—in sweetness of scent, in light, and love, and space.[8]

[6] This same word occurs again in *Le Christique* (1955), as a synonym for 'the Mystic'.

[7] 'The universal Milieu' is the name first applied by Père Teilhard to what he later called 'the divine Milieu' (pp. 128, 133, 134). See also above p. 110. Cf. The definition of the 'mystical Milieu, on p. 137, and (p. 141) the 'universal Centre'. Cf. *The Religion of Teilhard de Chardin*, p. 57

[8] 'It would appear that it is human love that opens the door by which divine love enters. According to Teilhard, however, the truth is that divine love uses human love as the door through which it forces its way into a being. (M. Barthélemy-Madaule, *op. cit.* p. 306).

I have thought to hear it said, Lord, that among those who serve you there are some who take fright when they see a heart that feels too acutely (just as they dread to see a mind that thinks too much). I cannot believe that such a fear can be justified; since, Lord, if a man closes his soul against the summons of the immanent Godhead, from what substance will he draw nourishment to keep alive the processes by which he claims to sustain his prayer?

Just as there is but a single matter created to maintain the successive growths of consciousness in the cosmos, so there is but *a single fundamental feeling* underlying all mystical systems; and that is *an innate love of the human person, extended to the whole universe.*

Like every natural force, that passion, as it develops, is liable to checks and perversions, to deviations. It can evaporate in futile poetry, it can be lost in naturalist mysticism, or take the degraded form of godless pantheism.[9] Nevertheless, it remains true that this is the only primordial, irrepressibly ebullient, passion in the human heart.

If, then, a man is to build up in himself, for God, the structure of a sublime love, he must first of all sharpen his sensibility. By a familiar contact, prudent but untiring, with the most deeply emotive realities, he must carefully foster in himself his feeling for, his perception of, his zest for the Omnipresence which haloes everything in nature.[10] Under this single tangible stuff, Lord,

[9] Later, p. 132, Père Teilhard speaks simply of 'pantheism'. In 1919, in *The Universal Element* we shall find him contrasting the 'Christian solution' and the 'pantheist solution'. See also *Le Milieu Divin*, p. 116. Nevertheless, on several occasions, he speaks of 'Christian pantheism', of 'true pantheism', of 'the pantheism of differentiation' etc. Pantheism represents for him an 'eternal mirage' and an 'immense temptation' which he observed in history and felt in himself. He longed, moreover, for the Christian to 'steal from the pantheist the fire with which he threatened to consume the world in a blaze that was alien to that of Christ.' (*Panthéisme et Christianisme*, 1920).

[10] It is faith in the divine Omnipresence, completed by the doctrine of the Universal Christ, that will provide the antidote to the temptation of pantheism. Cf. *Le Milieu Divin*, p. 114: 'The omnipresence of the divine is simply the effect of its extreme spirituality, and is the exact contrary of the fallacious ubiquity which matter seems to derive from its extreme dissociation'. Cf. pp. 116–17, 121–2, 130, 131; letter of 8 August 1919 on 'The need to worship an omnipresence' (*Making of a Mind*, p. 300). Later, in *L'Atomisme de L'Esprit* (1941)

you make yourself manifest to us and fill us with rapture; in this you gradually disclose to us the wonders of your existence among us.

Countless numbers of beings surround me on all sides: I like to feel the soft touch of their infinite contact and to lose myself in their boundless swarm.

Formerly, this throng of beings seemed to me incoherent and obtrusive. To an unenlightened observer, the atoms of this world seem cold and alien. They jostle and irritate us, they flit to and fro, they make us weary. They are like a heavy cloud over-shadowing life. I, too, have known the feeling of being stifled in their dust. The multitude of beings is an infliction hard to bear.[11]

From this I was released by the Vision of the Presence.

In contact with some particularly loved object, something pierced through the dark cloud like a ray of light. A translucent spot grew larger until it spread throughout the powdery opacity, and everything became not simply warm and diaphanous but wholly transparent. Everything formed a single limpid mass in which no division between things could be seen. Clarity reigned throughout.

At the same time, that transparency[12] filled my being, too; it penetrated into me, and made its way deep down within me, into depths whose existence I had never suspected; and as it did so it

---

he wrote: 'The thinking atom finds itself finally and for ever submerged in the omnipresence and omni-action of a supreme Consciousness' (*Oeuvres*, Vol, 7, p. 61); and in a retreat note (20 Oct. 1945) we find: '*Domine, fact ut videam*' *ut Te videam, ut Te* omnipraesentem *et* omni-animantem *videam et sentiam!* —Lord, grant that I may see, that I may see *You*, that I may see you and feel you present in all things and animating all.

[11] This is the theme of *The Struggle against the Multitude*, whose composition immediately preceded that of *The Mystical Milieu*. Cf. letter of 13 Jan. 1917, to Marguerite Teillard-Chambon: 'I didn't know, I'm ashamed to say, that Schopenhauer had already spoken of the misery of individuation. In a way, this concurrence flatters me and gives me more confidence. However per-nicious a man's influence may be, the importance it assumes in men's minds proves that it contains a precious element of truth, in which men have seen a correct reflexion of themselves'. (*Making of a Mind*, p. 168.)

[12] Transparency: an essential word in Teilhard's vocabulary. Cf. *Le Milieu Divin*, p. 131, 'The transparence of God in the universe'; p. 134, 'within this transparency he will concentrate himself to the point of appearing as a child'.

dissolved in its mysterious waters the plurality of my being and its dark recesses. I experienced an unbelievable relief in feeling that Another existed, and through him all things existed, deep down within me.

I feel now as though I were moving in some impalpable homogeneity made up of countless interfused presences. I can appreciate the variety and the different appeals of each one of these; but I can see them only as the changing tints of one and the same light or as areas of fragrance running through one and the same atmosphere. I can pass through them without emerging from the medium that unites them. Underlying the medley of inessential detail and surface charms, the Presence that spreads through all things is the only source that gives me light and the only air that I can ever breathe.

B: THE CIRCLE OF CONSISTENCE

The basic mystical intuition has just led up to the discovery of a supra-real unity diffused throughout the immensity of the world. In a natural development, this initial vision immediately becomes embodied in a further perception, closely akin to the first, in which we see that there is a universal substratum, extremely refined and tenuous, through which the totality of beings subsists.

In that milieu, at once divine and cosmic, in which he had at first observed only a simplification and as it were a spiritualization of space, the seer, faithful to the light given him, now perceives the gradual delineation of the form and attributes of an ultimate *Element* in which all things find their definitive consistence.[13]

[13] Père Teilhard had sought for consistence since his childhood. Cf. *Le Coeur de la Matière*: 'Consistence: without any doubt that was for me the fundamental attribute of Being'. He is fond of applying the word to the Absolute, to the Real, to Plenitude. Letter of 13 Nov. 1916: 'The realities of faith are not felt with the same solidity (*consistance*) as the reality of experience' (*Making of a Mind*, p. 145). Retreat, 1939: 'Who, oh who, will make God real for us, consistent!' Man, as a created being, in himself lacks consistence: 'Accept and love the feeling of being totally without consistence'. 'God, my consistence!' (Retreat, 1945). Cf. St Augustine, Confessions, Bk. XI, c. 30, n. 40, '*Solidabor in Te*' ('I shall take on consistence in Thee'). Cf. below, p. 128 'Now that I hold you, sovereign Consistence'.

And then he begins to measure more exactly the joys, and the pressing demands, of that mysterious presence to which he has surrendered himself.

Joy is above all the fruit of having come face to face with a universal and enduring reality to which one can refer and as it were attach those fragmentary moments of happiness that, being successive and fugitive, excite the heart without satisfying it. The mystic suffers more than other men from the tendency of created things *to crumble into dust*: instinctively and obstinately he searches for the stable, the unfailing, the absolute; but so long as he remains in the domain of outward appearances he meets with nothing but disappointment.

Even the most precious of substances have, each one of them, the rust or the worm that devours them.

Matter, so enthralling and so divine in virtue of its priority in the order of created things and of its persistence into life, dissolves, under analysis, into pure multiplicity.

Spirit can succeed in releasing itself only by detaching itself in the form of monads in which the unity, and hence the stability, of the world appear to be destroyed rather than perfected.

The cosmos itself, taken in its totality, breaks down into a vast agglomeration of individual self-centred particles whose paths cross and obstruct one another.

This crumbling away, which is the mark of the corruptible and the precarious, is to be seen everywhere. And yet everywhere there are traces of, and a yearning for, a unique support, a unique and absolute soul, a unique reality in which other realities are brought together in synthesis, as stable and universal as matter, as simple as spirit.

One must have felt deeply the pain of being plunged into that multiplicity which swirls about one and slips through one's fingers, if one is to be worthy of experiencing the rapture that transports the soul when, through the unifying influence of the universal Presence, it perceives that reality has become not merely transparent but *solidly* enduring. For this means that the incorruptible principle of the universe is now and for ever found, and that it extends everywhere: *the world is filled*, and filled with the Absolute. To see this is to be made free.

No longer need we be distressed by the mutability of individual beings, the detail of whose design is incessantly being built up and falling apart: nor by the exteriority of individual lives whose paths clash or are hidden from one another.

Beneath what is temporal and plural, the mystic can see only the unique Reality which is the support common to all substances, and which clothes and dyes itself in all the universe's countless shades without sharing their impermanence. He knows the joy of feeling that Reality penetrates all things—wherever the mysterious light of the Omnipresence had shone—even to the most hidden places of his own person—even into the very stuff of which his mental awareness, in the different forms it assumes, is made up. He soon comes to see the world as no more than the back-wash of one essential Thing whose pleasure it is to react upon itself, within the conscious minds it supports. To the mystic, everything is equally, and for ever, dear and precious. And yet at the same time the individual charms of each particular being have never seemed to him more delectable than from the moment when every least nicety and every trifling grace took on for his senses the rich colour and savour of some supreme incorruptibility.

Thus, like a rising tide, the mystical milieu has pursued its task of entering into and refashioning the Real. A moment ago it was no more than an ethereal glow that lit up the inner essence, common to all things, and now it is universal consistence, in which every one of us moves and has his being. It is not simply God diverting himself through the crystalline transparency of the world: it is he who constitutes and sustains its refractive power.

Hitherto, Lord, my attitude towards your gifts has been that of a man who, feeling that he is not alone, tries to distinguish what influence is acting upon him in the darkness. Now that I have found the transparent consistence in which we are all held, I realize that *the mystical effort to see* must give way to *the effort to feel and to surrender myself*. This is *the phase of communion*.

Gladly, then, I welcome, each in its due order and according to its own measure, every force and every charm, every form and every movement, everything that is great and strong—everything that stands and endures, everything that reaches out, and overflows its own limits.

Lord, that I might hold you more closely, I would that my consciousness were as wide as the skies and the earth and the peoples of the earth; as deep as the past, the desert, the ocean; as tenuous as the atoms of matter or the thoughts of the human heart.

Must I not adhere to you throughout the entire extent of the universe, must not my love drive its roots into every single thing, since it is through the entire extension of the world that you offer yourself to me, that so I may feel you and clasp you?

When I do so, I well know, I am repeating the outward gesture of the pagans and the wise men of the earth; and of those who see what I am doing more than one will shake his head and accuse me of worshipping nature.[14]

In order that the spirit may ever shine forth in me, that I may not succumb to the temptation that lies in wait for every act of boldness, nor ever forget that you alone must be sought in and through everything, I know, Lord, that you will send me—at what moments only you know—deprivations, sorrow. The object of my love will fall away from me, or I shall outgrow it.

The flower I held in my hands withered in my hands.

At the turn of the lane a wall rose up before me.

Suddenly, between the trees I saw the edge of the forest which I thought had no end.

A flame burnt up the paper on which my thought was written.

The testing time had come.

But it did not bring the unalleviated sorrow I had expected, of being pulled up short by the uncertainties and limitations of every single particular good. On the contrary, a glorious, unsuspected joy invaded my soul. And why was this, Lord, if not because, in the collapse of those immediate supports I came so dangerously close to accepting for my life, I knew with an unique experiential

---

[14] On more than one occasion Père Teilhard was to protest against the false interpretation of his work that he anticipates here. In a more general way, a letter of 8 Oct. 1933 refers, in connection with Buddhism, to 'cases in which the same appearances disguise contrary realities'.

certainty that I would never again rely for support on anything save your own divine consistence.

The power to appreciate and to open the heart is indispensable to the awakening and the maintenance of the mystical appetite. *But all the raptures they bring put together are not so effective as the icy chill of a disappointment* in showing us that you alone, my God, are stable. It is through sorrow, and not through joy that your Godhead gradually assumes, *in our sentient faculty*, the higher Reality it possesses in the nature of things, but which it is so difficult even for those who are most fully initiated to put into words.

That is why, if some day—if not before, it will at least be on the day I die—everything should begin to fall away from me, if some total catastrophe should tear down the structure, based on all the things I have sought for and loved, which makes up my life's work—then, when I see the naked form of your consistence rising up alone from the ruins, I believe that, with the help of your grace, Lord, the words that come to my lips will be the old paean of the ancient world, *Io triumpe!*[15]

---

[15] These last paragraphs bring out the role of our essential passivities, later to be emphasized in *Le Milieu Divin* and *La signification et la valeur constructrice de la souffrance*; see also below, pp. 130-1. Cf. letter of 9 April 1916: 'We have but one permanent home, heaven: that's still the old truth that we always have to re-learn—and it's only through the impact of sad experiences that we assimilate it. I don't know whether I told you how, while I was helping Boule in September 1914 to put away in safety the most valuable of the Museum's treasures, handling the fragility of human hopes with such a direct physical contact, I felt buoyed up by a sort of triumphant joy: because God, his Will, not to be attained by anything that grows less, and yet attainable in spite of every disaster and ruin, became manifest to me as the only absolute and desirable reality . . . And even now, in my bad moments, however awful the future that menaces our country, I still retain this triumphant joy, based on a conviction of the transcendence of God. Yes, even if, contrary to all expectations, the war should end badly not only for us but for the real progress of the world . . . even then, I would feel like repeating over all these seeming victories of evil, the ancient cry of the Greek festivals, *Io triumpe*'. (*Making of a Mind*, p. 98). Cf. Horace, Epodes, 9, 21 and 23; '*Quasi deum invocat triumphum*' (Pomponius Porphyrion, *Commentarii*).

C: THE CIRCLE OF ENERGY

1. *Passivity*. But I look for more, Lord, much more!

When your Presence bathed me in its light, I sought to find in it the supreme tangible Reality.

Now that I hold you, sovereign Consistence, and feel that I am carried along by you, I realize that hidden away beneath my yearnings was an unspoken longing not to embrace but to be possessed.

It is not in the form of a ray of light or of a tenuous matter, but as fire that I desire you; and it was as fire that I felt your presence, in the intuition of my first contact. I shall never, I know well, find rest, unless some active force pours down from you, to cover and transform me.

I pray you, divine milieu, already decked with the spoils of quantity and space, show yourself to me as the focus of all energies;[16] and, that you may do so, make yourself known to me in your true essence, which is *Creative Action*.

The first stage in the natural view of energies, consists in recognizing the existence of the countless transient activities that make up the web on which the universe is woven. It is only too easy to observe our dependence in relation to the objects around us. If we are, instinctively and as a matter of habit, to see the external world as a network of activities of which each being represents a knot, we must have a long-trained mind, and one that has received the grace that enables us to cherish our passivities.

Taken to the second stage, consciousness of cosmic energy penetrates into the region of individual immanence. It distinguishes, beneath the superficial autonomy of the soul, a central organic current—antecedent to, and foreign to, our freedom of choice—rather as though one could see, through our own personality, the track of the human phylum.

---

[16] The question of energy was to play an increasingly dominant part in Père Teilhard's thought. Cf. *L'énergie humaine* (1937); *L'énergie spirituelle de la souffrance* (1951); *La réflexion de l'énergie* (1952); *L'énergie d'évolution* (1953); *L'activation de l'énergie humaine* (1953).

In the third and final stage, the two earlier types of knowledge are fused together in the intuition of vast cosmic trails; in these whole groups of monads, linked together by transient forces, making up a system that tends to appear as an immanence, are organized and pursue their course under the influence of certain axial energies or collective souls.

From the purely scientific point of view, this deployment of interwoven forces mounts up into a formidable and alarming mass: superficially, it can be mastered and made use of, but, as a whole, it is too much for human industry or human thought.

Once again, it is for the mystic to carry out the task of taking possession of the world at that point at which it escapes from other men, and to effect the synthesis, which, if attempted experientially or on normal philosophical lines, can only bring failure or disaster.[17] The mystic was looking for the devouring fire which he could identify with the Divine that summons him from all sides: science points it out to him.

See, the universe is ablaze!

See how the starry depths expand in an ever-vaster magazine of assembled suns!

How, from either end of the spectrum, waves of radiation endlessly extend their range of shade and penetration.

How life draws from ever more distant sources the sap that flows through its innumerable branches.

How the soul is seen to be ever more lost in the determinisms of the universe, more difficult to descry at its centre, more ill-defined at its periphery.

How there is an endless increase in our perception of the hidden forces that lie dormant, of the seething multitudes of the infinitesimal, of the things that are so vast that, being unable to see more than one point in them, we cannot grasp their totality.

From all these discoveries, each one of which carries him deeper into an ocean of energy, the mystic draws an undiluted

---

[17] A characteristic remark in which we can see how Père Teilhard thought he stood in relation to the thinkers, scientific or philosophical, of his own time. It will be noted that the faculty he attributes to the 'mystic' is not simply cognitive.

joy. And he is always eager for more; he will never feel that he is as fully dominated by the forces of Earth and Air as his yearning to be subject to God's mastery demands.

In very truth, it is God, and God alone whose Spirit stirs up the whole mass of the universe in ferment.

What, then, are we to say of that truncated view that presents the creation to us as a far-distant, instantaneous act which long ago, in an initial phase that is now finished, produced the essences that the power of God now does no more than sustain and preserve?

The heart of the seer rejects that notion as unbearable.

The fact is that creation has never stopped. The creative act is one huge continual gesture, drawn out over the totality of time. It is still going on; and, incessantly even if imperceptibly, the world is constantly emerging a little farther above nothingness. The operation which raises it up and gives it form may well be infinitely broken up into the creatures in which the work it does is materialized and accumulated: but, ultimately, it is that operation alone—the supreme influence derived from the prime mover[18]—that subsists.

Through the whole breadth and depth of the cosmos, it is in truth the divine action that still moulds us, as it moulded the clay on the first day of creation.

Thus the mystic recollects himself in hallowed communion with the omni-operant Will. Delectably, he loses himself in the indefinitely renewed consciousness of his universal passivity.

All round him, there float, dense-packed, influences—some blessed, some hateful—that emanate from elements and minds.

[18] This goes farther than the classic notion of 'continuous creation', which is simply conservation in being. Cf. *Mon Univers* (1924): Creation 'is an act co-extensive with the duration of the world'; Address given in 1928: 'Creation never stops'. *The transformist paradox* (1925): God's creative action is conceived . . . 'as a *bringing to birth* of the successive stages of his work in the heart of things. It is no less essential, no less universal, no less intimate either on that account'. (*Vision of the Past*, p. 102, note) 'Evolution . . . is certainly not "creative" as science for a brief moment believed; but it is the expression of creation, for our experience, in time and space.' (*Man's Place in the Universe*, ibid. p. 231.) Cf. Pierre Smulders, *La vision de Teilhard de Chardin* (1964), pp. 57–70. (English translation, *The Design of Teilhard de Chardin*, Newman Press, Westminster, 1967)

Embedded in his organisms are the hereditary characteristics and inexorable processes of the flesh.

Forcibly directing the growth of his soul, there is his own personal temperament, the single, unalterable, passionate urge, to which, the longer he lives, the more obedient he will find he has been.

Ordered throughout his life by providence, there are the crises and encounters which his vocation has survived and in which it has matured.

There are forces that caress him, and penetrate him, and widen his being; and other forces, too, that rend, and shatter, and disorganize.

As my consciousness passes from one phase to another, a flicker of light illuminates now one, now another, of the many shades my bondage assumes: when that happens, why is it, Lord, that my heart gradually comes to linger with delight upon some rather than upon others?

What is there in suffering that commits me so deeply to you?

Why, when you stretched out nets to imprison me should I have thrilled with greater joy than when you offered me wings?

It is because the only element I hanker after in your gifts is the fragrance of your power over me and the touch of your hand upon me. For what exhilarates us human creatures more than freedom, more than the glory of achievement, is the joy of finding and surrendering to a beauty greater than man, the rapture of being possessed. So long as my movement and growth are dictated by my own desires, I can believe that I am my own master. But I do not feel your active influence so long as I follow its guidance. My ship seems to sail without rudder or sails. Yet when there comes a sudden squall of wind, when her way is suddenly checked, when she lies over on her beam-ends, then I feel the full strength of the force that holds me up. It is only in opposition to my own appetites, and only by conquering them, that your power, my God, takes on for my heart its complete reality, and stamps me to the quick with the beatifying imprint of its domination.

Blessed, then, be the disappointments which snatch the cup

from our lips; blessed be the chains that force us to go where we would not.

Blessed be relentless time and the unending thraldom in which it holds us: the inexorable bondage of time that goes too slowly and frets our impatience, of time that goes too quickly and ages us, of time that never stops and never returns.

Blessed, above all, be death and the horror of falling back into the cosmic forces. At the moment of its coming a power as strong as the universe pounces upon our bodies to grind them to dust and dissolve them, and an attraction more tremendous than any material tension draws our unresisting souls towards their proper centre. Death causes us to lose our footing completely in ourselves so as to deliver us over to the powers of heaven and earth. This is its final terror—but it is also, for the mystic, the climax of his bliss: it is our final entry, there to remain for ever, into the milieu that dominates, that carries us off, that consumes.

'*Io Triumpe.*'[19]

2. *Action.*[20] Just as the mystic, in following his innate appetite for the Universal, did not fall into pantheism, so, in surrendering to his preference for passivity, he does not sink into inertia. The very logic of his attitude (with the assistance of divine grace) prevents him from being tossed to and fro, like a drifting wreck, by the countless billows of causation.

Above all, he is immune from the perversion of loving suffering for its own sake, of seeking to suffer simply in order to suffer. In his eyes, the *only* charm of sorrow derives exclusively from its quality of being without any possible doubt, something *involuntary*, of representing eminently what is *in nobis sine nobis*. As soon as pain is no longer inflicted or introduced by circumstances, its heavenly radiance is extinguished for him, it resumes its natural ugliness, and he flies from it.

What is more, in virtue of the principle that we only really feel

[19] Throughout his whole life, Père Teilhard was constantly to return to the subject of death. Cf. *The Religion of Teilhard de Chardin*, Chapter 5. Meditation on Death, pp. 47-55.

[20] It will be noticed that in this essay action comes after passivity. *Le Milieu Divin* treats of them in the opposite order. But here too, pp. 136 ff., in 'the circle of spirit', we shall later meet a 'higher passivity'.

what we fight against, he reacts normally to the stab of any suffering, even sent by providence, that harasses and wounds him. He knows only too well that the more alive he is, the more active, the more tenacious in his advance towards happiness, the more strongly will he feel the mighty caress of the wave, the more completely will the ocean engulf him. The man who is passionately enamoured of the divine milieu will never surrender any essential part of himself, never let himself become less a man, never throw up the sponge when things go wrong: only in the last extremity will he accept suffering, and then only in so far as it is unavoidable. And when that is so, he will take it to himself as a heavenly bride. Thus the mystic is preserved from an ex-aggerated love of passivity by a very excess of that same love. In the bliss of feeling himself conquered by God, he instinctively stiffens his will against evil, and fights, through failures, to make his destiny triumph.[21]

This leads him, imperceptibly, to find in this spontaneous reaction a new way, more perfect than suffering, of adhering to the divine influence. And thereby he discovers, as he acts, that it is possible to effect *communion in action*.

God's creative power does not, in fact, fashion us as though out of soft clay. It is a fire that kindles life in whatever it touches, a quickening spirit. Therefore it is *by living* that we must de-cisively adapt ourselves to it, model ourselves upon it, identifying ourselves with it. The mystic is given at times a keen, obsessive, insight into this situation.

In the milieu of higher energy within which beings move, he then sees the free natures of men as independent nuclei, *un-absorbed*, with the power partly to isolate themselves from the divine forces that flow around them and lay siege to them. These nuclei, can, if they wish, insulate themselves against the radiation that seeks to penetrate and guide them. They can also, if they have received the light, resist its transfiguring action, or again, monopolizing it in their selfishness, allow its shadow to fall behind them.[22]

---

[21] Cf. *Le Milieu Divin*, pp. 62-3, Fontana, pp. 83-4, *Our struggle with God against evil*.

[22] To bring out the importance of individual freedom of choice and the

Any one who has the mystic's insight, and who loves, will feel within himself a fever of active dependence and arduous purity seizing upon him and driving him on to an absolute integrity and the utilization of all his powers. Such a man is pledged, in virtue of his inner vision, to an endless task of self-correction and self-development that exercises a delectable tyranny over his life. He can never rest so long as there remains the least discord between the vibration of his own being and that of the divine milieu: and yet how can one conceive that such an ideal harmony can ever be effected?

In order to become perfectly resonant to the pulsations of the basic rhythm of reality, the mystic makes himself docile to the least hint of human obligation, the most unobtrusive demands of grace.

To win for himself a little more of the creative energy, he tirelessly develops his thought, dilates his heart, intensifies his external activity. For created beings must work if they would be yet further created.

And finally, that no blemish may separate him, by so much as a single atom of himself, from the essential limpidity, he labours unceasingly to purify his affections and to remove even the very faintest opacities which might cloud or impede the light.[23]

What the soul has to attain, in fact, is not an annihilation of self that causes its own personal being to disappear, but an identification that will fulfil its being; and it is in order to do this that it

---

necessity of the option to be made by every man, was always to remain a leading element in Teilhard's thought. In this we can see the influence of his reading of Maurice Blondel's *L'Action*.

[23] On purity of heart, see *The Struggle against the Multitude*, above. Letter of 13 Nov. 1918: 'One can only be terrified at the crying need for purity the universe suffers from, and almost be beside oneself with longing to do something to supply it'. (*Making of a Mind*, p. 252.) 8 December: 'You know what is my dearest wish: that God, through Our Lady, may grant us so to share in her purity that we may really be able to serve, in our own small way, to regenerate the world.' (*Ibid*, p. 262.) The themes of purity and option are combined in a letter of 1 Feb. 1917: 'May our Lord make each of us a purifying leaven, in this universal, age-old, operation by which mankind is so mysteriously divided, through the activity of the Child-God, into the chosen and the rejected!' (*Making of a Mind*, p. 178.)

must not, in any part of itself, in its texture, or in its motions, be distinguishable from the clear and vibrant milieu into which it sinks.

As yet, the disappearance is not complete. The contours can still just be made out. A slight tremor betrays the imperfection of the union.

There must be still more perfect obedience.

The heart must open still more generously.

Purity must be still more intense.

There are no limits to this communion of an activity that strives to approach the perfection of its first principle: no limits to the right ordering of disposition, to the docility of the will, to the candour of mind and heart.

The mystic finds a joy no words can describe in feeling that through this active obedience (which is a very different thing from the passive acceptance that first satisfied him) he *endlessly* adheres *more closely* to the encompassing Godhead. Endlessly, the more perfect an *instrument* he becomes, the more does he *become one* with the creative Act. A little more, it would seem, and God, finding no resistance to his guidance in accordance with his designs, would no longer be able to distinguish the tool from his own almighty hand.

The truth is that the mystic is no longer much concerned with docility of will, or greater natural enrichment, or purity of soul, *in themselves*. He is completely absorbed for the moment in the idea of forming one with the universal Godhead. This attitude characterizes the first great cycle of his vision, which is on the point of reaching its conclusion.

Ever since he first discovered the mystical milieu in the halo of an intense emotion or in the magnification of an infinitely precious object of love, the seer has constantly seen all around him the development of an irrepressible homogeneity, in the depth of which superficial differences lose their sharpness. Once the mystic has reached this stage of his development, then, whatever he experiences, whatever action he carries through, wherever he goes, he never quits the same sublime and unchanging atmosphere that in all circumstances surrounds and dominates him. Whatever he does and wherever he is, he lives in a sort of *higher dream* in which the distinctions of practical life seem of minor importance and are blurred. Even though, in order to foster his vision, he is obliged to develop a vigorous perception of the immediate realities of life, he feels that their value is diminishing, and they tend to lose their importance for him.

This is the Cycle of the Homogeneous.

A further, complementary, phase is now imminent; in the course of this the uniform and supremely consistent principle of the universe will show itself capable of penetrating beings and 'absolutizing' them without either affecting their individual contrasts or suffering any change itself.

So we come to the threshold of the *Cycle of the Heterogeneous.*[24]

D: THE CIRCLE OF SPIRIT

The force that had been drawing the mystic towards the zone in which all things are fused together, now reverses its direction and brings him back to an exact examination of the experiential Multiple, *from the moment he realizes* that the higher element in which he longs to lose himself is not only the beatifying term of human activity but also, to some extent, its *product*.

Hitherto, he had hardly been able to distinguish, in the cosmic Godhead, anything more than a sort of unchanging Entity, and what mattered to him was to make as close as possible a *contact* with it. What he saw in the Creative Act, for example, to the almost complete exclusion of created things, was the creative energy which he felt flowing like sap into his life. In short, the movement of life was reduced, for him, to the opposition between *two invariables*—later to be followed by their almost complete conjunction—his own being and God, both in process of reaching unity *through the surface contact* provided by tangible things.

---

[24] In this we see the dialectical character of the development. In the first three circles (Presence, Consistence, Energy) the mystic was still confined to the 'cycle of the homogeneous', within which he could speak of 'forming one with the universal Godhead': that, however, was still a sort of 'higher dream'.

It was an incomplete view, sadly coloured by dualism, by an inability to enter into things and see their inner dynamism.

As soon as the light grows a little more brilliant, the seat of all action and communion will be revealed to the seer as being situated neither in the divine sphere nor in the created stratum, both properly so called, but in a special reality born of their mutual interaction. The mystical milieu *is not a completed zone* in which beings, once they have succeeded in entering it, remain immobilized. It is a *complex* element, made up of *divinized created being*, in which, as time goes on, the immortal distillation of the universe is gradually assembled. We cannot give it precisely the name of God: it is his Kingdom. Nor can we say that it *is*: it is in process of *becoming*.

As a result of this new insight the mystic is reinvigorated by the infusion into him of a life that had hitherto been somewhat alien to his soul. Now that man's labour interests him not simply *as an operation* that brings union with the divine act, but *as a work (opus)* which is a condition for the presence of God among us,[25] it becomes possible for him not only to *feel* the divine milieu but to *form* it, and to allow it to encompass him like a continually stronger light. Now that, in order to adhere to God, it is not enough for him to lend himself to purely *operative action*, but to *action* aimed at *achievement*, he has no difficulty, in his mystical drive, in making his own that insatiable ardour which gives the children of earth their passion for progress. While he was passing through the lower circles of his initiation, space, and matter, and energy, were each in turn divinized in his eyes. Now it is the turn of evolution.

1. *The Light that Inspires the Battle.* The first necessity is the liberation of Spirit.

Spirit is the goal towards which nature's age-long labours are directed. Everything that lives (and that may well mean everything that moves) is driven, from its very beginning, by an urge towards a little more freedom, a little more power, more truth.

---

[25] Père Teilhard was often to bring out, in various forms, this distinction between *operatio* and *opus*, though never emphasizing one at the expense of the other. Cf. the whole of the first part of *Le Milieu Divin*, etc.

Vaguely at first, and later with fuller consciousness of what it wants and what it lacks, each monad presses on towards the areas in which thought sheds its light.

We often ask ourselves the agonizing question, what force can be expected to keep in one common orbit, untiringly and without any disorder, the countless numbers of individuals who *pass through* life without making a success of it and without understanding what it means. What, then, is the driving force that insistently urges into the struggle so many wretched, unconscious living beings who seem to be attached to the earth by no appetite, no interest, and no useful purpose? Why should we, too, exhaust ourselves in an effort to succeed and acquire knowledge? Would not a *relaxation of effort* still give us enough to do for the moment and enable us to be happy?

The mystic, however, can see the profound and hallowed reason for his insatiable activity, for man's unswerving impulse towards the elusive Something that shines ahead of him. Throughout time, a task greater than individual lives is being achieved. An interest higher than individual successes is at stake. Spirit is coming to birth, the created foundation of the mystical milieu, the cosmic substance into which the Godhead among us is finally and for ever to be condensed. God, as he spiritualizes the world, is in process of penetrating it. A creative restlessness is stirring up the monads: such is the significance that the seer (particularly if he is a Christian) reads into the mysterious summons to perfect man and the enthralling hopes it raises; and such the intuition that gives him the nervous resilience of the conqueror.

Then it is really true, Lord? By helping on the spread of science and freedom, I can increase the density of the divine atmosphere, in itself as well as for me: that atmosphere in which it is always my one desire to be immersed. By laying hold of the Earth I enable myself to cling closely to you. What joy then possesses my mind, with what joy my heart expands! *The hunter's instinct*, which ever since my childhood sent me unremittingly in pursuit of things, never the same, which never led me to the goal I sought—that, I now see, is both justified and transfigured.

May the kingdom of matter, then, under our scrutinies and our manipulations, surrender to us the secrets of its texture, its movements, its history.

May the world's energies, mastered by us, bow down before us and accept the yoke of our power.

May the race of men, grown to fuller consciousness and greater strength, become grouped into rich and happy organisms in which life shall be put to better use and bring in a hundredfold return.

May the universe offer to our gaze the symbols and forms of all harmony and all beauty.

I must *search*, and I must *find*.

What is at stake is not my own satisfaction, nor my own well-being, nor even only my own life.

It is the survival and development of universal Spirit—of the Spirit which is not yet fully formed, nor *yet assured* of total *success*, but whose movement towards an ever greater degree of spirituality perseveres without slackening, of the Spirit that is quickened by the constant traffic of men's needs and their uncertainties.

It is the element, Lord, wherein you will to dwell here on earth.

What is at stake is your existence among us.

In the very first place, the perception of God present in all things presupposed in the mystic an intense zest for *the Real*.

A little later, adherence to God active in all things, forced him to develop as wide a consciousness as possible, *again of the Real*.

And now that he is making his way farther into the immanent God, he is tied, as a person, to an unremitting *fulfilment*, once again of *the Real*.

And this can mean only one thing, that man finds himself inexorably forced, by his passion for union with God, *to give* things *their highest possible degree of reality*, whether it be in his knowledge of them and his love for them, or in their proper being.

Lost though he is in his dream, the mystic is still a supreme *realist*.[26]

[26] Cf. letter of 10 June 1917: 'I'm tending to give still more prominence to the realism by which mysticism lives, and also to analyse more clearly the

The mystic is not, as some accuse him of being, a renegade or deserter, who does not share the earth's agonies nor its raptures. He, too, for all the infallibility of the dogmas he holds and the promises of paradise he has received, knows that he must fight to keep what he holds, and that he must seek if he is not to lose. He, too, even in his mystical domain, must work if he is to live; and he, too—he or others—may well die if his efforts go astray.

Here we meet a great mystery, but one that is constantly confirmed by experience: truth, even revealed truth, can be preserved only by being continually enlarged; or, if there are some minds that are excused that effort either because of their isolation or their exceptional simplicity, it is because others, close to them, take over in their place the task (indispensable even for believers if they wish to maintain their faith) of unremittingly clearing the road to thought and Life.

In his love for the Divine, which he sees welling up on all sides with each new advance effected by nature, the mystic flings himself with enthusiasm into *the battle for the Light*. It is agony to him to have his vision restricted. When evil fights back or lies across his path, he suffers torments. On the other hand, when the battle is won, he savours the heady brew poured out for its most faithful exponents by the *doctrine of might*. His vision does not prevent him from being fundamentally *human*; nevertheless, in addition to a more exalted motive for his desires, it provides him with a wonderful supplement for the inadequacy that constantly saddens human activity. Alone among men, the mystic is *certain* that the least of his labours is a κτῆμα εἰς ἀεί,[27] effective and enduring. For the mystic works within God.

One day, I remember, I could find no words in which to express the affirmation in which my life sought to be embodied. The wind carried off, or men's ears were deaf to, half of what I was able to say; and the rest, no one understood.

---

alternating movement that carries the soul away from (and in turn drives it back to) the Divine Milieu, homogeneous and essential, the vehicle being the particular determined forms of the real that we have to know and love and fulfil' (*Making of a Mind*, p. 195).

[27] An enduring possession.

It was then that I felt that all of us, all the many millions of us, crushed to suffocation on the surface of the earth, live here below, in the misery of being strangers to one another. The network of acts, and sounds, written or spoken, that links us together is crude and lifeless. It moulds us in only a rough and ready way, and it cannot faithfully transmit nor preserve our image. Nature is a bungler.

In the field in which Spirit ripens, when frost and hail have ruined the finest shoots and the plumpest ears, she still leaves trailing on the ground, after the harvest, a rich crop of energy and good will.

At that moment, I cursed progress. And in my disappointment I dreamed of a common centre into which all things would drive the most vital roots of their sensibility and energy; a universal Centre, living and benign, that would itself reinforce our desire to do what is right, when we are at a loss to express it, or preserve it, or realize it.

No being in the world could be deaf to or could reject the words which this infinitely sensitive milieu seeks to hear and transmit, for they would echo deep within every created being, mingled with life's imperative demands.

No untoward accident could destroy the seed that this infinitely conserving milieu had resolved to preserve and make use of. In its own time and place that seed would germinate, to bring joy to the spirit that conceived it.

Such was the dream that consoled my baffled longing for action.

It was then, Lord, that you offered my aspirations and my efforts the inner shelter of the divine Essence, so mysteriously incorporated in our universe, and that you said to me, 'I am at hand'.

'I am at hand, at the common heart of your own being and of all things, to welcome even the wildest of your longings and to assure you that not one single fragment of what is useful in them will be lost to God.

'I am at hand, changeless from generation to generation, ready to save for those who are to come the treasure that would otherwise be lost today, but which the future will inherit. One day I shall pass on to another, whose name I know, the thought that is in your mind. And when that man speaks and is heard, it is your voice that will be listened to. Do you yourself know from whom came the idea that excites you and which you cherish as though it were your own?

'It is I who am the true bond that holds the World together. Without me, even though beings may seem to make contact with one another, they are divided by an abyss. In me, they meet, in spite of the chaos of time and space.[28]

'I am at hand to fructify and ease your labours.

'But above all, I am at hand to take over your work and consummate it.

'You have fought long enough that the world may be divinized. It is for me now to force open the gates of Spirit.

'Stand aside!'

2. *The Fire that Comes Down upon Earth*.[29] Anyone who observes, simply as a scientist, the progress of natural evolution, often forms the impression that the part to be attributed in it to individual spontaneous actions is extremely limited. When one sees how living beings organize themselves, one would say that their role is confined to obediently following a particular direction inside the field of influence of an *outside* force that runs through them and builds up their structure. Individuals seem to *submit* to life much more than sustain and extend it.

This impression becomes the expression of an exact reality when the mystic passes from the domain of the natural liberation of Spirit by work into that of its divinization by grace, and finds in *supernaturalized* being the final and permanent atmosphere

[28] Cf. Ferdinand Prat, *La théologie de St Paul* (38th imp., vol. 1, p. 349): For St Paul, 'without Christ, all created things would be dispersed and fragmented and, in mutual conflict, would once again fall back into nothingness. It is Christ who maintains them not only in existence but in cohesion and harmony'.

[29] The fire-theme recurs in *The Priest* (1918) and in a much fuller form in *The Mass on the World* (1923, in *Hymn of the Universe*). See also the correspondence with Maurice Blondel in Dec. 1919, (*Archives de philosophie*, vol. 24, 1961, pp. 151–6). Letter of 30 May 1925: 'Pray that, come what may, I never let myself wish for anything but *The Fire*', and above, p. 128.

(half divine, half natural) in which he seeks to be enveloped, and which he himself can continually develop more fully.

The divine operation reigns in absolute sovereignty over the domain of sanctity.

For the seer with mystical insight into this zone of the Real, everything is ablaze. The universe has once more burst into fire.

At this stage, however, the initiate is not solely concerned, as he was in the circle of energy, with hastening to the blaze and losing himself in it *while still remaining himself*; the time has come when the created being's own substance, under the mastering influence of God, must become a constitutive element of the regenerated universe. What seeks to be effected is more than a simple union; it is a *transformation*, in the course of which the only thing our human activity can do is, humbly, to make ourselves ready, and to accept.

Fold your wings, my soul, those wings you had spread wide to soar to the terrestrial peaks where the light is most ardent. It is for you simply to await the descent of the Fire—supposing it to be willing to take possession of you.

If you are to attract its power to yourself, you must first loosen the bonds of affection which still tie you to objects cherished too exclusively for their own sake. The true union that you ought to seek with creatures that attract you is to be found not by going directly to them but by converging with them on God, sought in and through them. It is not by making themselves more material, relying solely on physical contacts, but by making themselves more spiritual in the embrace of God, that things draw closer to each other and, following their invincible natural bent, end by becoming, all of them together, one. Therefore, my soul, be chaste.

And when you have thus relieved your being of its burden of crude accretions, you must loosen yet further the fibres of your substance. In your excessive self-love you are like a molecule closed in upon itself and incapable of entering easily into any new combination. God looks to you to be more open and more pliant. If you are to enter into him you need to be freer and more eager. Have done, then, with your egoism and your fear of suffering. Love others as you love yourself, that is to say admit them into yourself, all of them, even those whom, if you were a pagan, you would exclude. Accept pain. Take up your cross, my soul.

. . . And now the Fire is with us: it has come down, as though upon a burnt-offering. Now the mystic has ceased to be *only himself*. Body and soul, he has become a fragment of the divine. Henceforth, as though through a sacred door opening on to the universe, God passes through him and spreads his radiance.

Seeing the mystic immobile, crucified or rapt in prayer, some may perhaps think that his activity is in abeyance or has left this earth: they are mistaken. Nothing in the world is more intensely alive and active than purity and prayer, which hang like an unmoving light between the universe and God. Through their serene transparency flow the waves of creative power charged with natural virtue and with grace. What else but this is the Virgin Mary?[30]

There was a time when, in his eagerness to accept the domination of God, the mystic found himself forced into action. Now, the process is reversed and the very excess of his desire for action weds him to a passivity of a higher order. Through seeking to possess and thoroughly cultivate the world (that so he may feel the presence of God), he has become an ascetic and a contemplative. Through seeking the development of his own nature he has found the rapture of feeling that suffering is dissolving his being, drop by drop, and replacing it by God. Through loving life, he has come to wish for death, since death alone can destroy his egoism so radically as to enable him to be absorbed in Christ.

So, for the third time, we cry again, *Io triumpe!*

E: THE CIRCLE OF PERSON

We have seen the mystical milieu gradually develop and assume a form at once divine and human.

[30] The same idea recurs in *Le Milieu Divin*, p. 134. See also, in connection with the Immaculate Conception, letter of 5 Dec. 1916, in *Making of a Mind*, p. 149.

At first, we might have mistaken it for a mere projection of our emotions, their excess flowing out over the world and appearing to animate it.

Soon, however, its autonomy became apparent as a strange and supremely desirable Omnipresence. This universal presence began by drawing into itself all consistence and all energy. Later, embodied in the great wind of purification and conquest that excites man at every stage in his history, it drew us into itself—so fully as to assimilate us to its own nature.

Sometimes, when I have scrutinized the world very closely, I have thought that I could see it enveloped in an atmosphere—still very tenuous but already individualized—of mutual good will and of truths accepted in common and retained as a permanent heritage. I have seen a shadow floating, as though it were the wraith of a universal soul seeking to be born.

What name can we give to this mysterious Entity, who is in some small way our own handiwork, with whom, eminently, we can enter into communion, and who is some part of ourselves, yet who masters us, has need of us in order to exist, and at the same time dominates us with the full force of his Absolute being?

I can feel it: he has a name and a face, but he alone can reveal his face and pronounce his name:[31]

Jesus![32]

The movement that first opened my eyes began *at one point*, in a person: my own person. As my powers of perception were aroused, that point expanded as though it would absorb all things. Very soon, however, it found that the process seemed to be reversed and that it was itself being taken over. Together with

[31] The idea of personal being was to play an increasingly important in the presentation of Père Teilhard's thought. It remained, however, entirely a matter of presentation. The idea itself already dominated his thought at this period.

[32] The repetition of the refrain 'Jesus' in this final prayer will be noted. Père Teilhard deliberately used the name 'Jesus' rather than, for example, 'Christ', as having a more personally evocative force, and because it gives the prayer a more intimate tone. See above, the final prayer in *Cosmic Life* (pp. 69–70).

all the beings around me I felt that I was caught up in a higher movement that was stirring together all the elements of the universe and grouping them in a new order. When it was given to me to see where the dazzling trail of particular beauties and partial harmonies was leading, I recognized that it was all coming to centre *on a single point*, on a Person: your Person:

Jesus!

In his superabundant unity, that Person possessed the virtue of each one of the lower mystical circles. His presence impregnated and sustained all things. His power animated all energy. His mastering life ate into every other life, to assimilate it to himself. Thus, Lord, I understood that it was possible to live without ever emerging from You, without ever ceasing to be buried in You, the Ocean of Life, the life that penetrates and quickens us. Since first, Lord, you said, '*Hoc est corpus meum*', not only the bread of the altar but (to some degree) everything in the universe that nourishes the soul for the life of Spirit and Grace, has become *yours* and has become *divine*—it is divinized, divinizing, and divinizable. Every presence makes me feel that you are near me; every touch is the touch of your hand; every necessity transmits to me a pulsation of your will. And so true is this, that everything around me that is essential and enduring has become for me the dominance and, in some way, the substance of your heart:

Jesus!

That is why it is impossible for me, Lord—impossible for any man who has acquired even the smallest understanding of you—to look on your face without seeing in it the *radiance* of every reality and every goodness. In the mystery of your mystical body —your cosmic body—you sought to feel the echo of every joy and every fear that moves each single one of all the countless cells that make up mankind. And correspondingly, we cannot contemplate you and adhere to you without your Being, for all its supreme simplicity, transmuting itself as we grasp it into the re-structured Multitude of all that you love upon earth:

Jesus!

And the result of this astonishing synthesis of all perfection and all growth that you effect in yourself, is that the act by which I possess you combines, in its strict simplicity, more attitudes and more insights than I have spoken of here, and more than I could ever express. When I think of you, Lord, I cannot say whether it is in this place that I find you more, or in that place—whether you are to me Friend or Strength or Matter—whether I am contemplating you or whether I am suffering—whether I rue my faults or find union—whether it is you I love or the whole sum of others. Every affection, every desire, every possession, every light, every depth, every harmony, and every ardour glitters with equal brilliance, at one and the same time, in the inexpressible *Relationship* that is being set up between me and you:

Jesus!

CONCLUSION

The experiences described in this essay are only *an introduction* to *mysticism*. Beyond the point at which I have stopped, the being in whom the higher cosmic milieu is completely *personified*, reveals, as and when he wills, the beauties of his countenance and heart. There are infinite degrees in the loving initiation of one person into another unfathomable Person.

I am not qualified to describe those sublime states.[33] All I have tried to do is to bring out their natural roots.

[33] We use the word 'mystical' in a number of very different meanings. Père Teilhard has here been trying, in the first place, to distinguish the root meaning common to them all: the natural sense that everyone, if he has the power of self-analysis, finds in himself, in degrees and under aspects that vary very widely, of an opening-out of his self onto the universe, onto the common basis—infinite, it would seem, to him—or the common source that he senses in it and which is accordingly 'mysterious' to him. The mystical sense, therefore, as the common origin of the words suggests, is the sense of the 'mystery' contained in everything (which is a mystery of unity).

There are, however, many degrees in the mystery: (a) that of the universe, for our natural reason; (b) that of the first source and the final end which reason postulates for the universe, beyond it; (c) the mystery again—for the Christian —that the Revelation of the one God in three persons opens up for him in faith; (d) finally, the mystery that God sometimes grants to the 'mystic' of

Of course, all who are admitted to the vision of Christ will not go through the different phases in the order I have described; but if they analyse their passion for the divine, they will see that they have proceeded through the circles, and that their love lies at the centre. In particular, they will recognize the role of the created thing in the sharpening of sensibility, which gives the warmth that Charity calls for, and the vast cosmic realities that give God his tangible and palpable being here below. *Amictus (mundo) sicut vestimento*—clothed (in the world) as in a garment. No one, I think, will understand the great mystics—St Francis, and Blessed Angela, and the others—unless he understands the full depth of the truth that *Jesus must be loved as a world*.

Moreover, from the humblest dawn of mystical thought, God is seen to be the only being that can maintain and direct it. Although, no doubt, we can by artificial means find some ways of briefly stimulating it, *the zest for life*, which is the source of all passion and all insight, even divine, does not come to us from ourselves. We are incapable of modifying those primordial depths of ourselves from which springs the force that animates us. All we can do is to accept ourselves as we are. It is God who has to give us *the impulse of wanting him*. And when the soul feels itself on fire for heaven, it still cannot, by itself, see what it lacks. It will see God only if God turns his face towards it: and a man

---

whom we speak in our 'mystical theology', in *passive* contemplation (the contemplation of which St Teresa of Avila describes a typical series of stages in her *Interior Castle*).

Starting in this essay from the first of these meanings and proceeding to disclose the second, Père Teilhard moves on, as a believer—and more markedly so towards the end of each of his 'circles'—to the third, that of Christian revelation. Here, in conclusion, he expresses his admiration for those mystical states which he says he is 'not qualified' to describe, but whose position he determines with great correctness.

The *mystical milieu*—which reappears later as the *divine milieu*, in a treatment that is more concerned with its spiritual nature than its natural roots—connotes essentially the 'bond' of that interaction, that personal dialogue between God and his creature, in which the creative action and the initiative of divine grace are constantly paramount, and constitute, for our natural action and our response to the divine summons, the ambience or 'milieu' in which we live, and move and have our being—of which St Paul first spoke, in his address to the Areopagus in Athens (Acts 17:28).

cannot even force another man to do that. And when, finally, the soul has distinguished the burning centre which has been seeking for it, it is powerless to follow up the ray of light that has fallen on it, and cast itself into the source. For it is written: 'No one can come to me unless I take him and draw him into myself'.

Mystical bliss is consummated in the consciousness of this gratuitous act, in other words of this supreme dependence upon God.

Qui potest capere, capiat.
Beaulieu-les-Fontaines, Oise. 13 August 1917

Creative Union

Père Teilhard himself tells us that this essay was not written for publication, but to provide a basis for discussion of his ideas, expressed in metaphysical terms, with official censors at some future date. He wrote from the front ('Making of a Mind', p. 209) to his cousin Marguerite Teillard-Chambon:

'8 October 1917: When I get back down the line, if God spares my life, I have almost made up my mind to make a start on an essay in philosophical synthesis (you'll smile to hear this ambitious plan) called 'Creative Union'. I think this essential if I am to make myself understood by those before whom I shall sooner or later have to defend or justify my ideas'.

Creative Union was finished on November 10th.

A year later, on 3 October 1918, he writes: 'From the "thinking" point of view, I'm hoping to get down in a few paragraphs, as an appendix to 'Creative Union', the various new points that have taken definite shape or defined themselves in my mind during the last year— for my own benefit, of course, and with an eye to future critics—and not for general publication'.

However, as he writes on 11 October 1918, he abandoned this plan:

'In any case, I've given up for the moment the appendix to 'Creative Union' about which I wrote to you. There would be too much to say; I'd rather wait until some new central aspect emerges from the various components'.

Moreover, this attempt, by a thinker who felt so compelled to 'picture' things to himself, to transpose to the metaphysical plane a concept derived from the 'physical' plane (in the old sense of 'natural philosophy') does not seem very happy. It is more a transposition into different language than a real transposition, and the idea it gives of the act of creation, transcendent and impatient of representation, cannot easily be reconciled with the Catholic dogma of creation ex nihilo.

Père Teilhard realized this; and in the years that followed he often returned to the theme, trying to find a way of expressing it whose orthodoxy would be less questionable. In the end he abandoned this metaphysical enquiry, feeling that the bent of his mind did not lend itself to it. (At the same time he continued to be interested in the problem, as we know from passages in 'Comment je vois' in 1948 and 'Contingence de l'Univers et goût humain de survivre' in 1953.)

Thus, on 25 April 1918 he notes, in connexion with his idea that to be is to be united (esse = uniri):

'The definition esse = uniri *would, it seems to me, be philosophically defensible. In any case it has the merit of being a fruitful definition and of being without doubt the law that governs the progress of being. Even if it is metaphysically questionable it has an undeniable practical value (as applied to growth:* crescere = uniri*)'. Again, on 3 October 1918: 'I must draw up, as an appendix to 'Creative Union', a summary of the new points I have established or developed during the last year. They seem to me principally the following: 1. An expulsive creative phase, necessary, perhaps, in order to base union upon a distinct efficient force . . . The origin of the Multiple would then have to be sought not in a sort of* opposition *(an organic reflex) but in a more contingent act'.*

And on 10 November 1918: ' "Creative Union" tended to reduce everything to a mechanics of union. There must, without doubt, be an expulsive phase:

(a) *either* per modum alicujus oppositionis organicae,

(b) *or . . .* efficientiae.'

Again, on 13 January 1919, he adds: 'If the expression is found more orthodox, instead of "union creates (creation = a sort of union)", we may say "creation unites" (Deus creat uniendo).'

In the 'Mon Univers' of 1924 (not to be confused with the essay of 1918, under the same title) he returns to the problem, and indicates more exactly how far his theory extends.

' "Creative Union" is not precisely a metaphysical doctrine. It is much more a sort of empirical and pragmatic explanation of the universe; I developed it to meet the need to reconcile, in a solidly coherent system, scientific views on evolution (now definitely accepted in their essence) with the innate tendency that urges me on to seek the divine, not by breaking away from the physical world, but through matter and, in some way, in union with it'.

CREATIVE UNION

I am proposing here to return to and set out systematically a number of ideas that will be found scattered throughout various essays I have written since January 1916 (in particular in *The Struggle against the Multitude*). I have, in fact, come to realize that these ideas only need to be brought together, to form a synthesis which constitutes '*a point of view from which to look at everything*'. I am anxious to establish this point of view more accurately, so that it may be critically examined, and made use of if it is thought worth while. As we all know, the conclusive force of a system lies much more in its capacity to explain (that is to say, to give unity to) the intelligible Real than in the proofs that can be given of its parts in isolation and, still more, of its fundamental basis— which latter is a postulate. I shall proceed, accordingly, much more by exposition than by discussion. A 'point of view' can be adopted and verified: it cannot be demonstrably proved.

The logic of the system, it will be seen, obliges me to put forward a number of paradoxical propositions: on the nature, for example, of Spirit, of non-being, of the future, etc. I do not think that these paradoxes are an indication that the theory I am offering is wrong. Completely lucid and 'orthodox'[1] syntheses are necessarily sterile and false *by omission*. On the other hand, certain obscurities or oddities that the Real forces upon our notice represent that unexplored but fruitful part of it from which further mental constructions will be developed. It is infinitely preferable to offer, *provisionally*, a mixture of truth and error than to mutilate reality by trying prematurely to separate the wheat from the tares. I have had no hesitation in following that Gospel precept, which applies equally to all intellectual enquiry and scientific progress.

[1] I am speaking primarily, it will be appreciated, of Scholastic orthodoxy. (Note by Père Teilhard.)

A: THE SYNTHETIC (COMPOSITE) NATURE OF SPIRIT

I accept, in the first place, as a presupposition to all that follows, that the universe is committed to *a Becoming*, which gradually constitutes it in its destined form, the most perfect elements of the world being produced in succession through the less perfect, starting from lower states of existence. No postulate seems to me to be based on a wider area of experience or on more exact critical examination—and none more certain, accordingly, still to be accepted by the scientists and philosophers of tomorrow —than that of evolution. And I am resolutely adopting it.

Secondly, I accept that the evolution of the universe has *an absolute direction*, which is *towards Spirit*. This second postulate, like the first, is derived from inferences and inductions too extensive to be considered in detail here. I shall confine myself to saying that, both *a priori* and *a posteriori*, the progressive spiritualization of conscious being is manifestly the only variable characteristic (the only parameter) that enables us to follow, both in direction and in height, the essential curve of Becoming through the labyrinth of individual evolution. It is refinement of psychism that determines the true, absolute, position of the monads in the ascending series of beings.

From this twofold fundamental postulate (the reality of an evolution, and the primacy of Spirit) it follows immediately that: *to explain the shape of the world means to explain the genesis of Spirit.* It is the secret of this genesis that the theory of creative union seeks to elucidate.

The originality of this theory consists in looking for the solution to the problem of Spirit in what is generally considered its most difficult aspect, which is the connexion between thought and the multiple and material.

It has always been noted that the organic characteristic of Spirit is that it appears coincidentally with, and in connexion with, a supremely complicated physical equipment. From the constitution of his protoplasm to his muscular and nervous tissue, the most spiritual being known to science—Man—is at the same time the being that is made up of the greatest number of parts. We may say that in our world psychic perfection varies in inverse[2] ratio with organic complexity and instability.

Materialists have seen in this remarkable contrast between the spirituality of the soul and the fragility of the organism a proof that thought is a subsidiary cosmic element, an epiphenomenon.

Philosophers of the Spirit, for their part, have resolutely maintained the essential dual reality (a reality at once supremely simple and supremely complicated) of the two principles which are coupled together in the rational being; they have never tried, however, to explain this surprising, and constant, association.

I hope to fill the gap between the two by accepting that the essential connexion found, in this world, between the spiritual and the multiple is not an insoluble philosophical riddle: on the contrary, it discloses to us the fundamental constitution of Spirit, from which that connexion is quite simply derived. The process is as follows:

Initially, we must see the formative energy of the world as grappling with an infinite tendency to crumble into dust, with a thing that is by its nature (and hence by its general trend) infinitely dissociated, a sort of pure multiple. The problem and the secret of creation consisted in reducing this power of dissociation and reversing its direction, in such a way as to produce progressively more synthesized monads. The more intimate the union effected between more diverse elements (that is, the more the Multitude was overcome) the more perfect and conscious the being that emerged. *Plus esse = plus, et a pluribus, uniri.* Soul, at all its degrees,[3] was born of this progressive concentration of the primordial dust. Animation is proportionate to union.

Consciousness, of course, should not be regarded, in this hypothesis, as no more than the result of elementary material properties brought into harmony with one another. The growth of being, following on the mutual fertilization of the monads, represents the appearance in the world of something *completely new.* The union of a pleiad in a monad of a higher order calls for a distinct recasting, and leads to the formation of a new substance,

---

[2] Père Teilhard inadvertently wrote 'inverse ratio' for 'direct ratio'.

[3] Atomic, vegetative, sensitive, rational (note by Père Teilhard).

formed on each occasion by a completely new principle of union (soul) enveloping an aggregation of earlier units. Ontological union (and the force of the adjective must be fully understood) is specifically *creative*. Creation is brought about by an act of uniting; and true union cannot be effected except by creating. These are two correlative propositions.[4]

When the advent of Spirit, properly so called, is close at hand, the mechanism of 'spiritualization' by union becomes easy to distinguish. In the higher animals, with large brains, the instability of the soul is at its greatest, because the very numerous elements that are constitutive of psychism are still loosely combined: the multiples from which being is born are not yet completely knit together, and the least thing can cause them to fall apart; when they are dissociated, their principle of union, which is *still itself tenuous*, disappears with them. In man, on the other hand, the organic components succeed in *centring themselves*,[5] and from that time a new spiritual substance appears in the world for the first time—the very centre of unification. In man the body (that is to say the ensemble of united elements) can disappear: the principle of his union, being strictly concentrated on one point, will survive the physical disappearance. As form that can be isolated from its matter—as a bond that can subsist with nothing to hold together—as a unitive force that can exist apart from the united whole—the human soul is incorruptible. At the same time it retains its solidarity with the Multitude that, *genetically* and *potentially*, never ceases to persist in it. Not only is the human soul without any doubt incompletely spiritualized (for there are

---

[4] This should be compared with *Mon Univers* (1924): 'Creative union is the theory that accepts that in the present evolutionary stage of the cosmos (which is the only one we know) everything happens as though the One were formed by successive unification of the Multiple, and were the more perfect the more perfectly it centralized beneath itself a more extensive Multiple. For the elements associated in a body by soul . . . *plus esse est cum pluribus uniri*. For the soul itself, the principle of unity, *plus esse est plus plura unire*. For both . . . it is to undergo the creative influence of God, *qui creat uniendo*. These propositions should be carefully weighed if they are not to be misinterpreted. They do not mean that the One is made up of the Multiple . . . but that the One appears to us only in succession to the Multiple, dominating it, since its essential, formal act is to unite'.

[5] Through reflexion: man thinks that he is thinking.

many degrees in stability of spirit), but it continues to need matter as a physiological environment, one from which it can draw nourishment, and into which, through the medium of the body, it extends its roots.

We may therefore conclude that if the most refined psychism coincides, in our universe, with the most complex material basis, then this is *by structural necessity*. As a result of the mechanism of evolution, *the One*, in the cycle of our creation, *is born on the multiple; the simple* is formed by giving its unity to what is *complex; spirit* is made *through the medium of matter*. Thus, in the process of becoming, organic complexity and psychic simplicity are not in opposition: the one, in fact, is the condition for the appearance of the other. There is no spiritual *unity* without the exercise of a unifying force: *unum nascitur uniendo*. The Multiple is the lower (and dispensable) side of the rational soul; and the soul is the point upon which Matter converges (and which can be detached from matter). Between the perishable souls of animals and man's immortal spirit, there is not exactly a hiatus: there is a transition from one to the other through a critical point. The rarefied becomes concentrated on one point, the section of the cone becomes the apex. We experience this ourselves in tangible form when we feel that we can recognize in ourselves that *thought* is *transformed sense-perception*.

Whereas the Kosmos, in Bergson's creative evolution, is seen as a radiation that spreads out from a central source, the picture of the universe we are introduced to by 'Creative Union' is that of a concentration, a convergence, a centripetal confluence that originates in some infinitely distended sphere. Although both evolutionary, each theory is the converse of the other.

It might appear that certain facts cannot be reconciled with this hypothesis of a world in process of continual concentration. The multiplication of living beings by reproduction, the jealously guarded and ever increasing autonomy of the monads, the divergence of animal phyla—surely all these mean not a reduction but a reinforcement of the Multiple?

It is not difficult to show that while these facts appear to contradict the theory of creative union, they fit in with it perfectly and even serve to *generalize* it.

If one considers it carefully, the proliferation of living beings no more represents a victory for number than the multiplication of crystals in a solution entails a numerical increase in the material units suspended in the liquid. The process of the psychic concentration of Matter is extended, no doubt, around each living being; but for the totality of things this extension represents a transition from a state of greater division to a lesser degree of fragmentation. The new multitude shows a reduction in relation to the former.[6] What is more, it is the condition necessary to a further simplification.

Souls are mistaken, in fact, when they imagine that they are made for autonomy and isolation. It is clear, indeed, that the work of individual deepening and folding back upon the centre is indispensable if the monads are to be completed; but that work is *ordered* to a higher fusion of the pleiad. Individuals are called to a higher unification, the need for which constantly plagues them— and we see evidence of this in their inability to find happiness and to develop in isolation. The great mass of souls, therefore, is not a sort of dust into which Life disintegrates: their totality constitutes the higher matter which is destined to be made one, to be created, beneath a new Spirit, heralded and prepared by their multitude. This is determined by the law of recurrence which governs the formation of beings.

It is not to be wondered at that all the roads that life tries in order to effect the synthesis of the Multiple are not equally profitable. Drawn by the same unifying force, beings choose different roads, some more direct, some less. Some of them come to grief in their attempts, or take a retrograde path. As the elements of Spirit make their way together towards their common goal, they suffer a disintegration—what one might call an unravelling—of their fibres. That is why so many phyla break away and give the illusion of a divergent evolution. This fragmentation is superficial and secondary. Basically, the whole of the world's psychism gravitates towards a single centre.

---

[6] As happens, for example, when water vapour condenses into mist or snow. (Note by Père Teilhard.)

B: THE REALITY OF THE CENTRE ON WHICH LIFE
CONVERGES

The fact that a pattern of convergence can be recognized in the process of universal becoming is sufficient in itself to demolish the Bergsonian notion of a vital *impulse* without any final purpose, of a *vis a tergo*. Such a dynamism, indeed, cannot but introduce into its principle a centre of divergence. One cannot see how it could produce the confluence of the elements it drives before it.

The force that creates the world can only be a *vis ab ante*, a force of attraction: what can we say about its nature?

(i) Is it a force completely submerged in the original Multiple, a loosely-knit affinity in the initial dust, in virtue of which the monads come into harmony purely by reciprocal action—in which case the centre of cosmic spiritualization would be *potential* and *immanent*, without actual existence or specific operation?

(ii) Is it, on the contrary, an energy that is extra-cosmic in origin (even though immanent in its term), animating material elements *ab extra* and fusing them together by the influx of a force that is external to them—in which case the centre that unifies the monads is *real* and *transcendent*?

This is, in fact, the problem of God expressed in terms of creative union. I propose to show that only the second alternative, that is to say the existence of a real and transcendent centre, is compatible with the mechanism of that union.

In the first place, the intervention of a specific energy that unifies the cosmos would appear to be indispensable if the smallest degree of association of the elements of spirit is to be even initiated. If we are not to contradict the logic of the system I am explaining, we must in fact admit that within the Multiple there is a mutual repulsion between the parts. If we observe that the monads around us are animated by positive, constructive, affinities, this is not in virtue of their origin in the multiple. It is due to the synthesis adumbrated in them by creative union. In itself, the Multiple is incapable of associating itself in groups or of progressing in being—since it is a power of dispersion (annihilation). This being so, it is obviously impossible to accept the spurious hypothesis of a multiplicity that contains its own principle of unification.

This first demonstration has the disadvantage of being a little bit 'up in the air' and too rigidly systematized. There is, however, another consideration that has the double advantage of resting on a wider experiential basis and of drawing its conclusive force from the practical demands of action at least as much as from the logical necessities of reason.

The centre of universal evolution must be real—and consequently transcendent—because if it were *only* potential (and immanent) the world would have no base from which to function, no consistence and, in consequence, no value—a conclusion that we cannot accept. Let me explain further.

The characteristic of a *convergent* evolution such as we have accepted is that Being appears in it—if I may put it so—'cantilevered': the world is without support at one end (when we look back, that is), since at that end it emerges from essential fragmentation. It is only through their forward impetus that things *hold firm*.

If, in these conditions, we could conjecture that *all* the forces of the universe worked harmoniously together to produce Spirit; if every higher form of being appeared to emerge from the co-operation of *all* the lower forces in pursuing a determined curve of progress; if, in other words, the cosmos behaved like a gigantic organism ordered in its entirety towards the production of souls—in that case we would be justified in attributing to the world a purely immanent power of growth, and we would not shrink from entrusting ourselves to it.

Experience, however, tells us, in the plainest terms, a very different story. In our universe, every higher form of existence appears within an energy that was there before but remains *unaffected, in its totality*, by the new formation it supports (organic life and physico-chemical forces, for example, or thought and organic life). From this it follows that the most spiritualized substance lies open to attack from—can be misled by—the lower forces that it has not, as it comes into being, completely mastered. For example, no factor in evolution known to our experience can make it clear that our human race *was bound to* succeed: nor is there any guarantee, immanent in progress, that can insure mankind for the future against any irrational cataclysm.

Faced with this radical contingence, any one who reflects on the problem will find that he must choose between two alternatives:

Either he must accept that he can find nothing in his environment that has the least claim to be called absolute, and agree that wherever he looks he can see nothing but a vast concurrence of chances (that, however, goes against both his most fundamental intellectual instinct and his indestructible need to devote himself only to a work that will en dure).

Or, on the other hand, if he wishes to salvage from the wreck his faith in the value of human effort, he will try to find outside the world a principle of fulfilment, in other words an extrinsic final purpose—a providence.

The only way out of this dilemma would be to maintain that a sufficiently great accumulation of contingencies can amount to a necessity. Since a very large number of attempts made in the same direction entail a certainty of success, one might say that the infallible success of the world (without which we cannot be intellectually or actively satisfied) results from the endless repetition of the Multitude's attempts to associate in groups; and this would relieve us of the necessity to have recourse to a directive force external to the world. To this I would reply that this process of 'multiple attempts' (which has ensured many partial successes in the course of life's transformations) cannot be sufficient to give evolution the essential stability that we are all compelled to recognize in it even though we cannot explain it scientifically. The 'infallibility of large numbers' may serve, at a pinch, to explain the success of *our* human race in the past, but it cannot dispel our anxiety for the future. And it is that reassurance that matters most to us.

Courageous, conscious, reflective, human life is impossible (by which I mean that it contains an intrinsic contradiction) unless Spirit—*our* Spirit—can have a guarantee of its success, and a promise of its future. That guarantee and that promise cannot be found in either the present or the future: only a power that is master of time and chance can give them.

That is why the centre towards which the elements of Spirit gravitate, under the influence of an attractive force that animates them—drawing them towards a unity that is to be theirs—can only be a transcendent Reality.

C: POSITIVE NON-BEING: THE QUASI-ABSOLUTE VALUE OF CREATION

Now that we have determined the nature of the peak of evolution, we may turn back to its base. What sort of reality should we attribute to the dust upon which creative union acts?

For a long time I thought that the increasing fragmentation into which things disappear when we try to trace them back *historically* (scientifically) to their source was only an appearance, the result of some 'form' or law of our minds. Just as we cannot imagine any limit to stellar or interatomic space, so we cannot see any absolute beginning to temporal series. We see everything around us extending into endless perspectives, because that is the way in which the Real breaks down under the action of our minds. That, I say, is the view I first accepted.

According to this hypothesis, it is clear, the ontological order of creation had nothing in common with the historical order of evolution. God, for example, could perfectly well have created the world in the state it reached in the year 1000, without our being any the wiser. Our experience, our science, would have continued none the less to carry the cosmic series indefinitely back into the past. The world of 1000 A.D. is conditioned by a network of antecedents, and science is concerned with discovering their threads, simply from the point of view of their mutual connexion, without prejudging their absolute reality.

This duality of the cognitive order and the real order has since seemed to me arbitrary and false. We have no serious reason for thinking that things are not made in the same pattern as that in which our experience unfolds them. On the contrary, that pattern may very well disclose to us the fundamental texture of Spirit.

In the theory of creative union, the imponderable Multiple

which evolution indicates as the original state of the cosmos, must be considered as having had a true, objective, absolute existence.[7]

What can we say about the nature of this primitive substratum of Spirit?

In the first place we should see it as an excessively impoverished and attenuated substance. Union, we must remember, does more than transform things and add to them. It *produces*. Every new union to be effected increases the absolute quantity of being existing in the universe. We should not, accordingly, think that as the principle underlying things there was some ὕλη, without form but complete in its consistence. As yet there was only an adumbration, a shadow, of being.

Even that is saying too much. When we speak of an adumbration or a shadow we imply some positive existence, and nothing can be positive that has not undergone an initial influence of union. Before there is any unification we can speak only of the negative (in its real form, which is pure Multiple). As we have already seen, the initial subject of creation was an essential power of dissociation and division. The *productio ex nihilo subjecti* did not consist in forming outright an infinitesimal being (an ε of being) destined to grow (as though the difficulty of making something 'out of nothing' were circumvented or conjured away) but in reversing the direction of this force of dispersion. If nascent being appears in an infinitesimal form, it is because it is still very close to its *point of total disunity*.

I am well aware that this concept of a sort of *positive non-being* as the subject of creation raises grave difficulties. However closely tied to non-being we may suppose it to be, the Thing, dissociated by its nature, required for the operation of creative union, implies that the creator found outside himself a purchase-point, or at least a reaction. It suggests, too, that the creation was not completely gratuitous but represents a work of quasi-absolute value. All this *redolet manichaeismum*—smacks of manichaeism.[8]

[7] On what follows, see introductory note to this essay.

[8] In as much as the Multiple is bound up with physical and moral evil, pain and sin are readily reduced to an effect of dissociation (either organic or deliberate), see *The struggle against the Multitude* and §F below (note by Père Teilhard).

True enough: can we, however, avoid these snags—or rather paradoxes—without offering explanations that are purely *verbal*.?[9] When we are speaking of God the truth lies between two series of approximations, of which one goes too far and the other falls short. We would without doubt present a very incomplete idea of the Godhead if we described it exclusively by *personal* attributes: some aspects of the supreme Being can be interpreted only in terms that I might call material and cosmic. It is the same with the creative act. If we try to make it too free or operating too much *in vacuity*, we may well make it unintelligible. Is there any reason why we should not admit that the necessary existence of absolute unity entails, as a secondary consequence, *ad extra*—rather as though it were its antithesis or shadow—the appearance at the opposite pole from being, of an infinite multiplicity?[10] To do so, I believe, would not be in any way to belittle either the Maker or his work.

D: QUALITY AND QUANTITY

There are two different ways of conceiving the 'dissociated thing' that serves as the basis of creation. One may, in the first place, assume that the initial Multiple is a heterogeneous, different throughout itself, so that its *pure multiplicity* is at the same time *pure variety*. The more we considered an extremely large segment of this thing, the more we would find in it different properties in an embryonic rudimentary state—in other words in a *converse* state.

We may also believe, however, that the original plurality is a pure homogeneous. In that case all the different varieties of beings would be born from different ways of union between identically similar elements. The closer the fusion between a

[9] A metaphysician would comment that it is more the expression 'positive non-being' that is a 'purely verbal explanation'.

[10] Thus there would somehow be two divine creative acts: the first, *quasi-organic*, concluding in the appearance of pure Multiple (= the effect in conflict with the divine oneness); the second, *quasi-efficient*, unifying the Multiple (= creation properly so called). (Note by Père Teilhard.)

greater number of elements, the more perfect the creature would be.

In the first case, there would have been, from the very beginning, a distinction between quality and quantity: but the two would vary in step with one another. In the second case, the *quale* would be a secondary consequence of the *quantum*: the latter view seems to fit better into our system.

However that may be, creative union, which sets up a direct relationship between the spirituality of the soul and the complexity of the body, thereby brings out an exact relationship (as yet more *empirical* than theoretical) between quality and quantity: *Plus esse = plus, a pluribus* UNIRI (p. 5) [= p. 155, above].

Just as the wider the base of the pyramid and the more acute the angle at the apex, the higher it is, so (in *our* universe) the created being is the more spiritual, the more closely it concentrates in itself a greater initial multiplicity.

This axiom entails a number of interesting corollaries:

(i) First, it shows that we must accept for the universe a *finally determined and invariable power of development*. Simply through the fact that the creative flux has covered a certain 'area' of the Multiple, the world is destined to attain a certain degree of spiritualization, this being a function of the mass of transformed plurality. This degree, which cannot be exceeded, is, of course, a theoretical maximum. In all evolution, in fact, we have to allow for failure, perversion and wastage—for evil. Not the whole of the mass summoned to union obeys the flood that urges it on. Side by side with quickening, spiritualizing forms of union there are others (as in crystals, for example) that paralyse, immobilize, materialize; and, what is worse, there are antagonisms, divisions, hatreds.

(ii) In spite of these inevitable losses, the spiritual perfection of the universe is still in direct ratio to the breadth of its material basis. Thus the simplicity of the soul, concentrated on a single point, is strangely linked to *the immensity of space around us*, an immensity that has been regarded by some as a useless extravagance and by others as a gesture of gracious munificence. We would be much more justified in seeing it as an organic condition of our faculty of thought. The whole of this vast cosmos, and all these countless treasures, were necessary for the concentration of our soul's complex essence: and it remains equally necessary that there should continue to be this hidden, underlying influx in order to provide substance for the wonderful synthesis of Spirit.

(iii) The staggering dimensions of the universe enable us to understand the limitless duration of evolution. In a system in which the perfecting of beings is effected not through 'drawing out' potential forces already implanted in them, but through the aggregation of pre-existing elements slowly seeking out one another through a Multitude, the *immensity of time* is a function of the immensity of space. The accumulation of centuries upon centuries is as necessary to the simplicity of the soul as the profusion of stars.

(iv) Quality, though born of quantity, is essentially higher than it. It would, therefore, be a mistake to allow oneself to be hypnotized by sheer number or to measure the strength of a force by the legions it recruits. *It is not multiplication that makes things greater* (since Multitude—quantity—pre-exist in nothingness): it is unification. A real multiplication, that is to say an operation that increased the *absolute* number of existing beings, would represent *a parte rei* a reversion to plurality, a division—in other words a decrease in the perfection of the universe. The true force is not that which increases number but that which reduces it.

E: TRANSIENCE. TRUE MATTER

Philosophers have always met great difficulties in trying to account for the interaction of beings. The problem of transience (with that of movement) is the *crux philosophorum*. Is this not to some extent their own fault, in that, like Zeno, they adopt a position in which the problem is insoluble? If we say that the monads are complete and self-contained, if we attribute no metaphysical value to the environment in which they are contained, it is obvious that we shall never be able to explain the influence that substances exert upon one another. Similarly, movement becomes *a priori* impossible if we break it down into fragments of immobility.

In the theory of creative union, the difficulty of transience does not arise, for the simple reason that the theory does not admit that things can exist in isolation. Since every being can subsist and hold together only through confluence with others, transience, far from being inexplicable, is the very condition for the monads' existence.

It may be urged that to side-step the question in this way is not to get rid of the problem but to transpose it to another context. We still have to explain the nature of a being which *is at the same time itself and something else*. To this I would reply that while this new problem may still be as awkward as the earlier, it has at least this advantage, that it is the *real* problem of the world: it is not a pseudo-problem, insoluble and barren, that arises from looking at things only from the point of view of a previously constructed system. I may add that if the mixed state of *incompletely in-dividualized*[11] beings presents obscurities for rational analysis, we can readily distinguish the cause of the obscurity: it derives from the inchoative nature of the universe. Whatever arguments we may bring forward, we cannot prevent the cosmos from being *in fieri*. Inevitably, therefore, in its present form, it can never be explained by theories constructed, as metaphysics constructs them, *for things that are completely made*.[12]

According to creative union, then, the transience of action results from the fact that the monads are caught up, enveloped, in a tenuous immanence that draws them all to itself. Far from being residual and decreasing, this common immanence is the dawn or adumbration of a Unity that is destined to become more and more fully realized. *The sum of the universe's transience* will

[11] It will be noted that, in the theory set out here, beings at present incompletely individualized are not beings *in process* of separation but beings moving towards union. According to the principle of creative union, the maximum differentiation (individualization) of the elements coincides with their unification in the universal Centre. (Note by Père Teilhard.)

[12] One might say that the physics of the experiential (the world of the continuous and the moving) is an *infra*-metaphysics (the laws of thought extend, strictly, only to things that are fixed and complete, in other words to things that *have attained their full reality*: reason, therefore, is *not* a faculty *practical* and *lower* in order: but its constructions hold good with full rigour only for a world more advanced than ours).

continue to increase until the time when it attains the value of an immanence that will embrace all things in a sort of common soul.

This was not the view that I tried to justify earlier in *Cosmic Life* (1916).[13] At that time I saw beings as held together principally by matter, so that, while fused together in their physical basis, they proceeded to disengage and isolate themselves in their spiritual apexes. I am now looking at it from a diametrically opposite point of view.

At a lower level than our souls, there are, no doubt, many interconnexions that we speak of as material. We hold together through the texture of the ether, through the impetus of the vital current; but these vast fundamental links should not be regarded as proceeding from our roots in matter. We should see them as the symptoms of far-reaching pre-spiritual union, effected, before the appearance of thought, by some sort of *formae cosmicae*: these latter being imposed on the Multiple by a breath from on high. The ether, life, and mankind(?) are great ill-defined souls, serving as a preliminary to more perfect forms of concentration. We should say that transience is *an effect*, not of *matter*, but of *Spirit*. What binds the monads together is not, properly speaking, the body, but the soul.[14]

Supposing, then, we have come habitually to *define* matter by these very properties of transience which are removed from it in its passage to Spirit—supposing we have always held that the *essence of the physical* is to ensure the interconnexion, the consistence, the fertility, of the world: in that case, we have to effect in ourselves a complete reversal in our attitude to the values of the cosmos. Conceding to the lower form of the 'material' only the attribute of multiplicity, we find ourselves obliged to recognize that *true matter* (in other words what we have always recognized and respected under that name) is *Spirit*.

This is a revindication of the attitude of those who instinctively revere the universal Milieu [15] and look to it for an answer to this

[13] See above, *Cosmic Life*, ch. 1-A.2. *Unity in the Ether*, pp. 19-22.

[14] On this question of 'the soul of the world', see below, the introductory note to the essay so entitled.

[15] It should be remembered that when Père Teilhard speaks of 'milieu' he

problem, no less than the centres of activity contained in it. Since Spirit has not yet completed its concentration but is still floating— in some part of it, and that the most precious—in a diffuse state among the souls that Creation brings together, it would be a great mistake to regard the value of the world as a monopoly of the monads we know. It is, on the contrary, the extra-individual, the inter-personal, that contains the hopes of higher union on which evolution lives. It is the milieu of the monads' mutual attraction and confluence that sustains their final centre of coalescence. Thus a certain 'intellectual materialism', by which I mean the according of a certain precedence *to the cosmic* over *the personal*, has the effect of leading to a more enlightened cult of the Spirit.

To many, I believe, this will be more than a moral solace. It will give them also a considerable intellectual satisfaction. Anyone who looks closely at the world cannot but be continually dis- appointed when he sees how beings crumble into dust. So far, the monads have been distressingly apt to break away from one another, to be alien and indifferent to one another. Almost with- out exception, they each follow their own road, freely and ego- centrically. Has the curve of my life anything in common with the fate of the insect scurrying at my feet? If the fusion of beings is effected through matter—which means that it has reached its maximum—then goodbye to our obstinate dreams of unity! Blessings, then, on the philosophy that shows us that the cohesion of things is destined to be completed in *the future*!

If it is not to flinch under the burden implied by so vast a hope, *the future* must be possessed of an extreme solidity. Spirit can inherit the stability of matter only if its own advances can find ahead of them an even more earnest guarantee than that which assured the success of the past: *the consistence of the future* is the indispensable condition for *the consistence of unity*.

The theory of creative union fully appreciates this necessity.

It sees the future taking the place of the past, just as Spirit takes the place of body. In duration, it is the future and not the past that

---

has at the back of his mind the 'divine milieu'; in other words he is thinking first, in St Paul's words, of God 'in whom we live and move and have our being'. (Acts 17:28.)

becomes the direction in which being attains solidity, density, stability. And the principle that gives coherence to the fluctuating and ambivalent multitude of contingencies is, as we saw earlier (pp. 160–2) the final purpose of providence; it is the influence of the transcendent Centre whose unerring action can infallibly guide chance towards its determined end.

Strong in this assurance, the creature can commit itself without hesitation to the apparent uncertainty of the morrow. Its head may reel at the thought that it is falling into emptiness, but in fact nothing could be more solid, more certain, than the ground on which it is advancing. If man believes with sufficient vigour in the force that is creating him, he will soon find that, for all its terrifying uncertainty, the future provides him with a solid footing as he advances. *Credenti, omnia convertuntur in bonum*—for the believer, all things are changed into good—for the future is like the waters upon which the apostle walked: the stronger our faith, the more firmly it holds us up.

The fact that the seat of transience in the universe is not what is *material* in beings but what is *spiritual*, entails an important moral consequence. It effectively determines the *direction* in which *love* should seek expression, and explains its too frequent lapses from grace.

Love seeks for union, in other words for contact with beings. When we ask how that contact may be established, we instinctively give the easy answer 'through matter', and too often we act accordingly. We all know that the purest affection can degenerate into a crude form of union; we have all grieved to see a relationship that originated on the highest spiritual plane gradually extend, unchecked, to the flesh. The majority of lovers, driven on by a passion to melt into one, to form but one, imagine that each can penetrate into the being of the other through ever more material expressions of love.

Experience plainly condemns this method of union, which always first disappoints and teases desire and then offers it a surfeit that brings a sense of futility and disgust. The theory put forward in this essay can readily explain this failure. Physical love can never achieve its aim, because the principle on which it relies, matter, is not a principle of contact but of separation. The

Multiple drives out the Multiple. The more, therefore, we try to meet on a lower sphere, the more we drift apart.

How, then, should we love another if we are truly to come together? The answer is, in Spirit.

The love that is directed towards the mutual spiritualization of the lovers, the love that does not seek to bring them together directly so much as to converge together upon the same divine Centre, that is the love, indefinitely advancing and endlessly renewed, within which beings gradually build up their unity.

This love, it is true, cannot and must not dispense with matter, any more than can the soul. Just as Spirit is never so enfranchised from matter as to be able to reject it, so every union of love must begin on the material basis of sensible confrontation and knowledge. It is a fundamental law of creative union that the fusion of spiritual apexes presupposes a coincidence of their bases.

The essential condition of happiness is this: progress in intimacy must be sought in the higher zones of being, where a more advanced *contact*—a contact that we might call *specific*—corresponds to *every higher degree* of spiritualization—one degree more in transience and true unification.

F: THE MORPHOGENIC FUNCTION OF MORALITY

From what we have already said, it is clear that love does not set up a no more than *extrinsic* relation between beings, whose term is a mere moral completion of each being by the other. Love is the conscious mark in us of the act that creates us by melting us into one. It is a factor of *physical* organization and *physical* construction.[16]

In consequence of this, the *social groups* whose formation it governs have a reality much higher than that of an association formed for economic reasons or for enjoyment: the collective units represent attempts, varying in the depth and distance to

[16] Père Teilhard often uses 'physical' in its original Greek meaning: $\dot{\eta} \phi\dot{\upsilon}\sigma\iota\varsigma$ = nature; $\phi\upsilon\sigma\iota\kappa\sigma\varsigma$ = pertaining to nature, or, we might say, organic. It is used as opposed not to 'supernatural' but to 'superficial, artificial, or simply moral'.

which they are carried, to make the Multitude of mankind raise itself to a *physical unity* higher—more spiritual—in order.

This coincides with the conclusion we reached earlier when we extrapolated the law of creative union. So long as a substance is still in a state of essential plurality (that is to say of unorganized multiplicity) we can be sure that it is incomplete and is going to produce, by a more advanced creation, purer and more concentrated being. Human souls are essentially legion, and a legion of undisciplined units. Their multitude, after having taken the place of other more diffuse multitudes, will have to come to an end in its turn. The sum of our souls is the potentiality (the 'non-being') of Some Thing, not yet made, which is to emerge from their mass.[17] Collective aspirations accompany and assist this organic work, greater than ourselves, which is effected in each one of us. It is the function of Morality to guide our free decisions into fruitful and obedient co-operation in this task.

Morality is generally regarded as a system of actions and relationships that are *biologically secondary*, less immediate and less physical than material or vital relationships. This is a great mistake. One has only to study, from the point of view of 'creative union', its role in the evolution of living beings, in order to see how profound is the morphogenic power of the Good. Through its two fundamental virtues of chastity and charity, practised in renunciation, the Christian moral system is strictly ordered towards the progressive unification of the living being.[18]

By fighting against the powers in the being that cause it to disintegrate, chastity maintains the elements of Spirit in their state of hard-won coherence, and carries them farther. *It unifies the monad in its own self.*

Conversely, *charity* is the force that stops beings from shutting themselves up in a self-centred folding-in of their energies, and makes them 'unbutton', open themselves and surrender themselves to one another: it makes them *find a centre outside themselves* and so enhance a higher centre of association. *It unifies the monads*

[17] This, in brief, is the theme of *The Struggle against the Multitude* (note by Père Teilhard.)
[18] The mystical body of Christ. See below, G, *Union in Christ.*

among one another, a role that is particularly godlike and providential in a world in which the appearance of intelligence inaugurated a crisis of autonomy and individualism.

From a purely natural and empirical point of view, life's further advances are seriously jeopardized by the very perfection of Spirit that their logical development has brought about. Intoxicated by their independence, the monads think only of living for themselves. Man's aversion from all promiscuous contact with his like, and his passion for his own selfish development to the exclusion of all else, are dangerous forces of disintegration; they sap the foundations of the world and attack the seed of unity it contains. Charity safeguards the development of the universe and keeps it to the true path of its progress. Moral effort is *the continuation in our souls of the same dynamic effort that gave us our bodies.*

If a being is to unify itself and concentrate in itself, it must break many pernicious attachments. If it is to make itself one with others and give itself to them, it must, in appearance, encroach on the most jealously cultivated private domain of its mind and heart. If it is to attain a higher life by centring upon another Self, it must destroy the preliminary unity in its own self. This means without a shadow of doubt that at all levels of being as it develops, the creative synthesis entails severance, every aggregation being accompanied by a segregation. Moral effort is necessarily accompanied by pain and sacrifice. That is why in every moral system perfection is bound up with suffering, and the highest form of life is reached through a death. Death (that is to say, disintegration) comes with every change for good or for bad. While, however, with some (whom it leaves permanently broken up and diminished) it is purely *ad mortem*, with others (whom, as it breaks them up, it compensates) it is a transition—the unique issue—that leads to the new life.

G: UNION IN CHRIST

The higher organic unity—the higher spirituality—towards which souls essentially tend, does not seem to be inaugurated in any of the specifically terrestrial associations we see taking shape around us. If we are to understand the true term of cosmic concentration (spiritualization), we must—as we would naturally anticipate—look for the answer in that same Religion whose moral teaching we saw to be so admirably in harmony with the laws that govern the development of the universe. Christianity answers that the term of the world is Christ.

Christ, it is true, is not the centre whom all things here below could *naturally* aspire to be one with. To be destined for Christ is a gratuitous favour of the Creator we have no right to count upon. Nevertheless it remains true that the Incarnation so completely *recast* the universe in the supernatural that, *in concrete fact*, we can no longer ask, or imagine, towards what Centre the elements of this world, had they not been raised up by grace, would have gravitated. Physically speaking, there is only one dynamism in the present world, that which gathers all things to Christ. Christ is the centre to which all the successfully realized, living, *elect* portions of the cosmos make their way, in whom each finds its being. In him, 'the plenitude of the universe', *omnia creantur* because *omnia uniuntur*—all things are created because all things are made one—and there we meet again the precise formula of creative union.

Simply to consider the human soul, analysed as a structure that is composite in origin (cf. §A), may well be sufficient in itself to induce our minds to build up the ontological system put forward in this essay. *Without* knowledge of Christ, this exposition would be extremely vulnerable and hypothetical, particularly in the extrapolation that led us to anticipate a spirituality, still to be realized, that is to be born from the sum of our souls. *With* knowledge of Christ, this almost delirious dream becomes to some degree a Reality known by faith. As the reader must have seen for some time, the philosophy of creative union is simply the development—generalization, extension to the universe—of what the Church teaches us about the growth of Christ. *It is the philosophy of the universe expressed in terms of the notion of the mystical body.* It was primarily as such that I myself came to grasp it, and it is only so that it can be understood: by striving to love and hold Christ in all things.

For the believer who has understood—in their full force and with no qualification—the words of St John and St Paul, Christ reveals himself at the heart of *every* being that progresses, as a Centre that is at once very near and very distant: very near, because he is, and it is his will to be, at the source of every affection; very distant, because the being cannot unite himself to Christ except at the term of a long process of perfection.

Precisely because there exists in all beings a common centre, scattered and separable though they are in appearance, they meet together at a deeper level. The more they perfect themselves naturally and sanctify themselves in grace, the more they come together and fuse into one, within the single, unifying Centre to which they aspire: and we may call that Centre equally well the *point* upon which they converge, or the *ambience* in which they float.

All these reachings-out that draw beings together and unify them constitute the *axis* of all individual and collective life. It is in virtue of that axis that we see that Christ has not only a *mystical*, but a *cosmic body*, the most impressive description of whose chief attributes we owe to St Paul—even if he never uses the actual term.[19] And this Cosmic Body, to be found in all things, and always in process of individualization (spiritualization) is eminently the *mystical Milieu*; whoever can enter into that milieu is conscious of having made his way to the very heart of everything, of having found what is most enduring in it. There, neither rust nor worm can penetrate; it is immune from the distress of misadventure; and there both action and love can make themselves felt by every being with the highest degree of immediacy and effectiveness.

At the term of the creative effort, when the kingdom of God has reached maturity, all the chosen monads and all the elect forces of the universe will be fused into God through Christ. Then, through the *plenitude* of his individual being, of his mystical body and his cosmic body, Christ, *in himself alone*, will be the heavenly Jerusalem, the new world. There, the original Multitude of bodies and souls—vanquished, but still recognizable

[19] These various ideas are treated in more detail, and vindicated, in *Cosmic Life* (1916) and *The Mystical Milieu* (1917). (Note by Père Teilhard.)

and distinct—will be encompassed in a Unity that will make of it one single spiritual thing.

All human endeavour, whether in action, in prayer, in peace, in war, in science, or in charity—all must press on to the building up of this blessed city.

Thus the philosophy of creative union culminates in a highly realistic mysticism. It originated in physical and biological observation, it proceeded by examining things from the metaphysical angle, and continues—still the same philosophy—into a moral and ascetical system, into religion.

Like the supreme Philosophy, with its roots in the ancient world, it is much more than a logical system that satisfies the mind: it is a unique way of living and of understanding everything.[20]

November 1917[21]

---

[20] Cf. the Soul of the World, p. 186, below.
[21] Dated November 1917, in *Forma Christi*. See below, p. 267, n. 16.

The Soul of the World

It is not very easy to see exactly what Père Teilhard had in mind when he used the expression 'the soul of the world', since the concept is ill-defined and varies from time to time. The same is true of the similar expression, 'the Spirit of the Earth', applied only to that part of the world which is offered in the first instance to our experience.

'I spoke of the Spirit of the Earth. But what are we to understand by that ambiguous phrase?' ('The Future of Man', p. 147.)

'But this Spirit, vaguely conceived as some sort of opposite pole to the energy of the physicist, still—and this was to be true for a long time—had no precise structure for me'. ('Le Coeur de la Matière'.)

We must understand exactly what Père Teilhard is trying to do. He has an intuition of the unity of the universe and of a unity, still incomplete, that is in process of being realized (evolution). On 12 March 1918, shortly after the date of the essay printed here, he notes: 'The soul of the world = unity in fieri'.

For Père Teilhard, as for the Schoolmen, there is no true unity without principle of unity: and to speak of 'principle of unity' is to speak of 'soul'.

Moreover, as he continually reaffirmed, this unity cannot be perfected without an Absolute. The supreme principle of unity is, therefore, God. (Père Teilhard almost always says 'Christ'. This is because, in the Christian dogma, it is through Christ and in Christ that the unity of the mystical body is realized: . . . 'I want to show that the life of Our Lord Jesus Christ flows through all things, the true Soul of the World'. Cf. below, 'The Priest', p. 203.

Here, however, we meet a complication.

Even from the natural point of view, the evolving world appears, to our reason, to converge towards a unity. Since the point of convergence is called Omega Point (ω) by Père Teilhard, and since the principle of unity active in it is also called ω, he is faced with the problem of the duality of the ω: one natural (which he sometimes calls omicron, o), and the other supernatural (identified with Christ, whom he calls ω).

Is there really an o, the natural soul of the world, subordinate and ordered to Christ-ω, intermediate between the evolving world and Christ? At first Père Teilhard was inclined to say that there was; later he rejected such a duality more and more decisively. That is why the soul of the world, in this sense of o, soon disappears from his writings. What caused him to affirm it in the first place, was, we have good reason to believe, the theology of the relationship between nature and the supernatural that he had no doubt been taught. In that teaching, the supernatural end (ω) was presented as a superaddition to a natural end (o), which it more or less supplanted. Père Teilhard gradually came to reject this theological concept, and so returned (though we may wonder whether he realized it) to the true patristic and medieval theology. St Thomas expressed this succinctly, when he said of the final end: non est aliquid naturae, sed naturae finis—*it is not in any way of nature, but the end of nature.*

Thus we first find Père Teilhard noting, on 31 December 1917, when he was writing the present essay: 'I think one could establish the existence, intermediate between the world and Christ (distinctio saltem rationis ratiocinatae, *a distinction at least of the ratiocinative reason*) of a natural cosmic entity (=the soul of the world), which is the natural form of the absolute in our universe': and then, as early as October 1918, writing: 'In "The Soul of the World", I accepted that there was in the K (=cosmos) a natural location (zone) of souls that was identified with X (= Christ). It would perhaps be better to see the ε (= the sum-total) of souls as forming a plurality, indeterminate in form, to which the X (= Christ) is superadded with no intermediary, even rationis. "On natural grounds" there can be no more than the "expectation" of a unification: without Christ, the K (=cosmos) would have no natural ω (omega). It would remain open'. (Cf. below, 'Forma Christi', §B, last paragraph.)

Finally, in the later writings, 'the soul of the world' was to merge into and even be identified with, the noosphere.

THE SOUL OF THE WORLD

Et vocabitur nomen ejus Emmanuel.
Between God and ourselves, there is a universal, created, Milieu: for Christians (who see through it without seeing it) it is transparent [translucent], for unbelievers (who can see only the milieu), opaque.

A: THE RIFT IN CHARITY

When the Church clashes with the unbelief of the godless or is torn by heresy, we who have the faith are accustomed to attribute her failure to a *defect* in the recalcitrant or dissenters. 'Christian morality', we say, 'was too much for them, or they were victims of pride. In rejecting or abandoning us, these men yielded to some tendency in their soul towards evil or towards the easy way out: they show a lack of energy, an undisciplined passion, a culpable obstinacy. They have been *disloyal to nature*, they have not loved the truth with sufficient generosity of heart and disinterestedness. That is why they have never found, or have lost, the Faith.'

That is what we say to ourselves when we meet unbelief.

It may be true that this critical explanation of the resistance offered by the world to the Kingdom of God is sufficient to account for many individual or collective crises in the history of Christianity. At the present moment any number of souls are still ignorant of Christ because *they do not love enough or* because they *love in the wrong way*. On the whole this dissent is of little moment to the apologist: for Christ, who came to save even earth's failures, cannot, for all that, be judged on the view taken of him by these poor creatures from the depth of their degradation.

A much more serious symptom, and one which highly complicates the problem—and the cure—of unbelief, is that we can see around us an increasing number of men of good will who cut themselves off from Christ precisely *through love*, because they *need and hope to love better and more fully*.

This is something we cannot fail to notice if we take the trouble to look.

Anyone, today, whose contact with unbelievers has not been confined to his textbooks—by which I mean anyone who has read their writings with a sympathetic mind or has been on familiar and friendly terms with them, and so learnt the direction in which their aspirations tend—will agree with me on this point: that we find, in the best minds our race is producing, this fear that Christianity is no longer *fine enough* to satisfy the desires that mean most to them. In so far as we can read the secrets of other men's souls, when even our own are more or less closed to us, we can see that there are among us sincere and *religious* men, men whose lives are spent in hard work and self-denial, who find that our dogmas no longer come up to the standard of their aspirations. Charity—natural charity—is not dead in these men; one cannot even say that it is beginning to grow cold. It is being *directed elsewhere*, towards some purer, more human, more exalted Reality, towards some passionately loved 'Antichrist'.

This *rift in charity*, is, I believe, one of the facts that characterize the life of the Church today, and it may well have important consequences for the religious state of tomorrow's world. Between Christ in the Church and the human ideal, something has broken down, something has come adrift, there has been a dislocation. There is a danger that the human heart may no longer be on our side.

How has this come about?

In this essay, I hope to show that the distemper from which we are all suffering has its origin in a misunderstanding between dogma and emancipated thought, centring on what, for lack of a better name, I shall call *the Soul of the World*.

B: CONSCIOUSNESS OF THE ABSOLUTE

There can be doubt that we are conscious of carrying within us something greater and more indispensable than ourselves: something that existed before we did and could have continued to exist without us: something in which we live, and that we cannot exhaust: something that serves us but of which we are not masters: something that will gather us up when, through death, we slip away from ourselves and our whole being seems to be evaporating.

If our soul were the only soul in the world, and if its knowledge summed up all the consciousness drawn from the universe, it would undoubtedly find that it is dominated and filled to overflowing by a Power beside which it is as nothing, and *with which*, nevertheless, *it is but one*. Bowed under the threefold bondage of its substance, its origin, and its progress in being, it would discover, without having to look outside itself, that it is itself infinitely greater than the sensibly apprehensible determinations and the free manifestations that make up its activity. Confronted by this masterful guest who, it felt, lived by virtue of the soul's being, the soul would be overcome by a profound and sacred feeling of awe.

Our soul, however, is not unique. It would even, no doubt, be a contradiction of the world's design and of the mechanism of union by which the world develops, to imagine it to be unique 'in natura rerum'. Souls are legion. But if we ask what lies *between* souls and holds them together, what *they have in common* that makes them into *a single living mass*, then we meet a great mystery; it is one that we are blind to, because our attention is always turned in the direction in which human beings appear to be isolated from one another and to wander restlessly like incomprehensible monads.

Souls do not form one solid block: if they did they would not react upon one another nor would they share a knowledge of the same universe. The sum, therefore, of their conscious individualities must be less than the whole quantity of being contained in their total. If we mentally extract and add up the perfections of all souls taken in isolation, we shall have no more than a phantom world. What we do will leave a *most impressive residue* that belongs to no particular soul but to all souls together.

What is this essential residue that makes the totality of the elements of the world to be richer than their sum?

Is it some reservoir of prime substance which is lent to all and takes a different form in each, without any part of it being broken up—something more like a body?

Or is it on the contrary (as is probable) the indication of a synthesizing and directing energy, that stirs up and impels creatures towards a higher state of unity—something more like a spirit?

Its precise nature, in fact, is of little importance.

What matters to us here is that its existence has to be accepted; that we, and all living beings, are grafted upon one and the same Reality as tangible as our own substance—and this whether we seek to arrive at the most highly concentrated point in our own person, or whether we extend ourselves to the measure of the whole of mankind. Whichever road we follow, we cannot withdraw from the superficial plane of day to day relationships without finding *immediately behind us, as though it were an extension of ourselves, a soul of the world.*

Since all time, the poets—the true poets—have felt the presence of the soul of the world, in the solitude of the deserts, in nature's fruitful breath, in the fathomless swell of the human heart. Everywhere it asserted itself as a living thing, and yet nowhere could they grasp it; and their loftiest inspiration was but the distress they suffered from its elusive presence.

Every age has seen a group of men on whom its light has shone with a special radiance and who have accorded it a devotion that amounted to true worship.

Every mystical system (as I have tried to show elsewhere—cf. *The Mystical Milieu*) has to some degree been fed from the never-failing spring within us of love for the great whole of which we are a part.

Throughout the centuries the soul of the world has constantly, from the manifold energy exerted by its magnetism, provided fuel for human enthusiasm and passion in their most intense form.

It has never ceased to produce within mankind a mighty current of pantheism, sometimes more conscious, sometimes less, directed towards itself.

Even so, with the passage of time, its radiating influence seems to become progressively more distinctly recognizable, and more and more indispensable for our intellectual and emotional satisfaction. It will not be long before no structure of truth or goodness can be built up without a central position being reserved for that soul, for its influence and its universal mediation.

Science's work of disclosing to us the inexhaustible energies of matter and the internal development of evolution has not been in vain; it has finally and permanently made us concentrate our attention on the virtues contained in the being that moulds us.

We owe a similar debt to the concept of the social state: by teaching men the strength of the links that unite them and the force produced by their union, it has opened their eyes to the hopes, as yet, maybe, ill-defined, passed on from one generation to another.

Philosophy, too, in examining the conditions of our knowledge and action, has found itself gradually obliged to build nothing that does not rest on the foundations of immanence.

In the light of this manifold illumination (which is perhaps simply the radiance projected by its own coming) the soul of the world is gradually emerging all around us, as an absorbing and inevitable Reality. Many, no doubt, are still blind to it; but those who can see how it is growing greater have no doubt but that the day will soon come when no human ideal will be able to continue to exist apart from it.

For it is not simply that the soul of the world must inevitably be accepted by our intelligence as a principle of existence and truth: the road to our heart, too, has been lying open to its domination for much longer than we could have suspected.

In that soul, everything works together to win the allegiance of modern man.

There is first, its quality as *Absolute*, which offers us, underlying the instability of beings and their tendency to crumble into dust, a principle of stability and unity that allows us to admire and love the beauties of the Earth, secure in the knowledge that in their attraction something solid and eternal is contained.

Its *Intimacy*, which penetrates and dissolves us, which makes its subjtance to be truly ours and truly within us, so that while it has sovereignty over us it is at the same time our own work.

Its *Greatness*, which cradles and encompasses us, which tangibly absorbs us.

Its *extra -* or *supra-individuality*, which allows us to give our energy to a life-work in which there is no ego-centrism, and which is radiant with selflessness.

And finally, its undeniable *mystery*, rich with promises that are already, in some obscure way, fulfilled.

We must make no mistake about this: A Divinity is being born among us. A new (and age-old) star is rising in the consciousness of man, and nothing can escape its magnetic force.

There are men among us who do not believe in Christ: they disclaim him in advance, because they suspect him of being hostile to the more immediate and more certain Absolute they can distinguish in the depths of their own being. In comparison with that term, Christ seems too distant—too easy to understand— too prone to lure us with the bait of a selfish and individual reward—he is at once too much of a man for them and not human enough to satisfy the pride of their ambitions.

There are others, however, who have faith in Christ: and these find the simplicity of their outlook on God hampered. Drawn in conflicting directions by the instinct inherent in their nature and by the obligations of their belief, they suffer the distress of a *dichotomy* in their outlook and action.

It is the appearance of the soul of the world that upsets and splits the primal force of love in us. It is that soul which causes the rift in charity.

C: GOD WITH US

Would it, in truth, be possible for the virtue of Christ to be exhausted? for his perfection to sink into the past? for the richness of his being to be powerless, in this new age, to satisfy the hunger of mankind?

No, indeed—a thousand times no!

But if we look for an explanation, it may well be that, in Christian teaching, the *contact* between Christ and the world is not sufficiently emphasized for the needs today; and this is for lack of a theory that is bold enough openly to *make plain* the *natural medium* in which the union of both is effected.[1]

The present postulate of the divine immanence, we should be careful to note, may be justified on two grounds.

In the first place, because, in real fact, we *experience* the presence 'ad intra' of a Reality more absolute and more precious than ourselves, which has the first claim on our veneration, and *in which alone* we can hope, when we die, to find a cosmic extension of our personality.

Secondly because, if God is to be God, he must bring about for us the *summum* of our intimate being, that is to say he must appear within us through some development and extension *of ourselves*, continuous and unbroken, since nothing can be more intimate to a being than its own self.

= there is a soul of the world and that if we are to be beatified it is through that soul that it must come about.

What then, are we to do to maintain Christ's primordial rights over us?

On the authority of the essential principles of Revelation, we must show that Christ and the soul of the world are not two opposed realities, independent of one another, and completely distinct '*in natura rerum*', but that one of those realities is the medium in which we are transformed into the other.

In practice, if not in theory, our Lord has been presented to our contemporaries too exclusively in the form of a *moral* complement—extrinsic, *particularist* and individual, promised to their personality. They have been given a picture of Christ, dissociated from the universe, as a detached fragment which brings men into conflict with one another. It is hardly surprising that

[1] Père Teilhard wrote in the margin of this paragraph: 'We have to establish (explain) the fusion, find the bridge between, *Everything* (in the effort of evolution, in substance) and *God who is in all things*'.

when the soul of the world, in turn, spontaneously entered into human consciousness, men should have seen it as a 'parallel', or as a hostile or more powerful, Absolute—as a new Messiah more to be longed for than the old.

The soul of the world is an inescapable reality, *more immediate*, in one sense, than Christ. To try to make men accept Christ without accepting or before accepting that soul is to reverse or destroy the ontological order of creation; it is to create a false appearance of duality in the aspirations of our hearts. We must, and this is urgent, restore things to their proper place, and no longer by-pass an essential stage in Christian apologetics and life.

Far from pushing Christ into the background, it is in Christ alone that the universe finds the guarantee of its consistence; and this is the first thing that we must be careful to make clear. The highest form we can attribute to the soul of the world is that of a spirit which is in process of developing its synthesis from a starting-point in the lower multiplicity of matter: in that form it holds together only through the unifying action of a centre which we must assume to be transcendent if we are not to see the hopes of the cosmos (and more particularly of mankind) vitiated by an incurable contingency. (Cf. *Creative Union*, November, 1917.) The Absolute we think we can feel within us must be accepted as fully absolute; otherwise the least jar may well cause it to fall apart in our hands. If we ask by what virtue it can attain permanent solidity, Scripture gives us a categorical answer in the properties it attributes to the incarnate Word—so magnificently enumerated by the Church in the Litany of the Sacred Heart: it is Christ who has the function of cementing the definitive concentration of the universe. The world, that is to say our substance, is centred on God *in Christo Jesu*.

Conversely, if Christ is to carry out the cosmic task entrusted to him, if he is to be constituted in the fulness of his humanity, it is absolutely essential for him to find support in the soul of the world and to use it as the medium of his action. That is the second point we now have to make clear.

Through the soul of the world, and through that soul alone

the Word, becoming incarnate in the universe, has been able to establish a vital, immediate, relationship with each one of the animate elements that make up the cosmos.

Through that soul, accordingly, and for all time, the humano-divine influence of Christ encompasses us, penetrates us, identifies itself with all the forces of our growth as individuals and as a social whole.

The soul of the world, whose life is drawn from the Word infused into it, is at the same time the purchase-point required for the Incarnation. It supplies ready to hand the matter destined to form the mystical body—and it is that soul, again, hidden beneath the countless multitudes of created beings, that envelops us in a living network charged with grace and spirituality.

Thus, in the most complete and comprehensive, and the most authentic, Christianity, the soul of the world and Christ are not in opposition: they carry their being further in the identity of one and the same Reality.

First, there is Christ: heir of all the attributes that make the world-soul our idol, of its so intimate interiority, of its so tangible greatness, its so intoxicating mystery. Loved and sought after as a world (*our* world) in which all is called to find salvation in all, the quest for Christ is safe from the twofold suspicion—damning in our eyes—of selfish interest or indolent indifference.

And then, on the other hand, there is this soul: enriched by the transcendence, the warm life, the personal beauties, of the Saviour—by the exactness, too, of his teaching. We know henceforth how we should cleave to it: through Christ's moral teaching, through purity, through charity and renunciation (cf. *Creative Union*). And we make our way to Christ with all the natural fiery enthusiasm that makes us fling ourselves upon creation.

Thus, in a communion with God through the world, is fulfilled the final longing that quickens the sense of religion: *to worship in ourselves something that is 'us'*. God with us! God does not give himself to the soul as some superadded good, some outside supplement. He does more, and better. He comes to us through the inner road of the world; he comes down into us through that zone in which our incomplete being is mingled with the universal substance. In that day-spring of ourselves, our consciousness grows bright with God, through a sort of internal metamorphosis of the created being, which allows us to attain the transcendent without having to emerge from ourselves. Without this divinization *by transmutation* of our being it would be impossible to explain why our faith attaches such inestimable value to every sanctified soul. Thus the Absolute of experience[2] is *the beginning of God in us.* We have both the right and the duty to give our allegiance to the soul of the world and to surrender ourselves to it. The contact we shall try to make with it is ordained for leading us to Christ: moreover, it cannot be fully realized objectively except in Christ.

D: MEDITATION ON THE WORLD

To conclude: the time has come when men will *a priori* turn away from any religion that offers them a God too cut off from themselves and from the earth, a God who makes us contemn the world or who appears completely other than the world. Before they consent to turn back to Christ they will insist more and more emphatically that Christ's call must be reconciled with the voice of the Being, greater than themselves, whose summons they hear deep within their consciousness. Surely, they will say, to grasp the former without knowing the nature of the latter, is to drop the prey and chase the shadow.

Can we say that we are really in a position to give a satisfactory answer to the questions that modern minds, haunted by pantheism, are asking?

For centuries we have studied closely and exactly the mysteries of the supernatural world, the relation between the Persons of the Trinity, the nature of the hypostatic union, the hierarchy of angels and saints, the mechanism of grace. We have built up and embellished with loving care a theologian's universe, a universe

---

[2] The context makes this expression understandable, even though, metaphysically and theologically, it is not sufficiently accurate.

of piety. Absorbed in this esoteric task of organization, we did not notice that we were rapidly ceasing to make any appeal to the mass of human beings: as far as they were concerned, we were building our city in the clouds.

The time has now come to consider, in a spirit of religious research, the relations that unite God to the elements of this world, and to the values of the universe.

The current of 'pantheist' (cosmic) mysticism is no stranger to Christianity. You have only to look at William James's *Varieties of Religious Experience*—not to mention R. H. Benson—to realize this. But we Catholics—and this is particularly true of our hagiographers—regard such types of spiritual attitude as inferior or questionable: we accordingly leave them out of account. Nevertheless, in the ecstasy of those Christians who have had the most sublime insight, a passion for the universe is undeniably apparent. We can afford to wait no longer: we must *explicitly Christianize* the compulsion that leads us to divinize the world.

In this essay I have tried to bring out the presence, between Christ and our souls, of a universal mediating reality: an intermediary which does not introduce a further gap between him and us, but removes one more division. This work will have to be tested and pursued, as every advance in the Church must be, in a quest shared by all and maintained in prayer.

Much has still to be done.

When we have shown the existence in us of a cosmic element divinized by Christ, we shall then have to go one step further. We shall be asked to make it perfectly clear to what degree this existence must, in the Christian view, be considered arbitrary. There is such a thing as the soul of the world. Is it, absolutely speaking, possible for it not to exist?

When that question is asked, we now confine ourselves to saying, 'God created through love', and we may add, 'through even greater love, God chose a world that would sin and would be redeemed'. Is that emotional explanation a satisfactory philosophical answer?[3] Creation, Incarnation, Redemption: each

---

[3] Père Teilhard added in the margin of this paragraph: 'Love must have an ontological foundation . . . (a function—a necessity—of union). Love is—is born of—a need for union. It does not *pre-exist*—create—this need'.

one of these, it is true, marks one degree farther in the gratuity of the divine operation; but are they not three acts, indissolubly linked, in the appearance of *participated being*? And does not that appearance itself meet a more exact need than the mere emotional requirement of a *Bonum diffusivum sui*?[4]

Who can say what we might find, in the light God sheds for us, if we enquired more often into those mysterious regions where the universe—the natural experiential face of God—is linked with the Infinite—if, above all, we looked with love.[5]

Whatever steps we take in this direction we shall never succeed, I fear, in effecting an absolute reconciliation between God and the World. Christ will always be *Signum cui contradicitur*. Of one thing at least, however, we may be sure: the line dividing the good from the bad will be drawn higher up, nearer the natural point at which it should appear—where egocentrism and self-denial part company. No one must be able to say that if he draws away from God it is in order to remain more wholeheartedly human.

Mourmelon-le-Grand
Epiphany 1918

---

[4] Père Teilhard notes in the margin: 'In the theological analysis of grace, we are primarily concerned with *overcoming* an apparent *opposition* between human action and the power of God—a theoretical opposition, belonging to the order of *social* relations. We do not try to bring God to light in the world of experience, or positively to divinize something that is within us'.

[5] The answer criticized here is not necessarily an 'emotional explanation', nor can one legitimately relate the idea of *Deus caritas* so closely to the neo-platonic idea of the *Bonum diffusivum sui*: even though the meaning of the latter expression can be strained to approach that of the former. Père Teilhard has taken the word 'love' here in a psychological sense without any correction by analogy. This is suggested by the use of the adjective 'arbitrary' in an earlier paragraph. The development of his thought was later to show that he was far from rejecting the Christian idea of love as emotional.

The Eternal Feminine

To Béatrix

In his attempt to construct a coherent and all-embracing synthesis, Père Teilhard could not neglect so powerful and fundamental a reality as love. In this essay he avails himself of Goethe's well-known expression 'Das Ewig-Weibliche' ('Faust', end of Part 2) (like a composer borrowing a theme and developing it in a series of variations), in order to express, in lyrical terms, his concept of the role of love in the universe, as the force that unifies and spiritualizes beings. At the same time he has in mind the Beatrice of the 'Divine Comedy'. As so often happens in Père Teilhard's writings, the phrase is extended to cover a variety of analogical meanings, from interatomic attraction, through human love, to love of God.

At the time of writing Père Teilhard was at Verzy (Marne) in the Rheims area.

THE ETERNAL FEMININE

I

Ab initio creata sum[1]

When the world was born, I came into being. Before the centuries were made, I issued from the hand of God—half-formed, yet destined to grow in beauty from age to age, the handmaid of his work.

Everything in the universe is made by union and generation—by the coming together of elements that seek out one another, melt together two by two, and are born again in a third.

God instilled me into the initial multiple as a force of condensation and concentration.

In me is seen that side of beings by which they are joined as one, in me the fragrance that makes them hasten together and leads them, freely and passionately, along their road to unity.

Through me, all things have their movement and are made to work as one.

I am the beauty running through the world, to make it associate in ordered groups: the ideal held up before the world to make it ascend.

I am the essential Feminine.[2]

In the beginning I was no more than a mist, rising and falling: I lay hidden beneath affinities that were as yet hardly conscious, beneath a loose and tenuous polarity.

And yet I was already in existence.

In the stirring of the layers of the cosmic substance, whose nascent folds contain the promise of worlds beyond number, the first traces of my countenance could be read.

---

[1] Eccl. 24: 14 where it is said of wisdom.

[2] In this first part, whose theme is taken from Proverbs 8:22–31, Père Teilhard presents love as a force of unification, a force that drives on to the realization of an ideal.

Like a soul, still dormant but essential, I bestirred the original mass, almost without form, which hastened into my field of attraction; and I instilled even into the atoms, into the fathomless depths of the infinitesimal, a vague but obstinate yearning to emerge from the solitude of their nothingness and to hold fast to something outside themselves.

I was the bond that thus held together the foundations of the universe.

For every monad, be it never so humble, provided it is in very truth a centre of activity, obeys in its movement an embryo of love for me:

The universal Feminine.[3]

With the coming of life, I began to be embodied in beings that had been chosen to be in a special way my image.

Step by step, I became individualized.

At first I was ill-defined and elusive, as though I could not make up my mind to be contained in a tangible form:

But then, as souls became more ready to enter into a richer, deeper, more spiritualized union, I became more differentiated.

And thus, patiently and in secret, was developed the archetype of bride and mother.

During this transformation I did not surrender any of the lower charms that marked the successive phases of my appearance—just as the heart of the olive-tree holds firm and sound when, with each new spring, it grows green once more.

I still held them within me, and taught them to bear the burden of a greater consciousness. Thus, as living beings approached greater perfection on earth, so (and yet always outdistancing their growth) I was able to stand before them, matching, circle for circle, the concentric zones of their desires, as the proper form of their beatitude.

Follow with your eye the vast tremor that runs, from horizon to horizon, through city and forest.

Observe, throughout all life, the human effervescence that works

[3] In this second part, the reference is to the forces of attraction, nctive throughout the universe, in its physico-chemical elements.

like leaven in the world—the song of the birds and their plumage—the wild hum of the insects—the tireless blooming of the flowers—the unremitting work of the cells—the endless labours of the seeds germinating in the soil.

I am the single radiance by which all this is aroused and within which it is vibrant.

Man, nature's synthesis, does many things with the fire that burns in his breast. He builds up power, he seeks for glory, he creates beauty, he weds himself to science. And often he does not realize that, under so many different forms, it is still the same passion that inspires him—purified, transformed, but living—the magnetism of the Feminine.[4]

It was within life that I began to unveil my face.

But it was man who was the first to recognize me, in the disquiet my presence brought him.

When a man loves a woman he thinks at first that his love is given simply to an individual like himself whom he envelops in his power and freely associates with himself.

He is very conscious of a radiance, haloing my countenance, which sensitizes his heart and illuminates all things.

But he attributes this radiation of my being to a subjective disposition of his entranced mind, or to a mere reflection of my beauty in nature's countless facets.

Soon, however, he is astonished by the violence of the forces unleashed in him at my approach, and trembles to realize that he cannot be united with me without inevitably becoming enslaved to a universal work of creation.

He thought that it was simply a partner who stood by his side: and now he sees that in me he meets the great hidden force, the mysterious latency, that has come to him in this form in order to lead him captive.

For the man who has found me, the door to all things stands open. I extend my being into the soul of the world—not only through the medium of that man's own sensibility, but also through the physical links of my own nature—or rather, I am the

[4] In this passage, Père Teilhard follows up the different stages of the 'tree of life' (cf. *The Phenomenon of Man*, p. 122) in all its various species.

magnetic force of the universal presence and the ceaseless ripple of its smile.[5]

I open the door to the whole heart of creation: I, the Gateway of the Earth, the Initiation.

He who takes me, gives himself to me, and is himself taken by the universe.[6]

In the knowledge of me, alas, there is both good and evil.

Man's initiation has proved too strong meat for him.

When he saw that *I was for him the universe*, he thought to encompass me in his arms.

He wished to shut himself up with me in a *closed* world for two, in which each would be sufficient to the other.

At that very moment, I fell apart in his hands.

And then it could have seemed as though I were the rock on which mankind foundered—the Temptress.

Why, O men, why do you halt in the task of hard-won purification as a summons to which my beauty was made?

I am essentially fruitful: that is to say my eyes are set on the future, on the Ideal.

The moment you try to pin me down, to possess me in some complete form, you stifle me.

What is more, you distort, you reverse—as you would a geometric pattern—my nature.

Since the true balance of life forces you continually to ascend, you cannot set me up as a lifeless idol to cling to, without falling back; instead of becoming gods, you revert to matter.

As soon as you fold your wings around me, you follow matter in its descent: for what drives matter down is the sterile union of its elements in which each neutralizes the other.

What you are grasping is no more than matter: for matter is a tendency, a direction—it is the side of Spirit that we meet as we fall back.

---

[5] Cf. Aeschylus, *Prometheus Vinctus* 90: 'the unnumbered laughter of the waves'.

[6] There is more in human love than two beings seeking to be made one. It entails, for them, contact with the whole of the universe and participation in the work of creation.

And your fall accelerates at a terrifying speed—as fast as the widening of the gap between your real appetites and the ever lower forms in which you seek for me.

And, when you, who are but dust, reach the term of your efforts, it is but dust that you embrace.

The more, O men, you seek me in the direction of pleasure, the farther will you wander from my reality.

The flesh, in truth, which operates as the pull of evil between you and the lower multiple (that reversed image of God) is no more than my inverted semblance, floating over an abyss of endless dissociation, that is, of endless corruption.

For a long time man, lacking the skill to distinguish between the mirage and the truth, has not known whether *he should fear me* or worship me.

He loved me for the magic of my charm and my sovereign power; he feared me as a force alien to himself, and for the bewildering riddle I presented.

I was at once his strength and his weakness—his hope and his trial. It was in relation to me that the good were divided from the wicked.

Indeed, had Christ not come, man might well have placed me for ever in the camp of evil.[7]

---

[7] The ambivalence of human love: we are summoned to follow matter in its ascent towards spirit, but, unhappily, we are only too prone to reverse our course and sink back towards matter. Such is the burden of sin in the unredeemed universe.

II

Et usque ad futurum saeculum non desinam.[8]

Christ has given me salvation and freedom.

When he said: *Melius est non nubere*,[9] men took it to mean that I was dead to eternal life.

In truth, by those words he restored me to life, with Lazarus—with Magdalen—and set me between himself and men as a nimbus of glory:

In making manifest that great virtue he defined, in fact, my true essence, and guided men, who had lost track of me, back to the true road I had trodden.

In the regenerated world I am still, as I was at my birth, the summons to unity with the universe—the world's attractive power imprinted on human features.

The true union, however, is the union that simplifies, and to simplify is to spiritualize.

The true fertility is the fertility that brings beings together in the engendering of Spirit.

If, in the new sphere into which created being entered, I was to remain Woman, I was obliged to change my form without impairing my former nature.

While my deceptive image continues to lure the pleasure-seeker towards matter, my reality has risen aloft, drawing men to the heights: it floats between the Christian and his God.

My charm can still draw men, but towards the light. I can still carry them with me, but into freedom.

---

[8] Ecclesiasticus 24:14.
[9] Père Teilhard's quotation is influenced by his recollection of the Pauline texts, *Melius est enim nubere quam uri* (1 Cor. 7:9) and *qui matrimonio jungit virginem suam, bene facit; et qui non jungit, melius facit* (1 Cor. 7:38).

Henceforth my name is Virginity.[10]

The Virgin is still woman and mother: in that we may read the sign of the new age.

The pagans on the Acropolis blame the Gospel for having disfigured the world, and they mourn for beauty. These men are blasphemers.

Christ's message is not the signal for a rupture, for an emancipation: as though the elect of God, rejecting the law of the flesh, could break the bonds that tie them to the destiny of their race, and escape from the cosmic current in which they came to birth.

The man who hearkens to Christ's summons is not called upon to exile love from his heart. On the contrary, it is his duty to remain essentially a man.

Thus he has an even greater need of me, to sensitize his powers, and arouse his soul to a passion for the divine.

For the Saint, more than for any other man, I am the maternal shadow leaning over the cradle—and the radiant forms assumed by youth's dreams—and the deep-seated aspiration that passes through the heart like some undisputed alien force—the mark, in each individual being of Life's axis.

Christ has left me all my jewels.

In addition, however, he has sent down upon me from heaven a ray that has boundlessly idealized me.[11]

It seemed good to him, in the first place, to give a new zest to the *natural* impetus of my development.

Faced by a mankind that never ceases to ascend, the part I have to play insists on my withdrawing to an ever higher level—held aloft, over the earth's growing ambition, as a lure and a prize—almost grasped, but never held. By its very nature, the Feminine

[10] In accordance with one of the fundamental data of the synthesis he was at this time beginning to construct, Père Teilhard sees in true union a spiritualizing force. Christ's revelation has shown us that the higher form of love is virginity.

[11] To idealize love is not to cut away its 'roots'. All that is best in the original impulse reappears in its higher forms.

must continue unremittingly to make itself progressively more felt in a universe that has not reached the term of its evolution: to ensure the final blossoming of my stock, will be the glory and bliss of chastity.

Countless are the new essences handed over by nature, from age to age, to life!

Under the influence of Christianity, I shall combine, until creation is complete, their subtle and dangerous refinements in an ever-changing perfection which will embrace the aspirations of each new generation.

Then, so long as the world endures, there will be seen reflected in the face of Beatrix the dreams of art and of science towards which each new century aspires.

Since the beginning of all things, Woman has never ceased to take as her own the flower of all that was produced by the vitality of nature or the art of man.

Who could say in what climax of perfections, both individual and cosmic, I shall blossom forth, in the evening of the world, before the face of God?

I am the unfading beauty of the times to come—the ideal Feminine.[12]

The more, then, I become Feminine, the more immaterial and celestial will my countenance be.

In me, the soul is at work to sublimate the body—Grace to divinize the soul.

Those who wish to continue to possess me must change as I change.

Behold!

The centre of my attraction is imperceptibly shifting towards the pole upon which all the avenues of Spirit converge.

The iridescence of my beauties, flung like a mantle over creation, is slowly gathering in its outlying folds.

Already the shadow is falling upon the flesh, even the flesh purified by the sacraments.

[12] This evolution of love will continue as long as the world endures, principally under the influence of Christianity, which has not yet borne its full fruit.

One day, maybe, it will swallow up even art, even science—things loved as a woman is loved.

The beam circles: and we must follow it round.

Soon only God will remain for you in a universe where all is virgin.

It is God who awaits you in me![13]

Long before I drew you, I drew God towards me.

Long before man had measured the extent of my power, and divinized the polarity of my attraction, the Lord had conceived me, whole and entire, in his wisdom, and I had won his heart.

Without the lure of my purity, think you, would God ever have come down, as flesh, to dwell in his creation?

Only love has the power to move being.

If God, then, was to be able to emerge from himself, he had first to lay a pathway of desire before his feet, he had to spread before him a sweet savour of beauty.

It was then that he caused me to rise up, a luminous mist hanging over the abyss—between the earth and himself—that, in me, he might dwell among you.

Now do you understand the secret of the emotion that possesses you when I come near?

The tender compassion, the hallowed charm, that radiate from Woman—so naturally that it is only in her that you look for them, and yet so mysteriously that you cannot say whence they come—are the presence of God making itself felt and setting you ablaze.

Lying between God and the earth, as a zone of mutual attraction, I draw them both together in a passionate union.

—until the meeting takes place in me, in which the generation and plenitude of Christ are consummated throughout the centuries.

I am the Church, the bride of Christ.

---

[13] The ideal term is a complete spiritualization of love and the total unification of its object.

I am Mary the Virgin, mother of all human kind.[14]

It might be thought that in this conjunction of heaven and earth I am destined to disappear as a useless handmaid, that I will have to vanish like a shadow before the reality.

Those who love me should dismiss this fear.

Just as participated being is not lost when it attains its principle —but, on the contrary, finds fulfilment in melting in God—

Just as the soul, once it is formed, does not completely exclude the countless elements from which it emerged—but retains, as essential to it, a potency for and a need for flesh in which to contain itself[15]—

So the Cosmos, when divinized, will not expel my magnetic influence by which the ever more complex and more simplified fascicle of its atoms is progressively more closely—and permanently—knit—

I shall subsist, entire, with all my past, even in the raptures of contact with God—

What is more, I shall continue to disclose myself—as inexhaustible in my development as the infinite beauties of which I am always, even if unseen, the raiment, the form, and the gateway.

When you think I am no longer with you—when you forget me, the air you breathe, the light with which you see—then I shall still be at hand, lost in the sun I have drawn to myself.

Blessed elect, you have only (think: is this not true?) to relax for one moment the tension that impels you towards God, or to let your glance fall the least distance short of the centre that enchants you, in order once again to see my image playing over the surface of the divine fire.

[14] It was the ideal love, the love of the Virgin—and that of the Church, too, of which the Virgin, in Christian tradition, is the perfect symbol—which drew God down to this world (the *Fiat* of the Incarnation; cf. *Le Milieu Divin*, p. 125, Fontana, p. 134). Claudel has on more than one occasion given lyrical expression to this mystical unity of Mary and the Church.

[15] A strictly Thomist concept. It should be noted (to avoid an error in interpretation that some writers have fallen into when commenting on similar passages) that Père Teilhard speaks not of the elements from which the soul is made, but of the elements 'from which it emerged'.

—And at that moment you may see with wonder how there unfolds, in the long web of my charms, the ever-living series of allurements—of forces that one after another have made themselves felt ever since the borderline of nothingness, and so brought together and assembled the elements of Spirit—through love.

I am the Eternal Feminine.[16]

Verzy—19–25 March 1918

---

[16] As they pass through each of their stages, the forces of love—the Eternal Feminine—are transformed, but they retain—in a purified form—something of each stage. Love will never disappear.

The Priest

On 26 May 1918, while on leave, Père Teilhard made his religious profession in the chapel of the novitiate for his province, at Sainte-Foy-lès-Lyon (where it had been established two years earlier, after the years of exile in England). Back at the front, in the area between Compiègne and Soissons, he wrote 'The Priest', which he finished on July 8th. On the 9th he wrote to his cousin, from the forest of Compiègne:

'Yesterday I sent you a notebook containing 'The Priest' (in the second part of the book, the pages at the beginning have been used for personal notes, more or less tentative, which I won't inflict on you). Tell me what you think of it. When I can get hold of a notebook, I'll make another copy for Père Vulliez-Sermet and, of course, for Guiguite'. ('Making of a Mind', p. 212.)

There are references again, in three other letters, to 'The Priest'. 'Forest of Laigue, 4 August: I'm writing from the same forest where, a month ago, I wrote The Priest'.

Chavannes-sur-l'Étang (Haut-Rhin), 3 October 1918:

'The day before yesterday I had a letter from Père Chanteur in which he writes about 'The Priest'. Once again—and unlike Père V.-S.—his reaction is primarily one of anxiety. He's obviously afraid (though he writes most affectionately) of seeing me fall into pantheism ... All the same, I've been anxious to let you know about this new warning I've had, so that you too may not engage yourself in a situation that may prove rather hazardous—or at any rate delicate' (Ibid, p. 244).

Finally, from Foussemagne (Haut-Rhin), on October 11th:
    '*The different reactions of Père Chanteur and Père Vulliez-Sermet
are more easily explained than you think. I realize that the tricky part
in my writings is not the blunt correction of formulas (easy enough to
look after) but the inspiration behind them and the general tendency.
Pray earnestly that it may always be the good spirit that animates me*'
(*Ibid, p. 254*).*

* (*Making of a Mind*, pp. 212, 244, 254.) Père Vulliez-Sermet's spiritual
insight gave him great authority both within and outside his order. Cf. Louis
de Lavareille, S.J., *A l'école de saint Ignace et saint François de Sales, Révérend Père
Vulliez-Sermet, S.J., 1860–1924* (Lyons, 1944). At that time Père Chanteur was
Provincial of the Lyons province.

THE PRIEST

A: CONSECRATION

Te igitur . . .

Since today, Lord, I your Priest have neither bread nor wine nor altar, I shall spread my hands over the whole universe and take its immensity as the matter of my sacrifice.[1]

Is not the infinite circle of things the one final Host that it is your will to transmute?

The seething cauldron in which the activities of all living and cosmic substance are brewed together—is not that the bitter cup that you seek to sanctify?

There is a way of looking at the world that allows us to see in it only an aggregate of disparate or antagonistic elements. All around us, it would seem, there is nothing but incurable division and innate hostility. The worthless is everywhere mixed with the precious—the wheat grows side by side with the tares. On all sides we see what is good for nothing, mere trash and rubbish.

You, my God, have given me the gift of discerning, beneath this surface incoherence, the living and deep-rooted unity that your grace has mercifully imposed on—instilled beneath—our hopeless plurality.

You have allowed me to overcome the illusion of appearances so that now I cannot look at things without seeing, both before and after their fragmentation (more real than, and yet subsequent to their multiplicity), the welding of the substantial bond—the soul of desire that is already concentrating its essence.

---

[1] Cf. The beginning of *The Mass on the World* (1923): 'Since once again, Lord—though this time not in the forests of the Aisne but in the steppes of Asia—I have neither bread nor wine nor altar . . .' (*Hymn of the Universe*, p. 19). To the Abbé Henri Breuil, from Tientsin, 30 Dec. 1923: 'I have got down to a little writing again . . . a new, quite different, version of "The Mass on the World" (or *The Priest*) which I wrote during the war—*ad usum privatum*, as it should be'. On 28 July 1918, three weeks after sending his cousin *The Priest*, he wrote to her: 'We're now resting, . . . I can say Mass'.

You have shown me the essential task of self-fulfilment in the plenitude of your incarnate word,[2] to which the world, through a chosen part of its *whole* being, is summoned.

For the man whose eyes have been opened, a tense current no words can describe flows from the repose and the busyness of the creature. The variety and mobility of the beings we meet seems to atomize (so our senses tell us) the power of the world. When all these rivulets of love and desire come to the surface, flowing together in one common aspiration, how vast will be the torrent, how irresistible its shock!

The whole world is concentrated, is exalted, in expectation of union with God . . . and yet it is pulled up short by an impassable barrier. Nothing can attain Christ except he take it up and enfold it.

Thus the universe groans, caught between its passionate desire and its impotence.[3]

Today, Lord, I can feel so strongly within me the cry of the weary multitude, seeking to win, in the divine, its right order and its repose.

I seem to hear, rising up from all creatures—both those that are imprisoned in inert matter, and those who are opening their eyes to the light of life, from those, too, who move and act in freedom—the universal lament: 'Show your pity for us, O you our

---

[2] Cf. below, p. 214: '. . . Such is the Pleroma of the world and of Christ'; and p. 223: '. . . to the whole cosmos of which you, Lord Jesus, are the plenitude'. This is the Pauline concept of the Pleroma (Col. 1:19; 2:9), at least as understood by many exegetes. Thus Pierre Benoit, O.P. (*Dictionnaire de la Bible, supplément*, fasc. 36 (1961) col. 164): 'It is legitimate, in this context, to take it as the pleroma . . . not only of the divine essence but also of the whole universe: both the Godhead and the cosmos being assumed through the medium of his body. By virtue of his Incarnation, crowned by the Resurrection, Christ, both God and Man, embraces in his plenitude not only God who is the source of salvation, not only men who are saved, but also the whole environment of man represented by the cosmos, including the angelic powers'. For a more detailed treatment, Père Benoit refers the reader to the forthcoming article *Plérôme*.

[3] Two things are emphasized together: the creature's supernatural vocation and its inability to realize it by itself. The allusion in this sentence is to Rom. 8:22: *Omnis creatura ingemiscit*, Cf. 8:19: *Exspectatio creaturae revelationem filiorum Dei exspectat.*

priest, and, if it be in your power, give us our fulfilment by giving us our God!'

Who, then, will utter, over the formless mass of the world, the words that will give it *one* soul?

What voice will overthrow the obstacle between God and creation which prevents *this One* from meeting with that other?

Let creation repeat to itself again today, and tomorrow, and until the end of time, so long as the transformation has not run its full course, the divine saying: 'This is my body.'

When Christ, carrying farther the process of his Incarnation, comes down into the bread in order to dwell there in its place, his action is not confined to the particle of matter that his Presence is at hand, for a moment, to etherealize.

The transubstantiation is encircled by a halo of divinization—real, even though less intense—that extends to the whole universe.

From the cosmic element into which he has entered, the Word is active to master and assimilate to himself all that still remains.[4]

Take up in your hands, Lord, and bless this universe that is destined to sustain and fulfil the plenitude of your being among us.

Make this universe ready to be united with you: and that this may be so, intensify the magnetism that comes down from your heart to draw to it the dust of which we are made.

When that moment comes, Almighty Father, I shall concen-

[4] Père Teilhard returned on more than one occasion to this notion of the 'extensions' of the Eucharist. He was careful, however, to make it clear that they are all completely 'dependent on the Eucharist', 'subject to the radiance of the consecrated host', 'under the influence of the host' (see below), etc. Cf. *The Struggle against the Multitude* (1917): 'Through the magnetism of his love and the efficacy of the Eucharist, Jesus Christ gradually gathers within himself all the power of unity diffused through the Universe'. *Le Milieu Divin*, p. 113, Fontana, p. 123-4: 'When the priest says the words *Hoc est corpus meum*, they fall directly upon the bread and directly transform it into the individual reality of Christ. But the great sacramental operation does not cease at that local and momentary event.' *Ibid.* p. 115, Fontana, p. 126: 'Grant, O God, that when I draw near to the altar to communicate, I may henceforth discern the infinite perspectives hidden beneath the smallness and nearness of the Host in which you are concealed.' Again, in *Le Christique* (1955): 'To the wondering gaze of the believer, it is the eucharistic mystery itself that is extended into infinity'. Cf. *Hymn of the Universe*, pp.46-50, *The Monstrance*.

trate in myself all the aspiration that rises up towards you from these lower spheres—I shall feel the full force of the yearning that seeks expression in my words—I shall look beyond the white host, accepting its domination, and with all the strength of my desire and my prayer, with all my power, over every substance and every development. I shall pronounce the words:

Hoc est corpus meum.

The divine work is accomplished.

Once again, through the priest, the formative power of the Word has come down upon the world, to overcome its nothingness, its wickedness, its futility, its disorder.

All the immortal monads converge upon Christ—but each monad, in turn, is to some degree the centre of the entire Cosmos, resting upon and at the same time supporting its fabric.

In virtue of this interconnexion, from which *nothing* is excluded, the whole of nature vibrates to the radiation of the consecrated Host. Every single atom, no matter how humble or imperfect it be, must co-operate, at least through what it repels or reflects, in the fulfilment of Christ. Every particle, every process, must, through some part of itself, appear in the definitive reality of Christ.

Thus, when I spoke those words, an organic unity, underlying every substance, was introduced into the isolated elements of nature. Superimposed upon all visible activity, a dominating force now guides individual movements in accordance with a higher plan.

The figure of Christ emerges: it takes on definition in the midst of our nebula of participated beings and secondary causes.

The universe assumes the form of Christ—but, O mystery! the man we see is Christ crucified.[5]

[5] Cf. letter of 30 July 1918: 'There's a prayer I'm fond of saying now, because it sums up what I mean: "Jesu, sis mihi mundus verus"—may all that is elect in the world be to me a channel for your influence, and be increasingly transformed, through my efforts, into you'. (*Making of a Mind*, p. 223) The same idea reappears in *Forma Christi*, towards the end of this same year, 1918: 'Around the radiant sun of love that has come to light up the world, there reaches out into infinity a "corona", seldom seen and yet the seat of the encompassing and unifying activity of the incarnate Word.'

The sacramental bread is made out of grains of wheat which have been pressed out and ground in the mill: and the dough has been slowly kneaded. Your hands, Jesus, have broken the bread before they hallow it.

Who shall describe, Lord, the violence suffered by the universe from the moment it falls under your sovereign power.

Christ is the goad that urges creatures along the road of effort, of elevation, of development.

He is the sword that mercilessly cuts away such of the body's members as are unworthy or decayed.[6]

He is that mightier life that inexorably brings death to our base egoisms in order to draw into itself all our capacities for loving.

That Christ may enter deeply into us we need alternately the work that widens our being and the sorrow that brings death to it, the life that makes a man greater in order that he may be sanctifiable and the death that makes him less in order that he may be sanctified.

The universe is rent asunder; it suffers a painful cleavage at the heart of each of its monads, as the flesh of Christ is born and grows. Like the work of creation which it redeems and surpasses, the Incarnation, so desired of man, is an awe-inspiring operation. It is achieved through blood.

May the blood of the Lord Jesus—the blood which is infused into creatures and the blood which is shed and spread out over all, the blood of endeavour and the blood of renouncement—mingle with the pain of the world.

[6] Cf. below, p. 214, where there is another reference to damnation. *Le Milieu Divin*, p. 148, Fontana, pp. 146-7: 'The total divine *milieu* is formed by the incorporation of every elect spirit in Jesus Christ. But to say "elect" is to imply a choice, a selection . . . It is precisely because Christ is the one who unites that he is also the one who selects, who separates and judges. The Gospel speaks of the good seed . . . but there are also the tares, the goats, the left hand of the Judge, the closed door, the outer darkness; and at the antipodes of the fire that unites in love there is the fire that destroys in isolation. The whole process from which the new earth is gradually born is an *aggregation* underlaid by a *segregation*'. Cf. *Ibid*. p. 148, Fontana, pp. 150-1: '. . . whether within Christ or without Christ (but always under the influence of Christ).'

Hic est calix sanguinis mei.[7]

B: ADORATION

Unde et memores . . .

Like an inner flame—sometimes free, live, and luminous, at others obscured but still burning beneath the ashes it throws off— the Divine now lights up all things for me from within.

Permeating the whole atmosphere of creation, God encompasses me and lays siege to me.

I kneel, Lord, before the universe that has imperceptibly, under the influence of the Host, become your adorable Body and your divine blood.

I prostrate myself in its presence, or better—much better—I recollect myself in that universe.

The world is filled by You!

O universal Christ, true foundation of the world, you who find your consummation in the fulfilment of all that your power has raised up from nothingness, I worship you, and am lost in the consciousness of your plenitude permeating all things.

We do not give you, my God, this plenitude, like parts that are added together to make a total: it is we who *submit to it.*

Your life is so much stronger than ours that it dominates us, absorbs us, and assimilates us to itself.[8]

[7] The whole of this section elaborates the symbolism of the bread and wine: work–suffering; life–death; joy–pain. Cf. 26th August 1923: 'I keep developing, and slightly improving, with the help of prayer, my "Mass upon things". It seems to me that in a sense the true substance to be consecrated each day is the world's development during that day—the bread symbolizing appropriately what creation succeeds in producing, the wine (blood) what creation causes to be lost in exhaustion and suffering in the course of its effort.' (*Letters from a Traveller*, p. 86.)

[8] A well-known Augustinian notion: *Panis sum fortium, nec tu me mutabis in te, sed tu mutaberis in me.* See also below, p. 214, 'had I ever imagined that it was I . . .' etc. There is a similar thought, in connexion with death, in *Le Milieu Divin*, p. 70, Fontana, p. 90: 'You are the irresistible and vivifying force, O Lord, and because yours is the energy, because of the two of us, you are infinitely the stronger, it is to you that falls the part of consuming me in the union that should weld us together'.

We are not the elements whose coming together constitutes you, but the fuel that feeds your fires.

It is not our development that brings about your consummation—rather is it your consummation that effects our fulfilment.

And nevertheless, Master, it remains true that we are the foundation necessary to your existence.

When you make us your own, you do not annihilate us, but jealously preserve all that is best in our natural qualities, in order to make of it the axis, the kernel, the support, of your growth. Under your action—which transforms and does not destroy—all that is good in us passes, for all eternity, into the perfection of your Body.

That is why I can henceforth, without quitting You, live and work in the fulness of beatitude.

You, Jesus,[9] are the epitome and the crown of all perfection, human and cosmic. No flash of beauty, no enchantment of goodness, no element of force, but finds in you its ultimate refinement and consummation. To possess you is indeed to hold gathered into a single object the perfect assemblage of all that the universe can give us or make us dream of. The unique fragrance of the glory and wonder of your being has so effectively drawn from the earth and synthesized all the most exquisite savours that the earth contains or can suggest that now we can find them, endlessly, one after another according to our desires, in you—you the Bread that 'holds within it every delight'.[10]

You who are yourself the *plenitudo Entis creati*, the fulness of created being, you, Jesus, are also the *plenitudo entis mei*, the fulness of my own personal being, and of all living creatures who accept your dominion. In you, and in you alone, as in a boundless abyss, our powers can launch forth into activity and relax their tensions, can show their full capacity—without being checked by any limitation—can plunge into love and into self-

[9] As in *The Mystical Milieu* and elsewhere, Père Teilhard delights in repeating the name Jesus. There are other instances later in this essay. Cf. p. 223: 'Lord Jesus.'

[10] The reference is to the words of the liturgy, taken from Scripture: *Panem de caelo praestitisti eis—Omne delectamentum in se habentem.*

surrender with the certainty that your deep waters are free from the reef of imperfection, the shoals of meanness, the current of perversion.

By you, and you alone, who are the entire and proper object of our love and the creative energy that fathoms the secrets of our hearts and the mystery of our growth, our souls are awakened, sensitized, enlarged, to the utmost limit of their latent potentialities.

And under your influence, and yours alone, the integument of organic isolation and wilful egoism which separates the monads from one another is torn asunder and dissolves, and the multitude of souls rushes on towards that union which is essential to the maturity of the world.

Thus a third plenitude is added to the other two. In a very real sense, Lord Jesus, you are the *plenitudo entium*, the full assemblage of all beings who shelter, and meet, and are for ever united, within the mystical bonds of your body. In your breast, my God, better than in any embrace, I possess all those whom I love and who are illumined by your beauty and in turn illumine you with the rays of light (so powerful in their effect upon our hearts) which they receive from you and send back to you. That multitude of beings, so daunting in its magnitude, that I long to help, to enlighten, to lead to you: it is already there, Lord, gathered together within you. Through you I can reach into the inmost depths of every being and endow them with whatever I will— provided that I know how to ask you and that you permit it.[11]

In this higher, mystical, climate suddenly disclosed to me by

---

[11] This is the classic teaching: God, who is 'his own being' is at the same time 'the being of all'. Pseudo-Dionysius, *The Hierarchy of Heaven*, IV.1 P.G.3, 177–8). Though incomprehensible and unattainable, he is at the same time intimately close. As 'principle and root of every creature', he is the Being who is eminently present. Cf. St Bernard, *De consideratione*, bk. 5, ch. 6, n. 13: '*Quid item Deus?—Sine quo, nihil est. Tam nihil esse sine ipso, quam nec ipse sine se potest. Ipse sibi, ipse omnibus est. Ac per hoc quodammodo ipse solus est, qui suum ipsius est et omnium esse.*—'What, again is God?—without whom nothing exists. As nothing can be without him, so he cannot be without himself. He exists for himself, and for all. And thus he who is at once his own being and the being of all, in some way alone exists.' (P.L. 182, 796A; *Opera*, ed. Jean Leclercq, vol. 3, 1963, p. 477). Cf. *In Cantica* sermo 4, n. 4 (P.L. 183, 708 AB; *Opera*, vol. 1, 1957, p. 23).

the consecration, the most diametrically opposed attributes meet and are combined in a perfection that oversteps the boundaries of our experience.

Our attachment to the legitimate allurements the earth offers us grows greater by being directed to an ever greater end (by which I mean the Body of Christ, the sole essential term of all created effort): thus it leaves behind all personal self-seeking and becomes identified with a rigorous spirit of detachment.[12]

By closing in upon the common centre of things, each according to its particular nature, the elements fall into a unity that absorbs them as it consummates them. The pains they take to differentiate themselves are in reality the measure and the instrument of their ultimate identification.

By growing less *in Christo Jesu*, those who mortify themselves, who suffer, and grow old, with patience, cross the critical threshold at which death is turned into life. By forgetting themselves, they find themselves again, never more to be lost.[13]

Christ is loved as a person: he compels recognition as a world.[14]

Of Christ's self-fulfilment there can be no doubt. He is immune from suffering. He has already risen from the dead. And yet we, who are his members, must continue, in humility and fear, in the excitement of danger, to work for the fulfilment of an element that the mystical Body can obtain *only* from us. Our peace of mind is underlaid by the exaltation of creating, in the midst of such hazards, an everlasting work that could not exist

---

[12] Cf. *Forma Christi*, below p. 262n: 'The effort of spiritual *attachment* to the natural universe is vitally essential; and it imposes a rigorous *austerity* on the souls of the faithful.' *Ibid.* pp. 261-2: 'Very often (in fact generally) the *two phases* of attachment and detachment are *fused together* in the concrete reality (the psychological unity) of a single *disinterested effort*. When man works to develop himself for God (to have a greater capacity for God), at the same time and by the same act his soul is personalized *in se* and depersonalized *in Christo*.'

[13] This teaching is set out at greater length in Part 2 of *Le Milieu Divin*: 'The divinization of our passivities'. See also *La Signification et la valeur constructrice de la suffrance* (1933) (*Oeuvres* vol. 6) and *L'Energie spirituelle de la souffrance* (1951), (*Oeuvres*, vol. 7).

[14] A typically Teilhardian phrase: it expresses the Pauline concept of the Pleroma.

without us. Our confidence in God is inspired and toughened by the human passion to conquer the world.[15]

Life and death, unity and plurality, element and totality, possession and quest, being and becoming . . . such is the Pleroma of the world and of Christ.

Sin alone is excluded. And yet, since to be damned is not to be annihilated, who can say what mysterious complement may not be added to the body of the Christ by that immortal loss?

Per quem omnia creas, vivificas, sanctificas . . . in Eo vivimus et movemur et sumus.[16]

C: COMMUNION

Panem caelestem accipiam . . .

Just as, when I turn my mind and reason to things that lie outside me, I have no right to dissociate myself from their destiny—so I cannot, in my personal being, escape from the Divine, whose dominating power I can see growing ever more supreme wherever I look.

Even had I ever imagined that it was I who held the consecrated Bread and gave myself its nourishment, I now see with

[15] This paragraph expresses both the assurance the Christian derives from his faith and his hope—since the risen Christ is the final victor—and the consciousness of the risk that threatens everything that has not yet been integrated into the mystical Body of Christ. The original emphasis that characterizes in this passage the twofold awareness in the Christian is that the feeling of risk itself contains a double element: a humble fear—and the excitement and enthusiasm aroused by the prospect of danger.

[16] It is thus that on several occasions Père Teilhard applies St Paul's words about the immensity of God. He is justified in so doing, in the light of the teaching of St Paul, and of tradition, on the cosmic function of the risen Christ. Cf. above, note 2. See also, for example, Bérulle, *Discours de l'état et des grandeurs de Jésus*, discours 2: 'The earth of our human race, living in Jesus Christ . . . is a new centre of the universe towards which every spiritual and physical creature tends'. (5th ed. 1639, pp. 152-3). *La Vie de Jésus*, 1, n. 21: 'Heaven and Earth, grace and nature, look towards you and tend towards you as to their whole and their centre'. (3rd ed. 1630, p. 29.) Cf. *Cosmic Life* (1916), conclusion, 'Jesus, the centre towards which all things are moving' (above, p. 70).

blinding clarity that it is the Bread that takes hold of me and draws me to itself.

That small, seemingly lifeless, Host has become for me as vast as the world, as insatiable as a furnace. I am encircled by its power. It seeks to close around me.

An inexhaustible and universal communion is the term of the universal consecration.

I cannot, Lord, evade such massive power: I can only yield to it in blissful surrender.

And first, my God, I entrust myself to the generalized forces of matter, of life, of grace. The ocean of energies that our weakness cannot control: upon which we drift—hardly conscious of our heading, hardly able to change our course—this has now become for me the comforting mantle of your creative action. That part of us which is *in nobis sine nobis*—in me, so large a part that my freedom seems to be lost in it—I can feel warm, animated, charged with the organizing virtue of your body, Jesus.

In everything in me that has subsistence and resonance, in everything that enlarges me from within, that arouses me, attracts me, or wounds me from without, it is you, Lord, who are at work upon me—it is you who mould and spiritualize my formless clay—you that change me into yourself.

To take possession of me, my God, you who are more remote than all and deeper than all, you take to yourself and unite together the immensity of the world and the intimate depths of myself.

I can feel that all the strain and struggle of the universe reaches down into the most hidden places of my being.[17]

But, Lord, I do not passively give way to these blessed passivities: I offer myself to them, actively, and do all I can to promote them.

I know how the life-giving power of the host can be blocked

[17] The threefold idea presented in this section should be noted. 1: the great part played by passivities. 2: the transformation of all things effected by faith, which sees the hand of God everywhere. (Cf. *Forma Christi*, C; *Le Milieu Divin*, pp. 135–6; etc.). 3: the transcendence and immanence of God, more distant than all, and lying deeper than all. (Cf. *L'Energie humaine* 1937, in *Oeuvres*, vol. 6 p. 183).

by our freedom of will. If I seal up the entry into my heart I must dwell in darkness—and not only I—my individual soul—but the whole universe in so far as its activity sustains my organism and awakens my consciousness, and in so far also as I act upon it in my turn to draw forth from it the materials of sensation, of ideas, of moral goodness, of holiness of life. But if, on the other hand, *my heart is open to you*, then at once through the pure intent of my will[18] the divine must flood into the universe, in so far as the universe is centred on me. Since, by virtue of my consent, I shall have become a living particle of the Body of Christ, all that affects me must in the end help on the growth of the total Christ. Christ will flood into and over me, me and *my* cosmos.

How I long, Lord Christ, for this to be!

May my acceptance be ever more complete, more comprehensive, more intense!

May my being, in its self-offering to you, become ever more open and more transparent to your influence!

And may I thus feel your activity coming ever closer, your presence growing ever more intense, everywhere around me.

Fiat, fiat.

In order to assist your action in me through all things, I shall do more than make myself receptive and offer myself to the passivities of life. I shall faithfully associate myself with the work you effect in my body and my soul. I shall strive to obey and anticipate your least promptings. My dearest wish, Master, is that I might offer so little resistance to you that you could no longer distinguish me from yourself—so perfectly would we be united, in a communion of will.[19]

[18] Later, in *Le Milieu Divin*, Père Teilhard re-emphasized the necessity for the 'pure intent of the will' (p. 133), 'There is no limit,' he says again, '*in respect of the intention* which animates our endeavour to act or to accept, because we can always go farther in the inward perfecting of our conformity. There can always be greater detachment and greater love' (pp. 138–9). Cf. note 20, and letters from Père Teilhard to Père Auguste Valensin, in *Archives de philosophie*, 1961.

[19] It will be noted that the strongest form of union Père Teilhard has in mind here is 'communion of will'. We find the same in St Bernard and St

And yet, Lord, you look to me for even more than this perfect docility. It would not, you see, exhaust the positive richness of my activity. It would affect only the *formal*—not the *material*—aspect of my work: and it is the whole of my being, Lord Jesus, that you would have me give you, tree and fruit alike, the finished work as well as the harnessed power, the *opus* together with the *operatio*.[20] To allay your hunger and quench your thirst, to nourish your body and bring it to its full stature, you need to find in us a substance which will be truly food for you. And this food ready to be transformed into you, this nourishment for your flesh, I will prepare for you by liberating the *spirit* in myself and in everything:

Through an effort (even a purely natural effort) to learn the truth, to live the good, to create the beautiful;

Through cutting away all inferior and evil energies;

Through practising that charity towards men which alone can gather up the multitude into a single soul. . . .

To promote, in however small a degree, *the awakening of spirit* in the world, is *to offer to the* incarnate *Word* an *increase of reality and consistence*: it is to allow his influence to increase in intensity around us.

And this means but one thing, Lord; that through the whole width and breadth of the Real, through all its past and through all that it will become, through all that I undergo and all that I do,

---

Ignatius Loyola. Cf. St Bernard, *De Diligendo Deo*, C. 15, n. 39 (*Opera*, vol. 3, 1963. p. 153), etc., where he shows that the union of will is the realization of the 'unus spiritus' of which St Paul speaks in 1 Cor. 6:17.

[20] Père Teilhard holds that the intention contained in the *operatio* (the act) is not sufficient, and that it may even become distorted if it does not extend to the *opus* (the work) which should normally be its fruit. Cf. *Le Milieu Divin*, p. 55: 'It is certainly a very great thing to be able to think that, if we love God, something of our inner activity, of our *operatio*, will never be lost. But will not the work itself of our minds, of our hearts, and of our hands—that is to say, our achievements, what we bring into being, our *opus*—will not this, too, in some sense be "eternalized" and saved?' And p. 60: 'Every man, in the course of his life, must not only show himself obedient and docile. By his fidelity, he must *build*—starting with the most natural territory of his own self —a work, an *opus*'.

through all that I am bound by, through every enterprise, through my whole life's work, I can make my way to you, be one with you, and progress endlessly in that union.

With a fulness no man has conceived you realized, through your Incarnation, love's threefold dream: to be so enveloped in the object of love as to be absorbed in it—endlessly to intensify its presence—and, without ever knowing surfeit, to be lost in it.

I pray that Christ's influence, spiritually substantial, physically mortifying, may ever spread wider among all beings, and that thence it may pour down upon me and bring me life.

I pray that this brief and limited contact with the sacramental species may introduce me to a universal and eternal communion with Christ, with his omni-operant will and his boundless mystical Body.

Corpus, sanguis Domini nostri Jesu Christi custodiant animam meam in vitam aeternam. Amen.

D: THE APOSTOLATE

Quid retribuam Domino . . .

And now, my God, that in and through all things you have made me one with you, I no longer belong to myself.

In obedience to the law that governs every plenitude in a universe that is still multiple and exteriorized [diffuse], I must—as must the adult life and the blazing torch—spread abroad the fire you have imparted to me.[21]

In a light that consistently grows brighter, you show me ever more clearly your Body—your personal and sacramental Body —enveloped in a 'corona' of living dust, as vast as the world: and I see how, under the spiritualizing current that flows from you, the elect portion of this dust concentrates with you as its focus, while what is left is expelled to roam the highways of the night.[22]

[21] Fire: see note 28 to *The Mystical Milieu*.
[22] Another reference to damnation. We find the same metaphor, more soberly expressed, in *The Monstrance* (in *Hymn of the Universe*).

I see your flesh extend throughout the entire universe, there to be mingled with it and so extract from it all the elements that can be made to serve your purpose. There is not a single atom that does not pay tribute to your totality, even though that be the prelude to its own destruction.

I realize at last that the totality of all perfections is the necessary basis for that ultimate mystical organism which you are constructing out of all things. You do not destroy, Lord, the beings you adopt for your building; but you transform them, while preserving everything good that centuries of creation have fashioned in them.[23]

= The universality of your divine attraction, and the intrinsic value of our human activity—I am on fire, Lord, to make known to all this twofold truth you have revealed to me, and to make it real.

Every priest, because he is a priest, has given his life to a work of universal salvation. If he is conscious of his dignity, he must no longer live for himself but for the world, as he lived whose anointed representative the priest is.

I feel, Jesus, that this duty has a more immediate urgency for me, and a more exact meaning, than it has for many others—far better men, too, than I.

Your call has innumerable different shades of emphasis: each vocation is essentially different from the rest.

The various regions, nations, social groupings, have each their particular apostles.

And I, Lord, for my (very lowly) part, would wish to be the apostle—and, if I dare be so bold—the evangelist—*of your Christ in the universe.*

Through my thinking, through the message I bring, through the practical activity of my whole life, I would wish to disclose and make known to men the bonds of continuity that make the cosmos of our restless ferment into an ambience that is divinized by the Incarnation, that divinizes by communion, and that is divinizable by our co-operation.

[23] This section brings out simultaneously the distinction between nature and the supernatural, and their oneness.

To bring Christ, by virtue of a specifically organic connexion, to the heart of realities that are esteemed to be the most dangerous, the most unspiritual, the most pagan—in that you have my gospel and my mission.

If men could only see that in each one of them there is an element of the Pleroma, would not that, Lord, effect the reconciliation between God and our age? If only they could understand that, with all its natural richness and its massive reality, the universe can find fulfilment only in Christ; and that Christ, in turn, can be attained only through a universe that has been carried to the very limit of its capabilities.[24]

To those who are seduced by the treasure-house of the Real and overcome by its immediacy—to these I would show the life of the Lord Jesus flowing through all things—the true soul of the world.

To those who are dazzled by the nobility of human endeavour, I would say, in the name of Christ, that man's work is sacred, sacred both in the submission of the will to God, and in the great task it accomplishes in the course of endless tentative efforts —and that task is the liberation, natural and supernatural, of Spirit.

To those who are indolent, unenterprising, infantile, or narrow-minded in their religious attitude, I would point out that man's development is essential to Christ for the formation of his Body, and that a constant *spirit of enquiry* directed towards the world and truth *is an absolute duty.*[25]

If you judge me worthy, Lord, I would show to those whose lives are dull and drab the limitless horizon opening out to

[24] The whole of this passage brings out Père Teilhard's awareness of the special character of his vocation, and also the apostolic importance he attached to it. On the fourth day of his annual retreat in 1940, meditating on the mystery of the Epiphany, he noted: 'Epiphany. *Stella: Jesus-Maria.* Grace: to follow *my* light—a special vocation'.

[25] Père Teilhard often refers to this duty of research understood in the widest and most profound sense. Cf. references in *The Religion of Teilhard de Chardin,* pp. 26-7. At the same time he pointed out the danger of a certain 'mystique of research', that claims to be self-sufficient: *Réflexions sur le bonheur* (1943), in *Cahiers Pierre Teilhard de Chardin,* No. 2, p. 69.

humble and hidden efforts; for these efforts, if pure in intention, can add to the extension of the incarnate Word a further element —an element *known* to Christ's heart and gathered up into his immortality.[26]

I shall remind those who are successful and fortunate that their success has an infinitely wider import than the satisfaction of their petty personality. They can, and indeed should, rejoice—but in Christ, whose plenitude calls for a certain completeness in their nature. And I shall teach these, even as they rejoice, to distinguish, side by side with the egoism that is centred on self, and the sensual appetite that relishes the pleasant, a *force* drawn from well-being and the widening of one's nature that can be added, in God, to their spiritual activity.

And above all, I shall remind those who suffer and mourn that the most direct way of making our life useful is to allow God, in his own good time, to grow within us, and, through death, to substitute himself for us.[27]

You know, my God, that I can now scarcely discern in the world the lineaments of its multiplicity,[28] for when I gaze at it I see it chiefly as a limitless reservoir in which the two contrary energies of joy and suffering are accumulating in vast quantities —and for the most part lying unused.

And I see how through this restless wavering mass there pass powerful psychic currents made up of souls who are carried away by a passion for art, for the Eternal Feminine, for science and the

[26] Père Teilhard is not forgetting non-scientists, nor overlooking the value of 'pure intention'. The same applies to *Le Milieu Divin*, which puts forward a spiritual teaching adapted to every Christian. See also below, pp. 258-9.

[27] See above, note 13. Père Teilhard's thoughts constantly return to death. Cf. *Le Milieu Divin*, p. 100: 'For all of them, in any event, the road ends at the same point: the final stripping off of the old by death which accompanies the recasting, and is a prelude to the final incorporation *in Christo Jesu*.'

[28] We find the same thought in *Note on the Universal Element* (appendix to *Forma Christi*): 'the man to whom it is given to see Christ as *more real* than any other reality in the world, he truly lives in a zone undisturbed by any multiplicity . . .' Cf. letter of 24 December 1915, referring to 'the blessed oneness of God, in which all things and all persons are achieved, with absolute certainty and permanence' (*Making of a Mind*, p. 84).

mastery of the universe, for the autonomy of the individual, for freedom of mankind.

From time to time these currents collide with one another in formidable crises which cause them to seethe and foam in their efforts to establish their equilibrium.

What glory it were for you, my God, and what an affluence of life to your humanity, could all this spiritual power be harmonized in you!

Lord, to see drawn from so much wealth, lying idle or put to base uses, all the dynamism that is locked up within it: this is my dream. And to share in bringing this about: this is the work to which I would dedicate myself.

As far as my strength will allow me, *because I am a priest*, I would henceforth be the first to become aware of what the world loves, pursues, suffers. I would be the first to seek, to sympathize, to toil: the first in self-fulfilment, the first in self-denial—I would be more widely human in my sympathies and more nobly terrestrial in my ambitions than any of the world's servants.

On the one hand I want to plunge into the midst of created things, and mingling with them, seize hold upon and disengage from them all that they contain of life eternal, down to the very last fragment, so that nothing may be lost; and on the other hand I want, by practising the counsels of perfection, to salvage through self-denial all the heavenly fire imprisoned within the threefold concupiscence of the flesh, of avarice, of pride: in other words, to hallow, through chastity, poverty and obedience, the power enclosed in love, in gold, in independence.

That is why I have taken on my vows and my priesthood (and it is this that gives me my strength and my happiness), in a determination to accept and divinize the powers of the earth.[29]

It was only a moment ago, my God, that I offered up my sacrifice 'upon all things'. And, in very truth, my yearning and

---

[29] Père Teilhard has in mind both ordination to the priesthood and profession in religion, the thought of which was the inspiration of this essay. It is a twofold epitome of the apologetical method and spiritual dialectic that are characteristic of his thought. Under the action of Christ, all things are weighed so that he may gather to himself the 'chosen part'.

my prayer then reached out to the whole cosmos, of which you, Lord Jesus, are the plenitude.

Nothing was excluded from the intention in my mind: and yet my eyes were turned above all to the grim battle-area where men, so close to me, have for four years been fighting and slaughtering one another.

Was there ever, my God, a humanity more like, in the shedding of its blood, to a sacrificed victim—more ready, in its ferment, to receive creative transformation—more rich, in what it unleashes, in energy that can be sanctified—more close, in its agony, to the supreme communion?

I speak to you, my fellow-priests, who share the battle: if there be any among you who are at a loss in so unforeseen a situation—with your mass unsaid and your ministry unaccomplished—remember that over and above the administration of the sacraments, as a higher duty than the care of individual souls, you have a universal function to fulfil: the offering to God of the *entire* world.

Going far beyond the bread and wine the Church has put in your hand, your influence is destined to extend to the immense host of mankind, waiting for him to come who will sanctify it.

You have the power—through your ordination—in a real way to consecrate into the flesh and blood of Christ the sufferings you see on all sides, and in which your priestly character makes it your duty to share.

You are the leaven spread by providence throughout the battle-field, so that, *by your mere presence*, the huge mass of our toil and agony may be transformed.

Never have you been more priests than you are now, involved as you are and submerged in the tears and blood of a generation —never have you been more active—never more fully in the line of your vocation.

I thank you, my God, in that you have made me a priest—and a priest ordained *for War*.

I am so conscious of my weakness, Lord, that I do not dare to ask you to allow me to share in this bliss. But I see it none the less clearly: and I shall proclaim:

'Happy are those among us who, in these decisive days of the creation and redemption, have been chosen for this supreme act, the logical crowning of their priesthood: to be in communion, even unto death, with the Christ who is being born and suffering in the human race.'

8th July 1918[30]

[30] Cf. p. 203.

Operative Faith

We find the first direct reference to the theme of 'Operative Faith' in letters that Père Teilhard wrote (on the 17 August 1918, and again on the 28th and 31st) to his cousin from the forest of Laigue, in the Oise.

In another letter, from Moyvillers (Oise), dated September 12th, he writes at greater length on the same subject, outlining a definite plan for the essay, but adding: 'My thought is feeling its way, and once again I'm trying to clarify it by talking it over with you'. ('Making of a Mind', pp. 228, 230, 232, 236.)

On September 27th, again, writing from Chavannes-sur-l'Etang, near Montreux-Vieux in Alsace (in the Dannemarie district) he says that he is 'rather absorbed in writing and copying out "Operative Faith"'. The manuscript was sent off to his cousin the next day, the 28th, and on the 29th he wrote again:
'Yesterday I sent you . . . my latest essay. I'm rather beginning to wonder whether I shouldn't, once again, offer it to Léonce with a view to publication (in "Recherches" for example). I feel that my own too individual ideas are represented in it only by that side of them that is generally applicable and certainly sound—in a form that minds in sympathy with mine will recognize as their own thought, without others taking alarm. But once again, I've become so accustomed to living "in my own universe" that I haven't much idea of what's strange or familiar to others. You must tell me what you think' (pp. 240–1, cf. p. 238).

We do not know Marguerite Teillard's reaction, nor whether the manuscript was in fact sent to Père de Grandmaison for publication in the 'Recherches de science religieuse'.

OPERATIVE FAITH

PREFACE

. . . And Peter answered him, 'Lord, if it is you, bid me come
to you on the water'. He said, 'Come'. So Peter got out of the
boat and walked on the water and came to Jesus; but when he
saw the wind, he was afraid, and beginning to sink he cried out,
'Lord, save me'. Jesus immediately reached out his hand and
caught him, saying to him, 'O man of little faith, why did you
doubt?'[1]

Fides substantia sperandarum rerum (Hebrews)

A: FEAR OF THE FUTURE

It is with reluctance that we allow our thoughts to dwell upon
the future.

Like nervous passengers in a ship or an aircraft who turn their
eyes away from the ever-moving emptiness of sea or air, we
generally shun the prospect of the future into which we are
launched.

Clinging to the apparently more solid framework of what has
already been acquired and of the past, we try—surrounded as we
are by relatively stable persons and things—to forget the bewildering domain of possibilities in which we are swallowed
up.

However, in spite of ourselves, the feeling of the uncertainty
in which we drift and of the inexorable force that drives us

---

[1] Matthew 14:28-31. All his life long, this was a favourite subject of
meditation for Père Teilhard. He frequently refers to it, particularly in his
retreat notes.

along, insists on making its way into our consciousness. However much we try to escape into the present, we are still haunted by the temptation to look overboard at what lies outside our vessel. The temptation becomes irresistible, and in the end we raise our heads and risk a glance into the future.

And then it is that we find ourselves hypnotized by a *double abyss*.[2]

The first abyss that opens up is that of *our fragility*.

From the direction from which we approach it, the Real that is still to come appears to us to be made up of an inextricable network of causalities (or antecedents). Looked at in isolation, the fibres of this shifting and tangled fabric seem, to all intents and purposes, to be firmly knit. Taken in groups, however, and in their combinations (and it is these alone that have any importance for life) they are found to be completely inconstant and instable. The least bit added to or taken away from the components, the least variation in the time or place of their coming together, is sufficient radically to transform the shape of the whole. The future seems to be completely at the mercy of the forces of *chance*. All the active reserves of the world seem to be caught up in a process that, given an infinitesimal difference of propulsive force (whose magnitude bears no relation to the results entailed), will end either in successful achievement or in utter waste. What, then, looking at it from where we stand, is at stake in this game of hazard, if not ourselves?

When we consider the intangible haze of chances through which we have to keep ourselves going and find our way, we feel the same trembling that possesses us when we stand, with no parapet to cling to, on a rock overhanging a sheer drop.

How did we ever manage to climb so high? What can stop us from falling? How can the countless determinisms by whose interplay we are formed have been able to combine, and how is it that at every moment of our lives they do not break away again?

Consider what infinite numbers of favourable encounters—

[2] 'Fragility' and 'contingence': i.e., what Père Teilhard was later to call 'inconsistence'. Cf. Retreat of 1945: 'To accept and love the feeling of utter inconsistence'; retreat of 1948: 'Yes: the dizzy abyss of fragility, of instability'

whose improbability increases in geometrical progression—must have been needed for the Earth to be formed, for mankind to develop, and for my own puny person to come into the world. Think, again, how slender, and ever more slender, are the threads from which my existence is woven, extending from the initial starting-point of the cosmic processes right down to the meeting of my parents . . . Had but a single one of those threads snapped my spirit would never have emerged into existence.

What was it that brought all these together, and what is it that now keeps them so?

If we look back, if we look downwards, we suddenly feel the agony of our extreme complexity; it seems as though we must fall apart, so *improbable* do we appear to be.

And yet we do not fall!

If we gently test out the machinery of our thought and our organism, we find that it is functioning: it was an illusion that made our minds reel for a moment. Existence still stands firm in us. We must continue to live.

That may well be true: but what are we to do if we wish to climb higher?

It is then that, after sowing doubts in our minds even about our past, a vivid awareness of the risks we run in pressing ahead, tends to paralyse the impetus that drives us towards the future. God above! how can we find our way through the countless roads in the void that yawns before us? The least false step in any direction can turn [divert] my course into a direction that is the complete reverse of what I wish—and, in particular, it can bring me into contact with entirely different forces, which can mean for me either safety or ruin.

I tremble when I contemplate the infinite variety of possible clashes that may be produced between me and the infinitely numerous and close-packed beings who haunt the region which I am about to enter.

Faced with such vast complexity and such extreme tenuity, how can I even begin to make a reckoning?

How can I pluck up the courage to take a single step, let alone to strike out boldly?

And yet, if I stand still, how can I fail to fall?

Wherever I look, farther than the eye can see, the future undulates like a treacherous, intangible, atmosphere.

The only fixed lines I can see are the inhuman trajectories of certain laws of probability. Just as chance arises from an assembled body of determinisms, so a determinism of the second order is born from the coming together of all chances. Nemesis, the goddess of the undifferentiated whole, she who knows no man's name and loves no man, who forbids good to exceed evil, who levels down and works to bring all things into one and the same circle—blindly, endlessly—she is the only power to whom I can turn my eyes and in whom I can place my hopes.

And yet, in fact, I have only to look at her and ice-cold fear drains the last of my courage. For, with her coming, I see that I have fallen into the heart of the second abyss whose depth shocks my eyes when I dare to peer into the time that stretches ahead of me—*the abyss of necessity lying at the bottom of the abyss of contingence*.

No part of me is free from necessity: it is incorporated into my substance and secreted by my activity. I rest upon it, and every decision I make strengthens its dominion over me.

On the one hand, there are the countless determinisms whose haphazard network is my support. These continue to live, hidden within me, like those vibratory impulses that capriciously combine to form a particle of matter, and, a moment later, separate and revert to their original dimensions. As the impermanent and unpredictable result of a thousand convergent forces, we are (as regards much the greater part of ourselves, which is neither initially free, nor freed later) subject to the combined laws of these elementary inevitabilities. This accounts for those tendencies in my nature that nothing can correct, for my innate virtues and defects, for the particular rhythm of my development, the various healthy or unhealthy processes that take place in my organism.

And this is not all.

Through the free action of the whole it forms, the more or less

ephemeral association of determinisms that constitutes me, is
obliged (by the very way in which it works) to envelop itself in
an ever closer web of compulsions. Every new decision I make
drives me along a road that I shall never be able to leave. It permanently restricts the field of possibilities open to me, and
confines my future to a narrower sphere. However anxious I may
be to do so, I can never take back the words I have spoken or
undo the folly I have been guilty of. Every decision is projected
into the formless, fluid, future, and there it closes water-tight
bulkheads that I cannot force. Our existence is imprisoned in
the irreparable: so irreversible duration insists.

The deeper we look into ourselves, the more numerous, we
see to our horror, are the fetters of the incurable and the irreparable. From all sides necessity creeps in to attack body and
soul. Every day it pushes out more tentacles into the fabric of
the future, initially so pliant and immature.

All these rigid lines into which we are forced share a common
framework: they all derive from the fundamental obligation of
living imposed on us without reference to our own wishes.
Moreover, they all converge upon one and the same unavoidable centre: death.[3]

Seen in the future, death is the epitome, and the common
basis, of everything that terrifies us and makes our minds reel.

It is the one great misfortune (*casus*), the supremely important
event that can be called down upon us by the most insignificant
decision on our part, or the most trifling accident.

It is a sort of punishment inflicted on us by Nemesis in return
for, and to make up for, the existence we have enjoyed.

It is the inevitable destiny (*fatum*) involved in our birth and
imposed as a limit to our lives.

Our eyes dwell, without ever being able to focus, on the dark
horizon that on all sides marks the boundary of the future—as
though we were looking at those pools of blackness between
the stars, from which there radiates (born in the supreme void

[3] Here Père Teilhard describes the dark side of death; later (pp. 241-2), in the
light of faith, death will be seen as the gateway into life. This is the constant
pattern of his reflection on death.

in which All moves) a more powerful pull towards the abyss.
What new hazards, what further compulsions, await us
beyond that darkness?

A man must have felt the shadow of death pass over him, if he
is to understand all the loneliness, the danger, and the terror that
each new advance into the future brings with it.

It is only when danger threatens—a danger in face of which we,
and all those around us, are powerless—that the future can be seen
by us distinctly: it is only then that we can see its two aspects of
capricious fortune and implacable destiny—an ocean that is at
once inconstant and stormy, in which we may be capsized and
founder—an ocean whose inconsistency is as uncontrollable as its
unleashed power.

Those who have not been within an inch of death have never
really seen what lay ahead of them.

Others—those whom an overpowering terror has forced
boldly to raise their eyes and look time straight in the face—have
often succumbed to fear, even in the middle of what was until
then a confident advance between the abysses on either side; and
in their consternation they may well have felt that they were
falling headlong.[4]

B: NATURAL FAITH

The most solid basis for our certainty is probably the principle
that 'the truth never disarms action'.

That being so, let us look at the apprehension we feel when we
become vividly aware of the hazards and necessities of the future:
it is an unhealthy apprehension, since it tends to disintegrate our
substance and slacken the sinews of our will. We may say, then,
that it points unmistakably to some ignorance, some faulty
perspective, in our view of the future.

From this we can only conclude that if we are to remain
faithful to truth and life, we must at all costs master our feeling
of dizziness: not, however, by closing our eyes, for such an

[4] One has here the direct echo of the experience of the war years.

attitude is not only unworthy of a man but also quite ineffective in bringing us reassurance: once we have looked into the void the feeling it inspires continues irresistibly to make its way into us through every fibre of our being. What we have to do is to fix our eyes firmly on the object which terrifies us. No matter what the cost, we must look at it without flinching, not trying to summon up some sort of passive resignation (stoic, fatalist, or merely supine), but reinforcing our conviction that the untamed element into which we are venturing can be mastered by our energy—that our energy will ultimately be able to stabilize its fluidity and master its determinisms.

We must, if we are not to sink back into despondency, and from that into inertia, succeed in imposing regularity and docility upon the future.

Moreover, there can be no doubt that it is *possible* to do so.

The fact is plain enough: so far, the universe has succeeded in making progress. The soul of man appeared in the midst of a chaos of chance; and this must mean that Spirit was able in some way to make improbability accept control, and to free itself from determinisms—at least in so far as the determinisms had to be made to yield in order to overcome chance. However unlikely it may seem to us, a direct '*pre-action*' on the future, and at least a partial emancipation from material mechanisms, are modes of action that do in fact exist in our universe. The utter bewilderment we feel as we stand on the threshold of destiny can derive, in consequence, only from an optical illusion or from failure on our part to understand some power contained within us.

Anyone who has more than a superficial interest in intellectual enquiry or to whom it is not simply a means to personal success, has felt that the fundamental problem is '*to discover the secret of advancing confidently and freely into the future*'; and it is the search for the solution to this problem that must inspire him.

Modern man has come to take it for granted that the best place to look for an answer to this secret is in *science*, in other words, in a clear knowledge of the laws of the universe. There are some who think it may be perfectly possible to work out the random possibilities so exactly, and elucidate the mechanisms of life so clearly, that chance, evil, and even death may one day be eliminated: they rely, in fact, on calculated action directed *from outside* on nature's mechanism. The scientist, not without some reason, holds that man will not be able to say that he is free until he has so profound and *rational* a knowledge of what makes up the future and what laws govern it, that he is in a position to control and direct them *infallibly*, making them work against each other—in other words, by turning against them their own determinism. He is certain, for example, that vaccines give us an undeniable power to check the progress of a number of diseases.

It is immediately apparent that if this great hope of scientifically mastering the future is pushed to the limit, it must presuppose a particular static and materialist view of nature. If knowledge of the elements that make up the future is to allow us to predict and control later forms of life, then we must admit that these forms contain no power higher in order than those we now experience: and that means that if we gradually make our way back into the past, the present universe contains nothing more than the primitive nebula.

Thus the man who relies on science does more even than fantastically extrapolate the curve of our present discoveries: he gives mystical assent to a philosophy or, more correctly, to a sort of religion. Adherence to the doctrine of salvation by science amounts to an act of faith. It is not with that faith, however, that the present study is concerned.[5]

The natural faith that I wish to analyse here is the faith professed by a class of thinkers—profoundly hostile to the worship of science, even though scientists by conviction—who believe they have found a way of influencing the Real still to come. This is a procedure very different from working out possible combinations and making mathematical calculations.

Since all time, there have been men who believe that instead of attacking determinisms through the use of reason and from outside, it would be much quicker and more effective to work upon them from within, by means of some living, mental influence.

[5] What does concern him is to refute 'scientism'—an exaggerated respect for science.

The 'scientist' has little time for such people who do not shrink from putting forward a psychical and voluntarist doctrine in opposition to the mechanical and intellectualist method of attempting to dominate phenomena. The great mass of the public regards them as visionaries. And yet—who knows?—may it not be the dreamers and the mystics who can show us the true road to freedom?

In its present, developed, form[6] the human doctrine that has recourse to an internal spiritual effort to free us from chance and the irreparable, derives from a common every-day experience expressed in the old saying: *Audentes fortuna favet.*

Fortune favours the brave.

That, indeed, is the law that popular good sense has extracted from an experience so lengthy and so venerable that, in comparison with it, science's analytical objections seem negligible.

There are men to whom success comes for no apparent reason, sometimes over a long period, because they are born 'under a lucky star'.

But there are others, too, whose boldness and tenacity enables them to bring chance to heel. A line of action pressed on with perseverance seldom fails to create around, and *ahead* of it, a current of favourable events.

Boldness determines fortune.

We may say even more: boldness forces the gateway into life.

Unlike hesitation, which dissociates bodily and spiritual energies and makes them vacillate, decisiveness in action increases, almost without limit, our power over the real. It 'increases our strength tenfold'. One might even say that it creates new energies, so vigorously is inertia aroused and so abundantly do friendly activities spring up around the man who is bold and determined—so unmistakably, in the muscles or the brain that strain in an ardent or desperate effort 'towards life', are new levels attained of physical strength and intellectual penetration.

[6] The magic that seeks to tame and subdue natural forces, conceived as animate, by incantations, can be associated with the doctrine of 'Progress through the will': but only, of course, if it is understood to be a rudimentary or degenerate expression of the doctrine. (Note by Père Teilhard.)

Every day of our life we can experience something of this nature.

With the evidence of these, and other similar facts we can understand why some men have believed they could see a new light dawning for their minds.

Who can say whether these limited and unco-ordinated experiences might not be transformed into a strict and general rule of action? Whether chance might not be like the air—intangible and elusive to too cautious a grasp, and yet safe and stable to resolute flight? Whether determinisms, inflexible in the routine conditions of our existence, might not, given a sufficient degree of vital tension, become pliable, and ready to combine in new properties?

It would, in truth, be altogether too much—though by no means unheard of—that man should have lived for centuries, bearing within himself—and even using in a bungling way—the weapon that could win his freedom, without understanding its universal effectiveness and range.

And then suddenly, when the human mind was struggling to make this great hope possible for itself, to make it reasonable, probable—a philosophy was at hand ready to accept, to generalize —demonstrate, almost—the truth of conclusions arrived at empirically.

According to a familiar form of idealism, matter and its inter-connexions do not exist in themselves, but result from a mechanization, a concretion, of thought. Matter is a fixation, an 'ankylosis', of Spirit, it is Spirit in an excessive state of fragmentation. All that would be required, therefore, would be a mental effort *sui generis* (individual or collective auto-suggestion) to re-animate the vast mechanism of the cosmos, and so to expel chance and death from this universe, now fully subject to Spirit. If we wish to win dominion over the future, all we have to do is boldly to bring the weight of our will to bear upon things, and at the same time to adjust the range and focus of our intellectual outlook in a particular way.

Such is the horizon, essentially practical and terrestrial, that opens up for natural faith: not only, we see, as a doctrine presented for its assent, but also as a result that may be expected from its operative power. Natural faith is above all an *operative faith*, and operative *here below*. The man who adheres to it *believes* that he can free the world *by believing*. And in so doing he adopts an attitude that is natural (naturalist) on two counts:

(i) First, because all he has in mind, and all he wants, is a transformation of the *experiential universe*.

(ii) Secondly, because he tends to make the human mind *itself* the agent of universal betterment, the Centre spreading through all things that is to exert a direct influence on the cosmos and so re-animate and vitalize it.[7]

Christian Science derived from a naturalistic and literal interpretation of the promises made to Faith by the Gospels: in a form that contains a curious mixture of revealed religion, it is precisely this method and this ideal that it offers its followers.[8]

For the Christian Scientist, it is true, the divine power intervenes as a necessary stage between human will and the effects produced by trust in Christ. Christ is the active milieu (the *medium*) in whom alone the Earth can become curable and faith become effective. However, this appeal to the supernatural would appear to be very largely nominal.

In the first place, the benefits hoped for from *faith-healing* are almost exclusively the alleviation of physical ills and an extremely 'Emersonian'[9] happiness. Secondly, the effort of faith demanded from the soul has all the characteristics of an auto-suggestion, into which Christ enters only as a fictitious figure, whose purpose is to

[7] The natural faith criticized here would be more correctly called 'naturalist' faith. Père Teilhard may well have had some particular writer in mind. The first of his two criticisms is directly applicable to H. G. Wells, and the same might perhaps be true of the second.

[8] Founded by the American Mrs Mary Baker Eddy, whose most important book was *Science and Religion* (1875; new edition, with *Key to the Scriptures*, 1910). At the time Père Teilhard was writing Christian Science had great influence, particularly in the U.S.A. and Great Britain.

[9] Ralph Waldo Emerson (1803-82) still exercised considerable influence in the first quarter of the twentieth century: he put forward the concept of an 'ideal Church' and extolled a 'moral sentiment' higher than any of the great figures that transmit it. His *Autobiographie* (based on his *Journals*, tr. by Régis Michaud) was published in France in 1914.

stimulate (set in motion) a force that is 'naturally' inherent in ourselves.

For these two reasons we may say, without injustice, that *faith-healing* is no more than a hardly disguised adaptation, in terms of the Gospel, of *man's faith in himself.*

Both faiths have the same power (and very real it is): no one can yet determine its *upper limits,* which are certainly much higher than science (and our more rash Christian apologists) are yet willing to admit.

Both, however, when we try to make them the instrument of our *final* salvation, fall a long way short of their goal. This is, first, because our wills, even working collectively, can do very little to influence in favour of our paltry ends the great driving forces of a universe in which all holds together and in which there are, without doubt, many other monads besides human souls. Secondly, it is because the brilliant hopes glimpsed by natural faith lie, in reality, on a plane completely different from that on which it pursues them; they are, therefore, completely out of the reach of natural faith.

C: CHRISTIAN FAITH

To read the Gospel with an open mind is to see beyond all possibility of doubt that Christ came to do more than bring us new truths concerning our destiny: he brought us not only a new concept of it, more exalted than that which we already had in our minds, but also, in a very real way, a new physical power of acting upon our *temporal* world.

Through a failure to grasp the exact nature of this power newly bestowed on all who put their confidence in God—a failure due either to a hesitation in face of what seems to us so unlikely, or to a fear of falling into illuminism—many Christians neglect this earthly aspect of the Master's promises, or at least do not give themselves to it with that complete boldness which he, however, never tires of asking of us, if only we have ears to hear him.

We must not allow timidity or modesty to turn us into drones.

If it is true that the development of the world can be influenced by our faith in Christ, then to let this power lie dormant within us would indeed be unpardonable.

We must ask ourselves, therefore, what pressure the believer should consider himself qualified, in the light of Christ's promises, to exert upon the future as it unfolds.

1. Fundamentally, the Christian has received from his Saviour the power of mastering fortune: that is to say he can so control the chances as to make them work in his favour. If that were not so, it would be impossible to account for the efficacy of prayer, and the saying *Credenti, omnia convertuntur in bonum* would be meaningless.

Scripture tells us this categorically.[10]

Thus I believe that disorder obeys my command, given in the name of Christ—the fluid becomes solid and stable.

To God, all things are possible.

The point, however, is this: how is that control realized?

We must picture it to ourselves as follows: it is just as though the *essential* single world we live in were, in spite of its unity, as multiple as the monads it contains. Even though the global progress of things is, in itself, one progress, we must recognize that it adds up not only to as many *different* aspects (that, of course, is inevitable) but also to as many variable [modifiable] individually isolated aspects as there are conscious minds. In virtue of some divine foreknowledge which controls the progress of the whole as a function of the freedom of each one, it is just as though there were, in the single event-system that determines the state of the universe at a given moment, as many *independent providences* as there are souls in the world. Thus each one of us has,

---

[10] Cf. Romans 8:28: *Scimus autem quoniam diligentibus Deum omnia co-operantur in bonum.* Cf. *Cosmic Life* (1916), p. 69: 'Everything, everything without exception, can, in the order of salvation, be of service to the monad of good will, *Omnia cooperantur in bonum*'. This same text reappears in *Forma Christi* as '*Credenti, omnia convertuntur in Christum*'. Cf. letter of 2 Dec. 1915: 'It's St Paul who tells us that, for those who love God, *everything* works together for the greatest good of the soul'. (*Making of a Mind*, p. 82.) It is this that gives the Christian who lives by faith 'the blissful consciousness of living in a universe super-animated by our Lord' (letter of Easter Sunday, 1927).

in reality, *his own* universe; he is its centre and he is called upon
to introduce harmony into it, just as though he were *alone* '*in
natura rerum*'.

In the light of this 'polyvalence' of the Cosmos,[11] which
enables prayer to exercise a *creative* pre-action on the *totality* of
phenomena, we can understand how each one of us, by confident
prayer, can modify *his own* future without necessarily interfering
with that of his neighbour—without even disturbing, in any
scientifically demonstrable way, the course of natural events.
Experimental science, whose field is confined to determinisms
considered in detail, cannot conflict with faith, which acts in such
a way as to modify the overall design of the tapestry without
breaking any individual thread.

Chance, that is to say unpredictable encounters produced by
the *collective* play of cosmic forces,[12] ceases, at the same time, to be
repugnant to reason. On the contrary, it represents God's role in
the direction of the world—or, we might say, it retains God's role
intact. It is through chance (and, may we say, at the opposite
pole to chance, through man's freedom) that creative power
enters into the universe—the power whose specific function is to
act by operating synthetically upon wholes—in other words by
controlling the *collective* play of causes.

Further, we now have an explanation of *the grossly excessive
influence* on our destiny exercised *by trifling deviations*. If it is true
that life's progress enables us to advance into something 'completely new', the importance of the events which develop us

[11] This doctrine of the 'polyvalence' of the cosmos is of cardinal importance:
failure to appreciate it opens the door to the crudest distortion of all Teilhard's
thought. Another essential distinction Teilhard makes, besides the one he
explains here, corresponds more or less exactly to the distinction the Epistle
to the Hebrews draws between the Kosmos and the Oikoumene (cf. Albert
Vanhoye, *L'Oikouménè dans l'Épître aux Hébreux*, in *Biblica*, vol. 45, fasc. 2,
1964, pp. 248–53): The Kosmos is the earth as it is now, the visible and material
world. The Oikoumene is the 'eschatological reality', 'the world of inter-
personal relationships'. Christ entered into the Kosmos through the Incarnation he humbly accepted: the triumph of Easter led him into the Oikoumene.

[12] This is a completely Aristotelian and Thomistic concept. Cf. A.-D. Ser-
tillanges, *Saint Thomas d'Aquin*, vol. 2, pp. 57ff: 'La Contingence dans la
Nature'.

spiritually cannot possibly be measured according to the rules, nor in the dimensions, of the material order from which we are even now being released. The degree of creative energy enclosed in an event can have nothing in common with its mechanical magnitude.

Finally, we see that the *disorder of the chance events* among which we move is purely apparent. The chaotic appearance of the future is due to our seeing the development of the universe 'the wrong way' or 'from the underside'. We are looking at a tapestry from the back, or playing a piece of music backwards. If we are to appreciate the harmony of events, they must be looked at 'in descending order'; we must, that is, start from the results to produce which they are set in motion. Looked at from this angle (that is, starting from God, who gathers us to himself) their undisciplined multitude falls into order: but, what is more, we can see how it is bound together in a final purpose (proportionate to our faith) which gives their fluidity a coherence higher than that of the Past.[13] In contrast with what we habitually feel, '*everything here below hangs together from on high*'.[14] The utter bewilderment we feel, whether we consider the improbability of what we were yesterday or the uncertainty of what we shall be tomorrow, is the result of a faulty analysis: it is the same mistake as that which causes our most heart-felt convictions to fade even as we entertain them, as soon as we try to reduce them *completely* to distinct motives, or that which upsets our most long-established equanimity immediately we try to rationalize the soundness of even our least important actions.

Once we accept that the world is 'pluri-providential', everything that lies ahead of us takes on clarity and stability. At the same time, we should note that this still remains hidden from those who do not wish to see; either (as we have already seen)

[13] Cf. *Creative Union*: 'The Consistence of the Future' (note by Père Teilhard).

[14] A quotation from Maurice Blondel. Cf. *Mon Univers* (1918), p. 281: 'The whole coherence and ontological value of the universe depends upon Spirit, which *knits* and *binds together* the elements of the world'. The criticism that, in Teilhard's view of evolution, the 'ascent' of the creature can only be secondary, is based on a complete misunderstanding. (Cf. Charles Journet, *Nova et Vetera*, 1964, p. 310.)

because it is only the *totality* of events that is influenced by faith, or because providence's adaptation of the visible universe to the requirements of each soul is effected in view not of a temporal success but of a success in heaven. Even if we believe with all our strength, fortune will not necessarily yield, as we advance, *in the way we wish*, but *in the way that must be*.[15]

2. This twofold character of faith operating on the uncertainties of the *future*—to harmonize the whole in preparation for a higher state—applies directly to the power it possesses, in the second place, of *overcoming* in the name of Christ the *forces of evil*, and more particularly *death*.

There is, no doubt, such a thing as the *faith that works miracles*: but this should not blind us to the true nature of our spiritual dominion over the cosmos. The *prodigy* amazes us because it asserts itself in the teeth of determinisms *over a limited area* and produces a 'local' reversal of the advance of time: but it has always been, and, it would seem, must necessarily continue to be, an altogether exceptional form of action. While it is an anticipation or a reflection of a form of life that transcends our own, it would not appear in any way to be the dawn of an earthly state of freedom and well-being. It heralds no millenium.[16]

Normally, as it habitually acts and can be relied on to act (which is all that concerns us here), faith does not break any injurious bonds that have been irreparably contracted in the past. All it does is to *integrate* them into a higher order. It forces them to work for good. It transforms them. It *absorbs* them. Sickness and error spell ruin to the small-minded, but the Christian, *if he has faith*, can make them enter into a combination from which *his* universe[17] emerges with more sanctifying power in it and

[15] This is the classic doctrine that prayer is always answered if it proceeds from faith.

[16] Père Teilhard thus dismisses any temptation to superstition and maintains the Christian in the purity of faith. On miracles, see *Les miracles de Lourdes et les enquêtes canoniques*, in *Études*, Jan. 1909 (vol. 118, pp. 161–83).

[17] This indicates the precise meaning we should attach to the title of two essays by Père Teilhard (1918 and 1924) both called *My Universe (Mon Univers)*. He means much more than the universe as he sees it and presents it to the minds of others: it it also his own universe, since every man has his own universe proportioned, so to speak, to his faith—as Père Teilhard explains here.

more of the divine. The Christian can make his own what is deadly poison to others, and assimilate it in such a way as to draw from it a new draught of life. It is in this sense alone that, through his faith, he conquers the inevitability of fate. And yet is not that victory in itself a resounding and unhoped for triumph?

We may therefore dismiss, with the religion of idealism and Christian Science, our dreams of a temporal release from suffering and death; the disorganization of our flesh is too firmly built into the *whole* of our past and the structure of the cosmos—we may even say it is too essential to our *true* spiritualization—for us to be able, or to have the right, to think of escaping from it. The further one progresses in life, the more one changes. And the more one changes, the more one dies. This is precisely the law that governs our development.

In spite of their sharing the same superficial appearance, so repugnant to our senses, there are as many sorts of deaths as there are souls; and some of those deaths are no more than a mere phase in the transformations of life. The whole difference that distinguishes them derives from the way in which the process of organic annihilation is influenced by faith—by the way in which it is physically converted by faith into a more or less direct ascent towards God. Only one effort, and it is one made possible by confidence in Christ, is worth making. It may be expressed thus: 'to believe so resolutely in the virtue of death that we can cause life to arise from the blackest depths of its shadows'.

3. The development in our soul of the *supernatural* life (founded on the *natural* spiritualization of the world by human effort) is, ultimately, *the field in which* the operative virtue of faith is *exercised*, *positively* and with no known limits.

In the material universe it is Spirit, and in Spirit it is the *moral* sphere, which are eminently the *present* centre in which life develops. It is into this flexible core of ourselves, accordingly, where divine grace mingles with the natural impulses of the Earth, that we have forcefully to direct the power of faith.

There, above all, we can count upon creative energy awaiting us, ready to transform us in a way that goes beyond anything that the eye of man has seen or his ear has heard. Who can say what

God might make of us, if we dared, relying on his Word, to follow his precepts to the uttermost, and surrender ourselves to his providence?

For love of our Creator and of the universe, we must fling ourselves boldly into the crucible of the world to come.

To sum up, we see that three characteristics distinguish the Christian achievement, as realized through faith:

(i) It is effected without distorting or destroying any individual determinism: events are not (as a general rule) diverted from their course by prayer, but integrated into a new form of combining the whole.

(ii) It is found not necessarily on the plane of natural human achievement, but in the order of supernatural growth in holiness.

(iii) God is, *in a real way*, the agent, the source, and the medium of its developments.

With this threefold reservation, which sharply distinguishes it from natural faith in its mode of operation, Christian faith is seen to be an extremely concrete and comprehensive 'cosmic energy'.

This faith does not, in the first place, consider that its power is confined to the higher zones of grace. Conscious of its ability to mould and enlarge the *physical system* of the universe, it resolutely enters into the domain of visible phenomena, in which supernatural being has its roots and from which it draws nourishment.

In order to handle and dominate these it neglects none of the natural means generally employed by man in his attempts to win his freedom. Through science, it seeks the cold, precise light that will enable it to distinguish the links in the chain of determinisms. Through the auto-suggestive power of the will, it tries to stimulate from deep within itself the dormant powers of its nature and personality. Working as industriously as though the whole of the future depended on the accuracy of its calculated predictions—straining with effort as though its only hope lay in its faith *in itself*—its single-minded behaviour illustrates the truth of the popular saying on which it bases its right to count upon God—God helps those who help themselves.

Christian faith is very different from the supine resignation of the Lutheran who leaves all the work to Christ. It jettisons neither the rational method of conquering the world, nor man's confidence in himself: on the contrary, it stimulates and inspires them. But, in conformity with *the law of the integration of the natural in the supernatural*, it superimposes itself on both. It comes as a reinforcement to the laboriously maintained foundation of human effort, to build upon it, direct it, organize and transform it. Its final role concerns the network of human feelers that venture out tentatively into the abyss of the new being still to be explored: to these it gives a sort of vital infallibility, the power to penetrate boldly into the Real, and the firm guarantee of a single, inflexible, direction.

Thus, just as does the creative power which it provides, faith *operatur uniendo*.[18] Under its influence, the elements cohere in a rigorously differentiated individual nature—and the individuals, in turn, communicating in one and the same divine Spirit, see their diversity melt away in a unity in which the form of the universe will be made complete—in which, that is to say, man's victory over the hazards of the future will be consummated.

If, in the name of Christ, we believe vigorously in our own power, we shall see the aimless meanderings of chance obediently accept our control. If we believe, the monotonous circle of nemesis will be shattered and from it a benevolent providence will emerge for us, a personal providence, orientated directly towards fuller being. If we believe, anything dangerous in the sap that runs through the world will no longer be poison to us, but will nourish our soul for eternal life.[19]

[18] See *Creative Union* (note by Père Teilhard).

[19] Cf. *Le Milieu Divin*, pp. 135–6, etc. Cf. letter of 12 Feb. 1919 on Christ 'who, when seen by the eyes of faith, animates the whole complex of exterior events and interior experiences. Is there any better way of understanding and enjoying intimacy with the divine than the knowledge that Our Lord is at the heart of all that moves us ' (*Making of a Mind*, pp. 282–3). Such, indeed, was certainly Père Teilhard's own faith. Cf. his letter to Père Auguste Valensin, 13 Nov. 1924, written on the very day on which he suffered the cruel shock of hearing of the first steps taken against him by Rome: 'Basically, I'm perfectly tranquil. Even this is only one more manifestation of Our Lord—it is another example of his operation—and so why should one worry?'

In very truth, Christian faith is eminently the transforming agent, the supreme organizing force of the universe. It is, ultimately, that faith which controls every chance and liberates all the powers of the Earth.

Now we know the secret, hitherto only glimpsed by men, of how we can bring a spiritual influence to bear upon our destinies. It consists in making Christ's hand reach out to us across the fluid medium in which we thought to founder.

D: THE WORK OF FAITH

If anyone is looking for an *immediate* alleviation of his suffering, and a *material* guarantee of his success in this life, then the hopes that may be realized by the action of faith, as just defined, will appear colourless and empty.

Is it not, he will ask, evading the question to transfer to a domain that is at present closed to us the results of a struggle whose only too palpable reality lies so heavy upon us? There can be little satisfaction, surely, in finding the secret of being happy after death, when what we are looking for is a panacea for our present miseries?

There is only one thing we can say to people who mourn their lost dream of material happiness—get down to work![20]

Christian faith, you say, seems to be working on something that has no real existence, to be building in the clouds? That is precisely because you have never tried, borne up by that faith, to launch yourself into that domain in which alone it allows you to see *as you move ahead*.

Here we have the mysterious bond that unites in our soul the faculties of seeing and acting: the higher reality of the supernatural world is apparent only to those who have the courage to make up their minds that it is true, and to set to work to build it

---

[20] Cf. *Esquisse d'un univers personnel* (1936): 'Instead of standing on the shore and proving to ourselves that the ocean cannot bear us up, we must venture out on its waters . . . We must take the chance of this bold gesture'. (*Oeuvres*, vol. 6, p. 110.) See also *Le Milieu Divin*, introduction, pp. 46–7.

up in themselves. The *vision of faith accompanies* (or should I say '*follows*'?) *the action of faith.*

Like other real objects, Christ is 'experienced'.

So long as we do not try to make our way to him without any hesitation, he will seem to us a phantom. As soon as we pluck up our courage to regard him as more real than all else, and to seek him, as he wishes us to do, above all things, he will become—through the external influence of his providence (which everyone is at liberty, from his own point of view, to deny except the man who is consciously its object), and through his unmistakable interior impact—through both these he will become the most substantial Reality that exists, the Reality that can show itself to be always, and indefinitely, more real.

Although all the phenomena of the lower world appear to remain the same (the material determinisms, the vicissitudes of chance, the law of work, the restless activity of men, the foot-falls of death), the man who *dares* to believe reaches a sphere of created reality in which things, while retaining their habitual texture, seem to be made out of a different substance. Everything remains the same so far as phenomena are concerned, but at the same time everything becomes luminous, animated, instinct with love.

Through the operation of faith, Christ appears, Christ is born, without any violation of nature's laws, in the heart of the world.

As soon as the believer has penetrated into Christ, the world loses for him its multiplicity, its dead weight, its rigidity, its bitterness.

The fragmented and turbid multitude of beings falls into a harmonious pattern, and dissolves into an organized, transparent entity. The terrifying inertia of mechanisms and wills lies so lightly upon us that we feel we have the strength to raise up and perfect the world. The hard-set mass of the cosmos suddenly allows itself to be moulded and blossoms out into exuberant life. The disorderly variety of phenomena takes on stability. Combining, in his activity, the most contrary forms of joy, the believer has the double happiness of acting effectively upon a pliable world that is now in full growth, and of resting upon the boundless security of the Absolute—and in all things he is in communion with God, whose power he makes his own and whose encompassing Presence he intensifies . . .

in Christo Jesu.[21]

But, once again, we must tell ourselves, 'In truth, I say to you, only the daring can enter the Kingdom of God, hidden henceforth in the heart of the world.'

It is of no use to read these pages, or other similar pages written twenty centuries ago, merely with one's eyes. Anyone who, without having put his hand to the plough, thinks he has mastered them, is deluding himself. *We must try to live them.*[22]

We must, in view of the practical uncertainty of the morrow, have thrown ourselves, in a true act of interior surrender, upon providence as our sole support—providence accepted as being as physically real as the objects of our disquietude; we must, in our suffering of the ills we have incurred, our remorse for the sins we have committed, our vexation over the opportunities we have missed, have forced ourselves to believe *unhesitatingly* that God is powerful enough to turn each and *every* particular evil into good; we must, despite some appearances to the contrary, have acted *without reservation* as though our being could make progress only when directed towards chastity, humility, loving-kindness.

We must, in the shadow of death, have forced ourselves not to look back to the past, but to seek in utter darkness the dawn of God.

Only a long and patient struggle can teach us the operative power of faith and show us what it can achieve.

[21] This theme was soon to be developed in *Forma Christi*, and later, at greater length, in *Le Milieu Divin*.

[22] The point emphasized, it will be appreciated, is the boldness of faith, understood in a very precise sense. This boldness is diametrically opposed to the Promethean attitude that some critics, distorting the meaning of such passages as this, have accused Père Teilhard of adopting. What he wishes the Christian to do is 'to make the most of the resources of his faith' (*Le Milieu Divin*, p. 73).

Only he who has fought bravely and been victorious in the battle against *the spurious security and strength and attraction of the past* can attain to the firm and blissful *experiential certainty* that 'the more we lose all foothold in the darkness and instability of the future, the more deeply we penetrate into God'.

Chavannes-sur-l'Etang
28 September 1918[23]

[23] Cf. p. 225.

Forma Christi

On 4 Nov. 1918 Père Teilhard wrote to his cousin Marguerite Teillard from Méricourt (Haute-Saône): 'I've finished drawing up a plan for my next essay, "Forma Christi"' ('Making of a Mind', p. 248); and on 8 December, from Strasbourg: 'We're still at Strasbourg, and I've fallen into a regular and studious routine of life which in some ways reminds me of my time in Paris. Except at night-time and for meals, I spend my time in the seminary by the cathedral, where a room has been placed at my disposal. I'm working on "Forma Christi"' (Ibid, p. 263).

Again on the 13th (p. 267): 'I've finished writing and copying out "Forma Christi". It makes twenty pages, very close-packed with thought, which seem to me an advance on what I've written so far (from the point of view of the way in which I see Our Lord present in this world).'

FORMA CHRISTI

Introduction

This new essay contains a restatement (since we shall soon be in 1919) of ideas that I have constantly, during the last four years, been trying to express. They relate to the synthesis, in the interior life of the Christian, of love of God and love of the world.

I am more convinced than ever that our generation understands Christianity in a way that is too *extrinsic* and too *individualistic*. Dogma, both as preached from the pulpit and as it enters into the consciousness of those who receive it: (1) is something up in the air, above the universe, and with no connexion with it; (2) it seems to impinge upon only *an insignificant part* of cosmic reality. To present the Christian God as in this way external to and (even quantitatively) less than, nature, is in itself, to impoverish his being. And this is doubly deplorable at a time when the noblest souls on our earth are filled with religious emotion by discovering the unity, the mystery and the immensity of the world of experience. While, for St John and St Paul in particular, *Christianity was essentially*[1] *a Cosmogony*, one might nowadays be justified sometimes in saying that we modern Christians can see and present to others only the didactic or disciplinary side of our creed. It is hardly surprising, therefore, that to many people who have been brought up on firm concrete realities the Christian revelation seems hopelessly frigid and unadult.

It is essential for us to get back to the soundest currents of Catholic tradition and at last offer men a theology in which

---

[1] To say 'essentially' is going too far, since the Christianity of St John and St Paul is in the first place a religion—a fact that Père Teilhard would obviously never dream of denying.

Christ will be seen to be linked with the development of the whole universe, a universe *as physical and as great* as he is. We must give them a Gospel in which moral teaching and the precepts of Christ are presented not simply as the guarantees of an *individual* reward, but as the road organically essential to the *collective success of the whole of life*.

It is time for our religion in some way to draw new youth from a substantial infusion of the Earth's passions and spiritual energies.

In what follows I shall try to show how this combination (retaining their hierarchical order) of all the powers of Spirit is demanded by the very nature of the total Christ, and that we can believe in this and try to realize it without doing violence either to the fundamental dogma of the gratuitous nature of supernatural or to the vital principle of detachment from the things of this world.

A: THE CHOOSING OF THE INSTRUMENT

Secundum potentiam (δύναμιν) *qua possit Ipse omnia sibi subjicere*. St. Paul. Philippians, 3:21.

When we are discussing the developments of the universe and its future, we almost always speak as though each new phase of being in the history of the world had the power to determine and bring about the next phase. On the whole, we instinctively picture the cosmos to ourselves as from its very beginning implying (necessitating), because of something in its original elements, a precise natural term.

This way of looking at things distorts the facts.

It is perfectly true, of course, that if we look at the universe from the point of view of its present concrete progress, we must conclude that it is directed towards a determined final end: if that were not so, it would crumble into dust. We must, however, realize that '*secundum signa rationis* (*ratiocinatae*)', this final purpose that embraces, co-ordinates and animates the general movement of things, is a creative influence, *that works downwards*, by which I mean that it operates by *gradually becoming more exactly defined*; it is the culmination of a *synthesizing* process.

In itself, before the final decision that recast all the successive moments of creation into a single continuous evolution,[2] each true phase in the growth of the universe (in the formation, that is, of Spirit) represents, in relation to the divine power, a real stage of indetermination—*a level*—at which the creative operation could halt or, at any rate, branch off along an infinite number of different lines.

The appearance of the human soul, as an autonomous and indestructible element of the world, is the supreme example of one of these levels of indetermination in the evolution of our cosmos. With man, we reach the end of one particular plane—a circle is drawn around the universe. The multiplicity of rational monads, '*in signo priori ad Christum*', constitutes a sort of *virgin matter*, adapted to numerous purposes, but requiring only *some* further unification of their plurality. It is *the flock without a shepherd*.

We know from Revelation what destiny God had freely determined for this Multiple, when he planted it to grow in the soil of this Earth. Men are called to form one single Body, in an intensely intimate divinization; and Christ's humanity was *chosen* to serve as the instrument of this unification in which the unravelled skein of all the fibres of the universe is woven into one. In Scripture Christ is essentially revealed as invested with *the power of giving the world*, in his own person, *its definitive form*. He is consecrated for a cosmic function. And since that function is not only moral but also (in the most real sense of the word) physical, it presupposes *a physical basis* in its humano-divine subject.

If things are to find their coherence *in Christo*, we must ultimately admit that there is *in natura Christi*, besides the specifically individual elements of Man—and in virtue of God's choice—some *universal physical*[3] reality, a certain cosmic extension of his Body and Soul.

[2] An evolution, that is, in which all the theoretically distinct parts have reacted upon one another (working down from the top) in such a way as to produce a single real whole. (Note by Père Teilhard.)

[3] Here, as often elsewhere, Père Teilhard uses 'physical' simply as opposed to 'juridical' [Cf. Christopher F. Mooney, S.J., *Teilhard de Chardin* and *the*

For us here below, this is the expression of *the mystery of Christ* that touches us most directly and intimately.

Around the radiant sun of love that has risen to light up the world, there extends into infinity a 'corona' that is seldom seen and that is, nevertheless, the seat of the encompassing and unifying activity of the incarnate Word.

Everything that I have written, here and elsewhere, presupposes the perception of, or is designed to bring out, this active light which, emanating from Christ, penetrates into us.

We should note, further, that there is nothing strange about this idea of a universal physical element in Christ.

Each and every one of us, if we care to observe it, is enveloped—is *haloed*—by an extension of his being as vast as the universe. We are conscious of only the core of ourselves. Nevertheless, the interplay of the monads would be unintelligible if an *aura* did not extend from one to another: something, that is, which is peculiar to each one of them and at the same time common to all.

How, then, may we conceive Christ to be constituted as the cosmic centre of creation?

Simply as a magnification, a transformation, realized in the humanity of Christ, of the *aura* that surrounds every human monad.

Just as one sees in a living organism elements, originally indistinguishable from the others, suddenly emerge as *leaders*[4] so that they are seen to be centres of attraction or points at which a formative activity is concentrated:

So (on an incomparably larger scale) the man, the Son of Mary, was *chosen* so that his *aura*, instead of serving simply as the medium in which interaction with other men might be effected *ex aequo*, might dominate them and draw them all into the network of its influence.

Even before the Incarnation became a fact, the whole history

Mystery of Christ, London and New York, 1966, p. 85: 'Perhaps the closest equivalent to Teilhard's "*physical*" in current theological usage is the word "*ontological*", which may be applied to whatever has existence in the present concrete order of things. "*Physical*" is thus *opposed* to all that is *juridical, abstract, extrinsic* to reality'.]

[4] Père Teilhard uses the English word 'leaders'.

of the universe (in virtue of a pre-action of the humanity of Christ, mysterious, but yet known to us through revelation) is the history of the progressive information[5] of the universe by Christ.

B: THE MAGNETISM OF CHRIST

Omnia traham ad meipsum.

The first consequence of Christ's being chosen as *Caput Creationis* is that we are *eminently drawn to him*. If we ask whether we can be *tangibly* aware of this pull from above, we are faced with a very nice dilemma.

If we say that we can—that (from the very nature of our emotional make-up) we can sensibly experience the desire to make our way to Christ as the single concrete centre of the present universe—then we are leaning towards the errors that have been condemned in the 'apologetics of immanence'.

If we say that we cannot—that the world is moving towards some term (real *or* apparent) other than Christ—then we make faith psychologically impossible, since no authority outside ourselves could have the right or the power to turn our hearts away from an end that makes a more direct emotional appeal to us than Jehovah.

There is only one safe course between Scylla and Charybdis: to admit that Christ is in a very real way the only concrete end awaiting the universe—adding, however, that his Being operates through extensions of his aura in which his divinity is not always equally embodied, and therefore manifests itself to us through a *gradual* and *creative* attraction.

This calls for further explanation.

It would seem that through a first surface of himself that he presents to us (the most external and most 'ambivalent') Christ acts upon our hearts as an ill-defined, impersonal, generic centre of universal union. When life in its lower stages is moving towards consciousness, when men are passionately striving for the

[5] The exact meaning of 'information' is examined later, p. 266 (note by Père Teilhard).

complete freedom and unanimity of their spirit, when thinkers and poets thrill with excitement at the emergence of a 'world-soul', it is in fact Christ whom they are all seeking—Christ who still keeps hidden his personal and divine being, but nevertheless Christ himself, who must be the *first object* of desire as the key-stone that holds together the effort of the universe—Christ who must *effectively* fulfil this natural function before he can reveal himself to us through the more intimate parts of his being, and, in those depths, undertake the supernatural work of our sanctification.

Under this *natural form* assumed by *his supernatural being in order* to enter into our universe[6] Christ arouses and claims for himself what we have agreed to call the natural demands of the heart of man. In his capacity as the centre of all visible things, he draws to himself—even though he is not yet recognized—the eyes of all who draw their appetite for life from the expectation and preparation of an age of light and peace.

This is the first step, common to all men, in Christ's magnetic power over souls.

Nevertheless, a vague uneasiness still survives in the hearts of those who faithfully serve the world, in spite of all their efforts to build up from nature a terrestrial ideal. This anxiety heralds a higher stage in their initiation; in it is expressed the still ill-defined attractive force that emanates from those circles of Christ's being which are still closed to them.

Until God speaks, however much the soul may reflect upon its appetites and desires, it can never discover the nature of the beatifying complement it seeks, *but has not yet risen high enough*[7] to grasp.

[6] If the *supernatural* term of the world did not at the same time 'round it off' *naturally*, it would leave the universe facing a void, and our hearts impervious to feeling. (Note by Père Teilhard.)

[7] It would appear, nevertheless, that before God's word has been spoken by an inspired Prophet, there already exists in men's minds a pre-formation, or partial divination, of the truths that are to be revealed. Otherwise, it would be difficult to explain the frequent appearance in ancient cosmogonies of the ideas of a divine Triad, a Virgin Mother, or of a just victim. Moreover, if dogmas were not 'in the air' at the time the Prophet is speaking, he would not be believed nor understood. (Note by Père Teilhard.)

The time comes, however, when God, speaking through the Prophets or his Son, allows his influence to be openly apparent. He manifests himself as living and personal—at once one and three. *Fides ex auditu.*

At that moment, if the soul holds to its faith, its hitherto vague desires *embody themselves* around the new truth. Accompanying faith in the revealed dogma, it feels coming down into it a clearly defined, conscious need for that dogma. All revealed truth, accordingly, including even the distant Trinity, is seen by the soul henceforth to be indispensable to its beatification.[8]

Thus the *felt* attraction of Christ—which was almost without form, no more than a general summons to rise higher, in the pagan soul—gradually grows richer in power in the Christian. Step by step, it models itself on the articles of the Creed, as these successively make their way from inspired utterance into obedient hearts.

Revelation CREATES *spirits to the degree that it enlightens them.*

It is, therefore, a mistake to distinguish in man two different attractions that influence him: one, towards a hypothetical natural end of the cosmos, and the other towards the supernatural end that awaits us in the presence of God. There is only *one single centre* in the universe; it is at once natural and supernatural; it impels the whole of creation along one and the same line, first towards the fullest development of consciousness, and later towards the highest degree of holiness:[9] in other words towards Christ Jesus, personal and cosmic.

---

[8] Without this appeal, belief in this supreme dogma would never go beyond the stage of being strictly an epiphenomenon in our interior life. (Note by Père Teilhard.)

[9] That is, first towards the fulfilment of the natural monads *in se*, and then towards their association *in Christo*. (Note by Père Teilhard.)

C: THE ESTABLISHMENT OF THE MYSTICAL MILIEU

In eo vivimus, et movemur et sumus.

For all its persuasive power, the growing magnetic force by which Christ draws us towards ever more intimate zones of his essence, is not sufficient by itself alone to attract us into his orbit.

If we are effectively to fall under the domination of Christ the centre of the world (*rex et centrum omnium rerum*) we must of our own free will open our hearts to him. If we are really to enter into the chosen universe that is marked off around the incarnate Word, we must *choose* to form part of it.

= Nothing, in the work of our 'information' by Christ, can be finally effected so long as we are not freely co-operating in its realization.

We may distinguish *two stages* in this collaboration of our freedom with God's creative and unifying action: through these two Christ's influence is brought to bear in turn on the *two halves* of our life, the *passive* and the *active*.

The first step in our acceptance (the acceptance of passivities) consists in recognizing Christ's function as the universal sanctifier, as the higher soul within all things. It is an *act of faith*—faith of the intelligence, which accepts a new illumination—faith of the will, which surrenders itself to the guidance it has received and the promises that accompany it.

That faith, whose influence, it would seem, cannot possibly extend beyond the strictest limits of our immanence [cannot be effective outside our own soul] is, in fact, extremely effective outside those limits.[10]

The first time a man says 'I believe', nothing outside his own soul appears to alter. In fact, through the words he has spoken, that man has produced a reaction in universal Reality. Hardly has he given his assent to revealed Truth, before all created powers are transformed, as though by magic, *in the circle of which he is the centre*. Natural forces, hitherto alien, hostile or ambi-

[10] Cf. *Operative Faith* (October 1918). (Note by Père Teilhard.)

valent, are without exception straightway charged *for him* with the influence of Christ. Suddenly, in fact, *his* individual world has entered into Christ's 'field of action'.

It is no exaggeration to say that immediately there is adherence to revealed truth, the whole impact of the world on the man who has experienced this conversion, *though it suffers no apparent change of form*, takes on Christ in its inner substance. It becomes physically animated by a new finality, *more interior* than all others. To the soul of the believer, who is centred vitally upon Christ, the whole impact of things (natural in their foundation, supernatural in their extensions) brings a contact with Christ; he feels in them the touch of Christ's hand. And the more firmly he believes in his omni-dependence in relation to Christ, the more concrete, dominating, and assured becomes the omni-action to which he is subject: *Credenti, omnia convertuntur 'in Christum'*.

In order to respond to this universal attraction whose formative influence surrounds it on all sides, the soul, in its turn, strives by the means naturally available to it, to make its way, actively and positively, towards Christ. First the soul acknowledges its faith in Christ's own action, then it devotes to Christ all the work that it can itself achieve. To faith it adds *right intention*. And so begins the second phase of Christ's invasion of his universe.

In virtue of the fundamental unity of our being and the world, we may already say of every upright man that everything he does on earth is ordered, more or less directly, to the spiritualization of the universe. The virtue proper to 'good will' is to harness this work for God, in other words, to make *all* progress (even natural progress and even in its *opus materiale*) we make in the development of Spirit serve the interests of the Mystical Body. Through its *intention*, which associates us with Christ as an active member, every effort we make reaches out, in its entirety, beyond ourselves: it makes its way to Christ, and serves him, living deep within us.

A moment ago, because we had faith, it was the universe that took on the function (even through its material energies) of transmitting Christ's action to us. Now, because our will is directed to the good, it is we in turn who will contribute, through everything we do, to securing for Christ his integral being.

Thus, through *the combined power* of faith and intention, a new world is formed for the Christian within things, without in any way changing the features of the old. At the heart of the universe a zone at once profound and simple is revealed to him, co-extensive with all created being. It is the zone in which

> *Quidquid patimur, Christum patimur.*
> *Quidquid agimus, Christus agitur.*

Whatever is done to us, it is Christ who does it; whatever we do, it is to Christ we do it.

Once we become conscious of this mystical atmosphere that extends on all sides, we feel the vast plenitude of the Incarnation being realized around us.

D: THE TWO PHASES IN THE GROWTH OF THE SOUL

> *Vivo ego—iam non ego: vivit in me Christus.* (Gal. 2:20).

Once it is at home in the mystical milieu, what must the soul do if it is to progress, to be continually more fully 'informed' by Christ? Is its primary duty to receive or to give? To enjoy or to suffer? To grow in accordance with nature's laws, or to accept annihilation? To empty itself of the world, or to drink its fill? to be attached to the universe or to scorn it? to live its own life, or to die?

The great difficulty in all interior life is rightly to reconcile the active and the passive.

If we are to offer as general as possible a solution of the problem of Christian ascetics, we must once again distinguish, *in our minds*, two phases in the growth of souls in Jesus Christ: the alternation and the combination of these phases accounts for all the contradictions we find in the behaviour of different saints.

The first phase is one of a *certain attachment to the world, a certain immersion* in the universe.

We must never forget that because a man turns to God it does not mean that he no longer needs to breathe, to take nourishment —to grow in stature in every way before his fellow-men. We must proclaim it from the housetops and in the places where men meet together: it is from the visible world that the soul draws the elements which grace divinizes! It is the use of tangible realities that (as a general rule) widens man's understanding, toughens his will, arouses his power to love. Normally, the soul that wishes to belong firmly to Christ must make ready in itself, as the basis of its supernatural perfection, an abundant matter for sanctification, a *rich nature*. Science, the arts, industry, social activity—all these are necessary if we are to offer worthy material for Christ's influence. None of these should be alien to the Christian, precisely *in his capacity* as a Christian.

Thus, supernaturalized man's first duty, both to himself as an individual and as an apostle to others, is so to make use of created things as to develop in himself, for Christ, a vigorous *self*. His first care—*similar*, though only apparently, to that of the pagan— must be to use human effort to extend in every direction that leads to spirit the still unfinished work of visible creation.

= Without hesitation, as a matter of duty, *in a religious spirit*, the soul, in the first stage of its evolution[11] in Christ, plunges into created things. There, it allows itself to be swept along by the life-giving passion for enquiry, for discovery and creation.

The soul that is true to life and to grace cannot continue indefinitely in this progress towards the full human development of its powers. It gradually becomes aware of the emergence from the very operation of its impulse towards 'self-hood', of a *hostile* component: this grows more dominant and will slowly reverse the direction in which the soul is moving. The form it takes is *predilection for detachment*.

The effort that the natural evolution of the world imposes upon those who work to build up the earth, is one of extreme self-denial and altruism.

It inspires them with an ardour to give their allegiance to an

[11] Though after a period of *retreat*, which allows it to develop its individual Christian outlook (the 'desert' period). (Note by Père Teilhard.)

ever vaster whole, and this brings with it an habitual disregard of anything petty and individual.

Finally, it makes them so conscious of the insurmountable barriers to be found in the restrictions of physical life that they dream of a death that will bring them release.

The result of these three lessons that the soul draws from its experience of the world is that it has *hardly arrived at the heart of things before it is ready to escape from them*. Having taken its fill of the universe and of its own self, the soul one day finds that it is possessed (and this is not through disappointment but as a *logical development* of its effort) by an intense need to die to itself and to leave its own self behind.

So begins the second stage in the soul's formation: the stage of *detachment*, or of *emergence* from the world.

Henceforth, working upon a solid natural basis, upon a vigorous natural capacity for growth and self-forgetfulness, Christ's activity (with suffering as its most important instrument) will take the form of *substituting Christ* for the soul (of 'ecstasizing' the soul). The time has come for the creature who is dominated by Christ when '*Oportet illum crescere, me autem minui*,' when 'he must grow greater, while I grow less'. This is the hour of the *specifically Christian* operation, when Christ, while preserving in man the treasures of human nature, empties him of his ego-centrism and takes his heart—it is a grievous hour for our lower nature, abandoned to those *forces* in the world *that bring diminishment*, but one full of delight for the man who has the light of faith and feels that he is being driven out of himself and that he is dying, under the compelling power of a Communion.

Wholehearted acceptance of the world for Christ, rejection of the world in Christ—all the different shades of holiness are contained in the innumerable permutations of these *two aspects of the breath* by which the soul lives—first taking its fill of possessing things, and then sublimating them in God.

1. Very often (in fact generally) the *two phases* of attachment and detachment are *fused together* in the concrete reality (the psychological unity) of a single *disinterested effort*. When man works to

develop himself for God (to have a greater capacity for God), at the same time and by the same act his soul is personalized *in se* and depersonalized *in Christo*.

2. Nevertheless, there is often also a *disjunction between the two components* (or at least a noticeable predominance of one over the other), and this imposes a pattern of oscillation on the movement in which we surrender ourselves to Christ.

(*a*) It is not uncommon to find in the history of *individual developments* a distinct phase of growth (coinciding, naturally enough, with youth) which is followed by a period of suffering and detachment.

(*b*) This reciprocating movement may recur several times in the course of one man's life, with a tendency always to become stabilized at a higher level, in a lesser degree of egocentrism (cf. below, 4); it is, however, only the reflexion on a smaller scale, of a much slower oscillation that affects *the very life of the Church.* The *first centuries* of Christianity, for example (think of the Desert Fathers!) were marked by a characteristic impulse towards penance and self-denial. It was Christianity's necessary initial reaction against pagan materialism, with a consequent unmistakable emphasis on the specifically Christian orientation. *Our own age*, on the other hand, seems primarily to need a rejuvenation of supernatural forces, to be effected by driving roots deep into the nutritious energies of the earth. Because it is not sufficiently moved by a truly human compassion, because it is not exalted by a sufficiently passionate admiration of the universe, our religion is becoming enfeebled; *even its capacity for detachment is impaired. We must have a great love for the world if we are passionately to wish to leave it behind.*

3. There is a predominance, more marked according to the period, first of one and then of another spirit, sometimes of greater and sometimes of less apparent austerity.[12] The Church,

---

[12] 'Separatism' would be a better word than 'austerity'—meaning a separation between the Kingdom of God and the world. The effort of spiritual *attachment* to the natural universe is vitally essential; and it imposes a rigorous *austerity* on the souls of the faithful. (Note by Père Teilhard.)

however, has so many children that even so she can, *at any moment* you choose, show us examples of all the individual types of holiness. There are always, no matter when you look, some souls in the Church who are more particularly committed to the area of development, others to that of detachment, either because they are actually moving from one *to* the other, or because a particular *vocation* stabilizes them in one *or* other of these two areas.

4. Finally, it is important to note that the series of variations (either in individual lives or in centuries of history) successively assumed in the Church by the *external form* of detachment never passes twice through the same points: *in its totality it forms a progressive evolution.*

In relation, more particularly, to the phase of attachment or immersion in the world, the level at which the soul has to seek its natural development certainly tends to become progressively higher. As creation becomes spiritualized, the earthly bread by which the higher part of man is nourished becomes less corporeal. To arouse and sustain their zest for living, the finest souls among us will continually and increasingly feel the need to turn towards purer and more generous-hearted interests. When that *drift* has gone as far as it can, one can imagine a mankind which (as happens with certain saints) requires only an extremely slight stimulus from sensible reality—a mankind naturally chaste and contemplative, in which individuals would almost at birth already be ripe for their 'depersonalization' in Jesus Christ. Only original sin, perhaps, prevents us from envisaging the full realization of such a hope.

To sum up (and this is what we must be sure to bear in mind) neither of the two components of the interior life (growth, and then diminishment, both natural, *in Christo*) can or should destroy the other. There are *not two opposed forms of ascesis*, one of development and the other of mortification. There are two phases with a capacity to combine in a flexible and dynamic equilibrium.

— sometimes in the (continuous) form of an effort instinct with detachment.

— sometimes in the (alternating) form of oscillations between active enjoyment and passive acceptance.

— sometimes in the (sporadic) form of peculiarly representative souls, whose totality is harmonized into a controlled (= human) and progressive whole.

The second phase, which makes man glory in his painful annihilation *in Christo*, is the more beatifying of the two. It is the phase that imprints upon the soul the definitive form of Christ.

We should never forget, however, that it is to the first phase that it owes its 'immediacy' and 'consistence'.

Jesus Christ *never establishes himself in a void*—at *Cana* did he not tell them first to fill the jars with water?—It is *by substituting his plenitude for another* that he wins us—that is, by taking *within us* the place of our own self, and substituting his own embrace for the universal embrace of created being *that encloses us*.

The tougher, then, we have woven the stuff of our personality, the more passionate will our consciousness of the great universe have become.

— and the more solidly, too, and completely will Christ be incarnate in us.

Even when it is (in some way) gathered up again into Christ, the soul is not lost to the Earth that nourished it. Borne up by the cosmic power of Christ, and united henceforth to the ultimate principle of created life, its radiating influence is more vigorously and profoundly active in beings that still have to be made holy.

Thus the two phases of the soul's development meet together in a common peak, and the soul finds itself *in possession, at the same time, both of Christ and of the universe.*

E: THE FLESH OF CHRIST

Now that we have determined how Christ's universal influence is manifested—is established—and then develops in each soul, we may take another look at the *general form* assumed by the universe, when, in each one of its elements, it has become subjected to the humano-divine attractive power of Christ.

Since the spiritual universe rests upon a basis of freedom, it does not, in its entirety, surrender to Christ's unifying action. *Pauci electi*—few are chosen. A portion of created being refuses to submit to Christ. Since this portion can find no natural centre of association outside Christ (cf. §A, pp. 252–4), it wanders aimlessly, indecisive and without unity, towards some mysterious opposite pole to Spirit. This is the damnation that banishes to *outer* darkness.

The rest, the faithful mass, gradually comes together in an organic whole, enveloped in the folds—both natural and supernatural—of Christ's cosmic being, of his *aura*.

What name shall we give to the physical influence exerted by Christ on his Mystical Body? To what sort of causality shall we reduce his quickening action?

When the schoolmen try more exactly to define the nature of grace, they compare it to an accident. They are, obviously, speaking analogically and use the term for want of a better. When it is applied to a state of grace, the word 'accident' simply means 'that which does not change the human essence of the soul'.[13]

The use of the word implies no intention of including in the same *positive* series both the divine life in us and, for example, the effect produced upon us by a physical sensation. A sensory state of soul is an *infra-substantial* accident; sanctifying grace is a *supra-substantial* accident. As soon as we leave the area of experiential

---

[13] Similarly, when we say that the Word is united to the Humanity of Christ *ratione Personae, non naturae* (in virtue of person, not of nature), it is to emphasize that the divine Substance remains unchanged in the Incarnation: it is not, in relation to the Word, to rule out an activity that concerns the organic intimate union of the Christ-Man—in other words *Persona* is *not* an *attenuation* of *natura*. The phrase has a negative rather than a positive significance.

Similarly, again, when *creation* is compared to an *efficiency*, the word brings out excellently the distinction between the Creator and his work (that is to say, it is excellent as a refutation of pantheism); but it tells us practically nothing about the nature of the process that links *uncreated being* to *participated being*: on the contrary, it introduces between them an *exteriority* in relation to one another that is surely exaggerated. (Note by Père Teilhard.)

relationships, our logical categories are no longer exactly applicable. They must be combined if they are to embrace supraterrestrial phenomena.

Subject to this express reservation, the word that comes nearest to a satisfactory definition of the universal influx of Jesus Christ, the Centre of the World, is 'information'. Christ encompasses his mystical members in a higher finality, order, law of growth, and even a higher sort of consciousness. Christ really *lives* in us. What more do we need in order to be able to say that, in a real sense, he informs us?

Christ, it is true, does not destroy nor dissolve us. He does not modify our nature nor wipe out our human personality—on the contrary, by melting us into himself he *completes our differentiation* as individual persons.

This restriction, however, should *not* be understood as an *attenuation*. It is quite the opposite, a *perfecting* of the concept of 'information'. If the life of Christ, when it takes possession of souls, allows them still to subsist as distinct beings within that life, this individuality they still retain derives from the fact that his influence is *superior* (*not* inferior) to that exerted by ordinary substantial forms.

In truth, Christ acts upon us *as a form*, and the *totality of souls* ready to receive it is the *matter* which interiorly (substantially) takes on form in him.[14]

If we carry further this idea that our souls stand as matter in

---

[14] *Figura Mundi*: the new universe, reformed in Christ, does not owe its make-up exclusively to the elements gathered together in it under the influence of Christ. It owes its form (should we say principally?) to the *individual* characteristics of the Chosen-Christ.

It may well be useless, therefore, to try to find for some of our dogmas (at least in their concrete mode of expression) a *reason* drawn from the general nature of being (created or uncreated).

These dogmas (or these modalities) are perhaps individual features (reflecting individual preferences) of Christ (for example, the *agony* of the Redemption).

The new universe must have certain very pronounced *free*, individual, characteristics, because it is fully realized in the sphere of a *person*. (Note by Père Teilhard.)

[The example chosen would not appear to be very happy. (Cf. the agony in the Garden of Olives: 'Not my will but thine be done'.)]

relation to Christ (more spiritual than they are) who is their soul, it is tempting to say that the Resurrection of the Flesh—taken in its literal, physical, sense—is a superfluous fantasy, quite apart from being a humiliating form of benefaction.

Why should we envisage this reappearance (not dogmatically necessary and debasing for our nature) of the obsolete part of our soul, the discarded chrysalis?

Is it because *an organic-multiplicity of spirits* is not sufficient in itself to form a matter, a body, a flesh?

There is here a double problem, and I shall not try to deal with it in its widest application. We want to know:

(i) whether we can conceive monads capable of organizing themselves into a whole, without *assuming* them to be *endowed* with a more or less disguised materiality.[15]

(ii) Or whether at least (even if we were to suppose that such monads were pure spirit before they united) *from the very fact of their association*, some equivalent of materiality is not produced.

We may answer that in the case of human monads the verdict, both of philosophy and of theology, is categorical: 'the mystical body of Christ is something more than a totality of souls; because, without there being present in it a specifically material element, souls could not be physically gathered together in Christ'.

Matter, it is true, is not the *formal* instrument of the union and interplay of the monads;[16] but it is matter that gives the things of this world their radical capacity of entering into higher or lower syntheses, under one and the same Spirit. The essence (the formal effect) of materiality would appear to be *to make beings capable of unification*. In this regard, there is no difference between the lower natural world and the new world that is being formed around Christ.

[15] That is to say, we must assume that there can be no pure Spirit other than God.* (Note by Père Teilhard.)

* The proposition put forward here is not Thomist in its literal expression, but it is to be found in many Fathers of the Church and theologians (including, among others, St Bonaventure).

[16] It is a common soul, not a common matter, that binds together the created multiple at the various stages of its evolution. (See *Creative Union*, November 1917.) (Note by Père Teilhard.)

If that is so, if every collective soul is born in *our* world through the instrumentality of a body, then Christ can consummate our unity in the Centre *that stands firm above us*—the Centre, that is, which is his Spirit—only if he first encloses us in a material network *underlying* our '*esse corporeum*'. If he is to be the soul of our souls, he must begin by being the flesh of our flesh.[17]

Hence the importance of the Eucharist.

Now let us look at a human soul at the moment of death. Deprived of its bodily element, it should, in the natural course of events, wander through the cosmos with no precise attachment, ready to enter in many forms of combination but committed to none (cf. p. 252).

The Resurrection benefits such a soul in two ways, contributing both to its happiness and its completion.

(i) First, it gives it the natural joy *it cannot do without* of again belonging to *a* universe.

(ii) Secondly, it brings it the supernatural grace of being called, in its quality as universe, to rejoin Christ and become integrated in him.

This gives us some indication why the effective Resurrection of the body is postponed until 'the end of the world'. The restoration of the flesh is a phenomenon cosmic rather than individual in order. In virtue of the very essence of materiality, *to raise up a single body from death* is the same, for God, *as to reconstitute a world*.[18]

In fact at no time have there ever been souls wandering in complete isolation. From the very beginning of time (through a mysterious anticipation or pre-action—a notion we must always bear in mind), and from the first Easter morning in actual reality, 'Christ is risen'. Since all time, therefore, souls, as they leave this world, have been passing, without any break, into the cosmic train of his body; and there they find the refuge of a new universe

[17] In other words we grow *held between* his flesh and his soul. (Note by Père Teilhard.)

[18] Père Teilhard noted in the margin of this passage (starting with 'We may answer that in the case of the human monads'), 'a bit off the mark' ('*Pas très au point*').

that receives them. Even before death were they not already, through grace and the Sacraments, moving in its nascent spheres?

We may well be amazed when we look at our world.

Beneath the uniform drabness of man's restless activity, *a cleavage* runs through the *whole* universe, *from the high peaks of the soul right down to the roots of matter.*

On one side, through a vast total made up of infinitely small efforts, through the accumulated effect of rightly directed intention and devotion to the Eucharist, an indestructible world is being built up by our souls and bodies, sheltered by the Flesh of Christ.

On the other side, an aggregation of disconnected, *uninformed* monads is still held together by the terrestrial forces of life and matter; but, at the first breath of death that dust will be scattered.

22 December 1918

Note on
the 'Universal Element' of
the World

The whole of this note, attached as an appendix to the manuscript of 'Forma Christi', has been crossed out in pencil.

Père Teilhard was evidently dissatisfied with it; as would appear, too, from the existence of a new essay entitled 'The Universal Element' in which, only two months later, he treated the same subject.

NOTE ON
THE 'UNIVERSAL ELEMENT' OF
THE WORLD

The special bent, or attitude, of the cosmic mind (of which the pantheist mind is *only one particular form*) consists essentially in a modification (change) undergone by the concrete being of the world (τὸ *esse rerum*), as seen by the intelligence. Whereas, as a general rule, men turn their attention to the individual, plural, forms of things, the 'cosmic' mind (which enjoys a cosmic vision) is primarily aware of *their common basis*. This basis seems to it to become continually more luminous, real, and individual—so much so that the particular determinations of concrete things tend to interest the soul less and less, as though they were dissolving into a higher entity. This transformation (or manifestation) of the universal stuff of the world, we should note, is an experienced psychological *fact*; in other words it is an intuition, pre-intellectual in order and is not the fruit of a chain of reasoning. It is basically, therefore, beyond the reach of criticism: *it exists*. However, when we try to explain this—when the man who has that intuition tries to interpret and rationalize his feelings—we find ourselves very much at a loss. However the explanation may be expressed, it is generally wrong because the terms it uses are pantheist.

In the language of pantheism, the 'universal element' we glimpse is sought for in the direction of matter, or is, at least, conceived *by analogy with matter*. There are idealist forms of pantheism that are highly spiritualized; but even to these the unique substance is no more than a refinement of the astral matter of the theosophists, or the physicists' ether. Pantheists see universal Being *as a basis* which has the capacity to manifest itself in an interplay of shifting forms, but which is at the same time strictly independent of the subsistence of those forms. The Absolute is an *Amorphous* from which everything emerges and in which everything is lost again. Individual determinations have no absolute value. The 'seer' can devote himself to the search for the *basis of things*, can wrap himself up in it and be absorbed in it, without any logical need to concern himself with the laborious progress of evolution.

Note: this paragraph is too cut and dried. In fact, in addition to *materialist pantheisms* (which look for the 'universal element' in a plastic or *informable principle of the world*) there is a whole category of *spiritual* pantheisms (which believe that this element may be found in a plasmatic or *informing* principle—vital or intellectual—of the universe).

One can, for example, conceive a theory in which universal Being could be seen in the form of a soul which is the Soul of the World, in process of being formed from the sum of all individual souls—these being particles of it. This theory differs from the theory I am adopting only in this respect: it regards the universal Centre of the world as *entirely* immanent, and the monads that concentrate around it are (or rather become) entirely divine as they join it.

If we start from rational principles such a theory must be rejected.

One might perhaps add that, for all its apparent appeal, *it does not* fundamentally *satisfy* the mind's 'cosmic' impulses. In fact, the universal element glimpsed in the 'cosmic vision' is not only something that is everywhere present: it is also, and primarily, something *Absolute*. This 'absolute' character, it would seem, is essentially lacking to a mere sum-total of contingencies, which is what a World–Soul, purely immanent *and* in a real process of becoming, must be.—? Spiritual pantheisms (as defined above) can, it is clear, admit an *absolute* Form (a 'Word') into their universe, only if they attribute to that Form a certain transcendence (by making it emerge from the stream of evolution).

23 December 1918

In this interpretation of the 'fundamental vision' it is the *lower* stuff of beings which is regarded as divine; and nothing has *true* existence except that stuff. Everything, therefore, is substantially divine . . . On the other hand, however, everything—if we go far enough back—sinks into an abyss of indetermination and of pure multiplicity (comparable to the prime matter of the scholastics). Pantheism is philosophically catastrophic; and the seer who hoped that it might teach him to make palpable contact with the Divine, finds that he is grasping a handful of dust.

The doctrine developed above (in *Forma Christi*: see also *Creative Union*) enables, I believe, the 'cosmic-minded' to justify their fundamental vision of universal Being without falling into these errors. It teaches, in fact, that the entitative formula for every created being $(E_1 . E_2 \ldots E_n)$ is as follows:

$$E_1 = (e_1)X$$
$$E_2 = (e_2)X$$
$$\overline{}$$
$$E_n = (e_n)X$$

$e_1, e_2 \ldots e_n$, being the individual nature of each being; and X representing a determination *higher in order* than the individuality of the monad—a determination *common to all monads*—which constitutes the monads as *elements of a determined universe*.

If the universe is regarded in relation to its term (the total Christ, *in casu*), it is not in fact an aggregate, but an organic whole of a higher entitative order than that of the elements considered in isolation. The universe's own particular form, therefore, must be impressed upon each monad by some determination higher in order than the degree of being found in the monads considered separately. That is the function of this universal element, X, *the principle of super-individualization* '*quo unumquodque ens perficitur, entitative, sub ratione adoptionis suae in tali universo*'—'by which each and every being is perfected, entitatively, in virtue of its reception into such a universe'.

In our universe, X is the penetrating influence of Christ-ω, of Christ-'*Forma-Mundi*'.

If we admit the existence of the *universal element X*, it is evident that the mind's 'cosmic aspirations' are satisfied, in a way that answers the requirements of dogma, of philosophy, and of practical life.

In the first place, *X* is not an epiphenomenon, a local and partial adjunct. It is an entitative influx, recasting and re-forming *all the lower degrees of being* in the monads it acts upon (in conformity with scholastic teaching about the *'Analogy of Being'*). It can, therefore, be grasped in the whole of everything, giving every individual object its final value, significance, and consistence.

In spite of this 'final' purpose, and this universal intrinsicism, *X* does not destroy the natures it envelops (cf. p. 266),[1] but completes them. Unlike the pantheist universal element, it enters into things *in proportion* to their degree of differentiation, spiritualization and sanctification. *The more dominating its position* in the monads, *the more fully are they realized 'in unitate universi'.* When the *common basis* of beings predominates over individual forms, so far from causing them to disappear, it accentuates them still more. One might say that it is born from the *confluence of their accentuation*.

Thus, instead of being, as it is in pantheism, a lower universal basis—the matter of Matters—the universal element is seen to be *the higher Centre common to all developments, the Form of Forms*.[2]

The man to whom it has been given to enjoy *the 'cosmic vision'*, no longer vague but distinct (that is to say to see Christ as *more real* than any other reality in the world, Christ present and growing greater in all things, Christ the final determination and formative principle of the universe), that man may truly be said to live in a zone into which the confusion of no multiplicity can penetrate, and in which, nevertheless, the work of universal fulfilment is the most actively pursued.

---

[1] In *Forma Christi*, above, p. 266.

[2] Is not this precisely the definition of the *Word*?

— In short, one may say this: instead of looking for the *universal element* in an *informable principle* of the world, we should recognize it in an *informing* supreme *principle*. If that principle is not operative, we immediately have multiplicity. (Note by Père Teilhard.)

Let him but be shown once more the inaccuracy or the error in the terms in which he is trying to embody his experience— and, in all patience, he will seek for another form of expression. But his vision will remain with him.

22 December 1918

The Promised Land

Shortly after finishing his 'Note pour servir à l'évangélisation des temps nouveaux', Père Teilhard went on leave, and then returned to his regiment in the village of Goldscheuer, in Baden. It was there that, in a few days, he wrote 'The Promised Land'. In this he was trying 'to determine just what remains to us from all the effort we put into the war, in the disappointments of peace', and 'to show that it's the awareness we acquired, for a moment, of the spiritual strength contained in unity'. 'Not without some hesitation,' he sent the essay to Père de Grandmaison 'not so much for publication—I've no illusions about that—as in order to get his advice and let him see what definite line of thought I'm adopting'. (Letters of 15 and 19 February, 1919, in 'Making of a Mind', pp. 283, 285.) In the event, 'The Promised Land' was to remain unpublished. On March 5th, Père Teilhard wrote to Marguerite Teillard, again from Goldscheuer:

'I've had a long letter from Père de Grandmaison. 'The Promised Land', of course, will never be published—I expected that. At any rate, Père Léonce takes my views seriously—and that's something achieved already. I realize that in this last essay I've attributed considerable importance to human views of progress—which obviously lays it open to a good many objections. I wrote back to Père de Grandmaison at equal length; and I believe that my position in this matter remains pretty clear' (p. 289).

THE PROMISED LAND

— And was peace, then, no more than this?

— The peace that all through these long years was the brilliant mirage always before our eyes.

The peace that gave us the courage to hold fast and to go into the attack because we thought we were fighting for a new world.

The peace that we hardly dared to hope might be ours, so lovely it seemed . . .

And this is all that peace had in store for us!

After five years of darkness, the sun has at last risen over the battlefield.

And when we look around us, eager to welcome the first signs of a universal spring, the face of the Earth seems to us as drab and cheerless—even more cheerless, some of us say—than when autumn had stripped it bare.

For a moment men knew real emotion, they were united, they were raised above themselves, in the defence of a common cause; but danger has no sooner relaxed its grip than they have fallen back into their jealous, self-centred, isolation. Draw up war's sorry balance-sheet and what do you find: much corruption, much shameless exploitation, much utilitarianism, and underlying it all a deep and shocked disgust at so much evil suffered or inflicted to no purpose.

What, then, was the point of so much generous effort? Why did we fight so well?

Is it because all the hard work life obliges living beings to undertake is simply a perpetual snare, one disillusionment following upon another, so that no progress is ever made?

That would be a terrible fact to have to accept.

For if progress is without doubt illusory, then nothing in fact has either the right or the power to make us hold firm to our human task. The sensible thing to do is to follow the line of least resistance and maximum enjoyment.

We thought that peace would lead us into a happy land. And so far, alas, all we have found is disappointment, and even (if we drink the dregs of our bitter draught) something much worse than disappointment: *doubt*.

Doubt, a fundamental doubt that questions the very value of human action, haunts our minds, and its shadow lies heavy on our courage.[1]

Before the fog of commonplace experiences and narrow personal interests closes down on my horizon—while I still retain the last impressions of an existence that in a few months' time will seem to be a dream—in this cold Rhenish plain where the expiring life of the battlefield lingers on in the occupation of enemy territory—I asked myself the key question:

'By condemning or justifying our confidence in the betterment of man, should the results of the war logically destroy or intensify our zest for action?'

Here, step by step, are the considerations that clarified my thought.

First, there came into my mind the multitudes of lives which the war, after purifying them in the furnace of trial, carried away to regions beyond our range of vision.

Then I remembered the long series of those whom I had seen with my own eyes gradually become masters of their souls in the sacrifice of self they made for a sacred cause—until finally duty called for their whole being.

I multiplied my own experience a thousandfold, by as many thousands as would be needed, I suppose, to equal the hecatombs sacrificed in all the battles we fought, put together.

And then I remembered our dead.

All these heroic lives seemed to me to escape from the earth, under the breath of war, like sparks blown by the wind from the blacksmith's fire. And I might have understood that the reason

[1] The doubt that questions the value of action was constantly to reappear in Père Teilhard's writings. His answer to it was the doctrine of irreversibility.

we suffered was in order that this glittering shower might burst forth, had I but been able to see the living flame with which the souls of the fallen were to be made one.

But that flame cannot be seen from the earth. It shines in another sphere of our universe.[2]

It was then that I had to recognize that the heavenly glory won by our fallen friends could not be *precisely* the compensation for which I was looking—the compensation that would give me fresh heart *as a man* to accept the losses suffered during these last years by our generation.

We must, I fear, admit that a harvest of the elect—however real and final the use it makes of our sufferings—cannot be the *immediate* reason that justifies all the effort we have made and all the blood that has been shed.

Because—*Earth comes before Heaven*—and: *Life comes before Death.*

If our earth is to produce a richer crop of souls, greater in number and holiness, one thing above all is necessary: the soil of the field in which they grow must be made more fertile, and the stem that bears us all must be strengthened.

The impulse set in motion by the war was a deep-rooted instinct to preserve the race and add to its greatness. Can we say that peace is bringing us the happiness of satisfying that instinct?

The perfecting of the lives lost to us cannot give us the only answer we await to the horror of all the evils we have suffered: only one thing can do that, an unmistakable betterment of life on earth, here below.

Either the final purpose of the universe is almost entirely beyond our grasp, or a great terrestrial effort (by which I mean not an effort made by an isolated individual but one that involves three-quarters of mankind) must be matched by a result of the same order—that is, of the terrestrial order.

Can it be true that nothing good and durable has been introduced by our patience and heroism into the hereditary stock from which all the souls that follow us will be born and develop?

[2] The same idea is found earlier in *La Grande Monade*.

If we think about it seriously, we shall see that the whole future of mankind's effort is covered precisely by that question.

Time and again during the war I told myself, to keep alive my courage and the joy of battle, that our work, in some hidden way, was a collaboration in a great visible enterprise.

It seemed to me impossible that the upheaval of nations in which we were taking part, should not serve to produce a better organization of the world. On the whole, the *dominant forces* in nature *work for good*: otherwise, how could life ever have cleared the way that led to man? And it is ultimately the *best* that profits from any freedom accorded to the elements to follow the course indicated by their desires. History teaches us that, by and large, the world emerges from the melting pot on every new occasion in better shape.

In the present case, the conflict seemed to be a clear-cut choice between might and right. We seemed, in the thick of the fighting, to be witnessing what was without any doubt an attempt by mankind to concentrate upon an ideal. Never had men fought for such immense and such selfless ends. This great tumult was indeed the smelting of a precious alloy that discards the dross.

But beneath the rejection of noxious elements we thought, did we not, that we could distinguish the first outlines of a new organization of mankind taking shape—what one could almost call the birth of a soul. The war was a crisis of growth. The youthful envelope of a new humanity could be seen beneath the cracks of the old husk.

For five years I lived in this belief in the value of the war; and even now, for all the disillusions of peace, I still have faith in life. The power that during millions upon millions of years of vicissitudes finally perfected the human brain cannot have exhausted its strength and vigour.

Our blows have gone home; our efforts have borne fruit—even here below. The world *is* better because we shed even our life's blood to resist evil. And, if the call came, I would enlist again under that banner.

But have I the right to impose my belief upon others?

That part of our history which is patient of measurement is so short that it is impossible to prove geometrically to the wilfully blind pessimist that *we are* in fact *ascending*.

What can we say to such a man that will make him accept the reasonable probability of our vision and bring him to share our faith?

The pessimist will not agree that *this time* our patience has succeeded in making the world organically superior.

Can we not show him at least that we have won the right to hope?

No one, I imagine, will deny that during the war a considerable portion of mankind went through *a unique psychological experience*.

Never since man existed, probably, has so large a number of individuals been governed by so strong a common compulsion.

We know that a proliferation of many types of vice was one of the results of that ordeal; but those were no more than waste-products or parasitic growths; for all their glaringness, they were only *secondary* effects.

What was the essential effect produced by the extraordinary stimulus of those circumstances, upon the healthy, soundly-rooted, part of our race? How did the central core or axis of human life react?

There can be no doubt that the reaction was an *extraordinary release of spiritual energy*.

In widely different orders—economic, industrial, moral—we have witnessed the production of efforts that intelligent men would have said were impossible to realize in normal times.

Under the pressure of an urgent and noble common necessity, men have displayed a capacity for hard work, for selfless enquiry, a strength of will, a devotion, that until then they hardly suspected they possessed.

Wherever the radiating influence of the sacred cause was most active, men found a power of union, an impulse of common feeling, a capacity for sacrifice, that for a moment swept away all differences and multiplied their energies tenfold.

During the war, men without any doubt attained (at least for a few moments) *a domain of higher spirituality* in which their individual faculties were magnified and ennobled in the carrying out of a collective enterprise.

They felt more free, and stronger, in the consciousness of *Some Thing that encompassed* and *transcended them* all.

That is the central fact that, amid all the uncertainties and heart-burnings of peace, we should retain as the permanent lesson of the war.[3]

Is it rather fashionable now to ridicule the notion of a hallowed unity? to laugh at the brevity of its life? to emphasize the renascence of human ill-will? to insinuate that all these fine appeals to an international ideal are no more than a cloak for the intrigues of politicians and financiers?

Deep within myself, and because I have felt its power, I *know* that a real and specifically new wind has just breathed over the soul of man. Moreover, I cannot believe that man could, even for a moment, have crossed the threshold of that zone where effort brings solace and unity, without retaining for all time the beginnings of a *habitus*, a vague nostalgia. Once again, however, I keep to myself a conviction that is not imposed by the facts.

Supposing, then, we admit that this fine emotion we experienced when we stood by at dawn in the front line has indeed vanished without trace from the earth.

Insignificant though the event may seem, to prove my point I shall confine myself to the single *undeniable* fact that *for a moment* mankind was the better for having lived for a few months under the influence of a common ideal: for this, I claim, is all we need if we are to be able to retain intact, and even give new life to, our confidence in the value of human effort.

To share in a hallowed unity, even for a split second, is enough

[3] The preceding pages recall the experience analysed by Père Teilhard in *La Nostalgie du Front*. At the same time they bring out his optimism, based on a forward-looking line of thought that already, at the very moment of the catastrophe, is alive to the progress which it will help to serve.

to enable us to glimpse the future promised to our species, and to
find the road that will lead us to it.

So long as we had not been tried and tested, we could reasonably ask whether there still remained a reservoir of vitality in
the human stock.

The history of the earth shows us certain animal forms
stabilized permanently in their type. Since the most distant ages
they have always been exactly the same, as fixed as chemical
substances, while all around them any number of new forms were
being born and dying out.

Had not we, too, the latest comers into life, become like those
animal forms, destined, like them, to stagnate at our present
stage?

Our minds and our hearts, eminently the seat of life's progress
—had they not exhausted their power of development? Were
we justified in envisaging new forms of growth for the human
race?

The war gave us the answer to this anxious questioning of
ourselves, by releasing from the depth of our nature a living
spring of moral intensity and beauty.

It would be false to despair of our future on earth, to deny the
treasures still hidden in the human soul, for, if only for a very
brief moment, we have seen and touched and known those
treasures.

No, my fellows, we are not a withered branch on the tree of
life !

When it came to the test, abundant resources were found in the
storehouse of our being. *In a practical experiment*, short but conclusive, we were able to measure the evolutionary reserves, the
potential, of our species. *We are still a long way from having
released all our energies.*

But what is needed, to call up those energies from the depths in
which they are stored, to rouse them from their slumber?

The war exerted upon us an activating force, a force of mutual
attraction and cohesion *directed against evil and for only a moment*:

now another cause must emerge to direct that same force *permanently* and *towards good.*

The defence of sacred interests aroused in us, as a temporary reaction, the consciousness of all working together in a task as great as the world itself: now the pursuit of a positive ideal must give us that same consciousness, never to be lost.[4]

Is it, in truth, impossible for love to create among us the soul of union that fear made palpitate with life?

Here we come to the heart of the lesson taught us by the war: *the condition of human progress* is that men must at last cease to live in isolation; they must learn to recognize *a common goal for their lives* (a goal set before them for ever in their heaven, transmissible by education, attainable and perfectible by disinterested research)—and the fiery energies still undoubtedly smouldering in men must be *fanned into flame and directed in common towards that end*—not in an individual, nor in a national, nor in a social, but in *a human effort.*

This common higher goal, this longed for ideal, whose magnetism is to bring us together and make us more perfect, *exists*, we need have no doubt, *in natura rerum*: for, if there is one principle that is verified by universal experience, *it is that every hungry mouth has, somewhere, its own bread waiting for it.*

All that matters for mankind is to be faithful in the effort that will win the nourishment prepared for us.

There are, of course, hazards to be faced as we pursue our task. Just as an individual can ruin his life, so (though with much greater difficulty) can a whole race.

Of one thing, at least, we may be certain: we have all the strength necessary to complete the work of Spirit upon earth. Our future is in our own hands.

And now, after reasoning as a man, I shall speak as a Christian. The ideal upon which the energies of human life must converge if they are to grow, is already with us: *we know it*—for

---

[4] On more than one occasion Père Teilhard was to draw up in similar terms the programme for a true peace, to be understood not in a negative but a positive sense: not as a mere negation of war, but as its transformation.

thousands of years its clarity has shone upon us: it is Christ, the King and Centre of Creation.

Why is it, then, that his action is not giving greater warmth to our hearts; why is it taking so long to produce a general 'convection current' towards him, in which mankind will be raised up and informed?

For some centuries there was reason to believe that the human race was on the point of grouping itself upon Christ as its Centre; and then this progress towards the organization of the world *in Christo* seemed to hesitate and slow down.

What lack, then, in the inhabitants of the earth must be made good, if Christ is to draw them to him and inform them—more completely, until we have the totality of a single world—more profoundly, until we have the unity of a single life?

What we are failing to do, perhaps, is to offer to Christ, in our nature, this greater soul—fully terrestrial and human—that was, for a while, instilled into us by the imminence of an extreme common danger.

Had Christ come down upon earth in the time of Abraham or Moses, we can well imagine that—apart from a miracle—men (precisely as St John expressed it) would have failed entirely to understand him. Their natural soul, the stage they had reached in their humanity, would not have been capable of receiving him.

Are we not witnessing a similar inability?

If Christ has not, as yet, aroused in men the great impulse towards him that his dignity is building up for him, may it not very well be because *the natural disposition* of men (taken as a whole) which should allow them to respond to what is most active (or at least most final) in the influence of the incarnate Word, is not yet sufficiently mature?

Men still lack *a sense*, without which they cannot see the full beauty of Christ and feel the full force *qua sibi omnia possit subjicere*: the sense of the unity they are summoned to constitute, and of the universe which contains them.[5]

In order finally to triumph on earth or at least (if it is true that

---

[5] Père Teilhard's apologetics relies more on the natural value of man and his development, than on some lack which Christ's action makes good.

mankind is to come to an end in a great spiritual schism)[6] to reign in his fulness over the elect portion that has chosen his side, Christ, I imagine, is waiting for the human race to raise itself, by a natural effort which he assists, to *the degree of higher moral being* that will make every man fully conscious of all things; in other words, he is waiting for them to be *fully men.*

Under whose influence will this wider consciousness of our existence and our duties ultimately be developed in us—for we as Christians must devote much of our apostolic care to fostering that influence?

Will it be produced simply by the combined action of Christ (whose love will inspire our work) and of terrestrial discoveries and upheavals (which will gradually enlarge the circle of our ambitions)?

Or will it come about quite differently? Will some *intermediate ideal* between Christ and our race be developed, in the form of *a terrestrial enterprise* to be safely achieved—an ideal by which 'spiritual' men will feel themselves magnetically drawn: that ideal being a more tenuous form of the attraction exercised by, a natural reflection of, a *dawn* heralding the coming of, Christ the only Centre of the universe?

No man can tell us, nor in fact do we need to know the answer. The road will open up as we advance. It is enough for us to know that the *way* ahead *is clear.*

Come, then—life still retains its beauty. Since the great conflict from which we are emerging has enabled us in the end to understand our vocation and to feel the vigour of our youth, we must not grieve at the cruelty of war nor the anticlimax of peace.

For all the dullness and drabness that have returned to life, for all the contradictions in a society that is again fragmented, I shall patiently take up once more my everyday tasks, guided by the

---

[6] Cf. *The Struggle against the Multitude:* 'Under exactly *the same appearances,* the two opposite principles draw to themselves their faithful, leading them either *to simplicity or to the Multitude*' (above, p. 113). *Faith in Man* (1947, in *The Future of Man*, pp. 187-9). *The Phenomenon of Man*, pp. 288-9.)

light that I saw for a few brief moments, when millions of us, in one body, felt ourselves united, through life's deepest roots, in a great cause.

I shall advance into the future with the new strength of my twofold faith as man and as Christian: for, from the mountain peak, I have seen *The Promised Land*.

Goldscheuer (Baden), February 1919

The Universal Element

Père Teilhard wrote to his cousin Marguerite Teillard-Chambon, from Goldscheuer (Alsace) on 19 February 1919, and after telling her that he had finished 'The Promised Land', continued: 'I've already begun, and got well into, 'The Universal Element', for which, as you know, my ideas were already completely in order. It won't be long, but clear and full of substance. It will, I think, be the most central exposition of my ideas I've yet produced; and so I'll be able to make good use of it to let people know and assess my position, in a private *way. I find it interesting to look back on the road I've travelled since three years ago (exactly), when I was writing 'Cosmic Life'. I find that I'm now concerned with just the same problems and see them in just the same way— but I have them much straighter in my mind and have a better grip on them'. Three days later, on the 22nd, he writes: 'I'm sending you by this post a little notebook containing 'The Universal Element'. You'll find that, basically, there's not much that you're not familiar with'. There is another reference in a letter of the 28th, again to his cousin: 'When I was writing 'The Universal Element', I remembered some things that Françoise once said to me—when she was already a Little Sister—about the unique and beatifying importance that the reality of God had assumed in her life—and I felt that I understood that we were fundamentally much more like one another than I had thought before. The only thing was that she was following a road where the realities of the world were much more obscured or left behind than happens with me'. ('Making of a Mind', pp. 285, 286, 288.)*

THE UNIVERSAL ELEMENT

Unum est necessarium

I

Existence

Many men (or all men, one should perhaps say, if they analysed themselves more carefully) feel the *need* and *capacity* of apprehending a *universal physical element* in the world, which establishes, at all times and in all things, a relationship between themselves and the Absolute—both in them and around them.

This element can be glimpsed (by minds that are sufficiently receptive or informed) as *a common fringe* on the outskirts of each of the great operative processes or main directing energies of our life.

(*a*) It sustains and carries further (in the form of a vivid feeling of omnipresence) the feeling we experience of the Real and of our own reality.

(*b*) It constitutes the essential value, the absolute kernel, which, if we are to have the courage to act, we need to feel present in everything we do.[1]

(*c*) It represents the stable and incorruptible zone in which we take refuge from the vicissitudes, the hazards, the precariousness, the losses, we meet on the immediate plane of existence.

Our perception of the Universal Element does more than *touch on* all our interior experiences, once they are taken far

[1] This need would not appear to be an illusion. For my own part, without any interior 'faking', I can say that I feel it distinctly—so much so that it seems to me that life would be a real factual contradiction, its emergence into consciousness would destroy it, if reflexion led us to the conclusion that all our actions were *completely* contingent. (Note by Père Teilhard.)

enough and analysed in sufficient depth: it also has an urge to invade them (or, which comes to the same thing, to emerge from them) in such a way as to force us to take exclusive account of a Unique Essential (*unum necessarium*) in whose activity we are included.

Beneath the absorbing influence of the universe that envelops us, beneath the personalizing activity of successful human achievement and the centrifugal effect of sorrow—*something that is unique in essence can be distinguished*, and we feel an urge to *transport ourselves into it.*

Throughout life, there thus takes place in us, *in the order of concrete action and physical reality*, a psychological phenomenon that is exactly analogous to the *logical* abstraction by which we apprehend the *Ens ut sic*, and probably as essential to the mind as that function, with which indeed it may well at times have been confused. Thus there develops in souls that have an unusual capacity for this special intuition, a specifically characteristic psychic state—'*cosmic consciousness*'.

For a mind that is in this state of cosmic consciousness the basis of things (a certain, ill-defined, basis, that is) tends to predominate over the detail and to obliterate the plurality of beings. It appears to such a mind that concrete Being itself (τό *esse rerum*) becomes individualized and takes on consistence, beneath the experiential Multiple. The shimmer of a sort of precious fabric can be distinguished beneath the accidental determinations of existence. A new unique tint spreads out at the heart of the now transparent universe.

Cosmic consciousness is often born and periodically comes to life again, in crises when the mind is gripped by an extremely vivid feeling of presence. Such a state of exaltation, however, is not essential to its life.

In its normal state, and completely dispassionately, a soul can act 'habitually' with the breadth of view (characteristic of the cosmic consciousness) which enables it to do everything *cum respectu ad omnia* and to see all things *sub ratione universi*.

If it is to make so constant an appeal to our minds, and to dominate them so powerfully, the Universal Element cannot possibly be an illusion, a *figmentum mentis*. Somewhere there must be *something* that corresponds to cosmic 'abstraction' and consciousness.

What name can we give to this mysterious Reality?

II

The Nature of the Universal Element

A: THE PANTHEIST SOLUTION

A first answer—the most obvious and the only one generally entertained—is the *pantheist answer.*

From the pantheist point of view, everything in the universe is seen to be radically One, Absolute, and Divine—either because the universe is born from an involution (deduction) of thought, or because it emerges from an evolution of matter.

Everything that exists is (or becomes), in the whole of its self, identical with God.

Understood in this sense, the Universal element embraces all (*comprehensive* and *extensive*[2]—individually and collectively); and everything becomes indistinguishably identified with it (more or less directly).

(i) On the one hand, no peak of the Absolute rises above the multiple elements of the world (= it is *absolutely immanent* in them).

(ii) On the other hand, it tends to absorb them completely (with nothing left of their individuality) in itself (= it is, strictly, the only thing *that exists*).

— either because the mutual opposition of the parts of the universe represents only a transient illumination, at the end of which the various individual determinations must revert to being dissolved in *the Homogeneous.*

[2] Père Teilhard indicates on his manuscript that he is using the Latin adverbs *comprehensive* and *extensive*, by accenting the final vowels.

— or because their differentiation and the progress they make are used for building up a consciousness, a universal soul, in which every elementary consciousness is destined to be lost.

= in the monist view, the Absolute is *integrally convertible* into its fragmentary elements, and *vice versa*.

The pantheist universal element may rationally be criticized, on the ground that, by combining in itself two contradictory properties (necessity and contingence) it is something *unthinkable*.

What is more to the immediate point, and belongs to the same order of ideas as that with which we are now concerned, is the further objection that it does not meet the demands of cosmic consciousness, even though it is nevertheless presented as alone capable of satisfying its desires.

What, in fact, is cosmic consciousness? It is, essentially, the need for, and joy in, *union* with *Another* (this Other being the universal element).

But there can be no '*Other*' (and, even more certainly, no higher Other to whom one can *give oneself*) when all the parts are equal in dignity, and associate together in virtue of a mutual attraction that is completely absorbed in their mass.

Nor can there be any 'union', when the term of conjunction is strictly single. Union presupposes, up to the very limit of its perfection, *duality beneath unification*: otherwise it completely changes in nature and loses all its attractive force.

By reason, therefore, of the two most essential characteristics of its nature (total immanence, absolute monism) the pantheist divine cannot be the universal element which experience reveals to us.

Pantheism cannot satisfy a truly cosmic mind.

This conclusion may seem a paradox. It will, however, astonish only those to whom the search for the universal element appears a specifically pantheist concern and enterprise.

In reality, cosmic consciousness is a psychological fact much more ancient and surely established than any philosophical system. To realize that this is so, one has only to think of the poets, thinkers, visionaries, whom it has for centuries been inspiring—followers of the most diverse philosophies and religions.

What I would like above all would be to show, just as I feel, that it reaches its full and *legitimate* development in Christianity.

B: THE CHRISTIAN SOLUTION

The Christian who is animated by cosmic consciousness, must hold above all else that God, the only Absolute, is essentially distinct from creation.

Nevertheless, if he is to be *able* to love and worship God 'with all his heart' he has a need that will take no denial to apprehend the divinity under the form of a universal element.

What physical relation, between the transcendent Absolute and the universe, what emanation or influence, can he find that will satisfy, without doing violence to his faith, his impassioned vision of a supreme 'cosmic' Reality, present in all things? How can he reconcile in his mind the law of his Church and the law of his heart?

Let me point out three successive stages which I *myself in real fact went through*, before I arrived at a satisfactory solution of this interior problem of making one's way to God *in all the sincerity and fulness of a soul that is irrevocably 'cosmic'*.

(i) The first 'universal Reality' that offered itself to my mind, in the domain of divino-terrestrial forces, was the *Will of God*, conceived as a special energy instilled into beings to animate them and order them towards their end.

If the Will of God is seen with sufficient intensity and realism it positively transforms the universe. It animates and softens all that we suffer; it stimulates and directs all that we initiate; it abolishes chance. It makes it possible for us to live, physically and for ever, within the divine Unity: that unity comes to us through all the influences to which we are subject—and we, in turn, through our obedience, become the instruments, we become an extension of, even members of, that unity.

For a long time this was the only vision that filled my life, as giving me God, universally immediate and tangible.

Gradually, however, I came to feel that the divine Presence of which I was thus assured did not come up to the measure of my experience or satisfy my desires. I was eager for something more —and I felt that *there must be something more*—in the universe, between God and myself, than a perpetual and universal contact in self-surrender and action.

Through the Will of God, universally seen and apprehended, I was becoming (and all things were becoming for me) *instruments* of God. What I wanted was to see that I was in some way, in virtue of my religious faith, an *element* of God—and to see all things share that quality with me.

(ii) Thus I found it necessary to give greater precision to my first approximate explanation of the dogma and of my own instinct, and so to accept *God's creative action* as the universal element.

In that new form, I could already see God as entering the sphere of external experience in which we move. Animating the great natural currents of life and matter, he penetrated into my own personal essence and into the development and growth of all things. He was the soul of everything that moves, the support of everything that exists. This stage corresponded more or less exactly to the views developed by St Ignatius in his meditation *ad amorem*.

Here again, however, I soon came to feel that something was lacking in the terms I was using to express the Reality, the intimate quality, of the Universal Presence experienced.

Even when seen as the supreme cause, God was still too separate from the world to satisfy me. Even when involved in his creative action, I was still not, in relation to God, the extremely lowly *element* that I felt myself to be—that I wished to be. And, on his side, God was still not the higher element, infused into the universe, through which the Absolute entered into my body and spirit.

For all God's intermixture with my being through his almighty action, there still remained between him and me a hiatus, a void, an icy gap, representing the distance that separates necessary from participated being. I felt that I was *not united* to him but *juxtaposed*.

With creative action, in fact, I still remained in the domain of *efficient causality*. What I was looking for was a flow of *formality* from God into myself, through the medium of the world.

(iii) It was only after writing an essay entitled *The Mystical Milieu* that I arrived at a conclusive explanation of what I felt. At last I found within myself the name that Christianity gives to the universal Reality I had worshipped so long: it was '*the cosmic influence* [life] *of Christ*'.

However, before explaining this unusual expression, I must add a comment of the philosophical order on the way in which we should conceive individuals in the universe.

As a result of the more restricted necessities of practical life, we have become accustomed to considering persons (monads) as the natural, complete, units into which the world can be broken down. When we speak of 'a soul', we believe that we are thinking of an independent reality, co-terminous with itself, separable *in its identity* from other souls and even from the universe. This pluralist concept may well be most inaccurate.

Certain though it is that Peter and Paul are two definitively separate and contrastable beings, *so long as we remain on the social plane of present-day mankind*, it is equally probable that if we consider them as situated *in the total universe*, neither of them can attain his full personality, his full significance, his full determination, except within the general design of the world. And this probability would become a certainty, if we knew that, in virtue of its nature, the universe was moving towards a *total end*. If such an end does in fact exist, then every being (in as much as it is *essentially* an element of such a universe) has its own particular essence crowned by a certain quality, a certain *form* (common to all) which makes it an integral, rightly adapted, part of the single Whole with which it shares a natural harmony, '*qua constituitur elementum talis Universi*'. We must say of every man that he contains in himself, besides a body and a soul, a certain physical entity that relates him in his entirety to the universe (the final universe) in which he reaches his fulfilment.

This is because, strictly speaking, there is in the universe only one single individuality (one single monad), that of the whole (conceived in its organized plurality).[3] The unity or measure of the world, is the world itself.

Once we have understood the nature of this *'cosmic composition' of created being*, and have appreciated the closeness and universality of the ties it forms with the Multiple, Christ's features take on an extraordinary sharpness and immediacy—and the meaning of Scripture is given incomparable clarity and depth.

We know from what St Paul and St John tell us that Christ is the Centre of Creation, the Force that can subject all things to itself, the term by which all things are informed.

What can we learn from those names given to Christ, if we look back at what we have just been saying?

The answer is unmistakable: that in every creature there exists physically (in virtue of Christ's having been chosen to be the Head of the Universe), *besides* the individual material and spiritual characteristics we recognize in it, a certain relationship that *all being* has to Christ—a particular adaptation to Christ of created essence—*something of Christ*, in short, that is born and develops, and gives the whole individual (even the 'natural' individual) its ultimate personality and final ontological value.

In virtue of even the natural properties[4] of the Universal Centre, the mystical Body of Christ is haloed by a *cosmic body*, that is to say by *all things* in as much as they are drawn by Christ to converge upon him and so reach their fulfilment in him, in the *Pleroma*.[5] We can live and act, immersed for ever in this living atmosphere co-extensive with the world. It is through and within the organic unity of the total Christ, it is under his *formal influx*, that God's will and his creative action finally come through to us and make us one with him.

In our world, when it is supernaturalized, the Universal

---

[3] This in no way obliterates lower individualities or persons, for these belong to another order. (Cf. below, §III, p. 299.) (Note by Père Teilhard.)

[4] God, as the only supernatural being, has, strictly speaking, no natural property. What Père Teilhard seems to mean by this expression is the properties of the Universal Centre in their relation to nature.

[5] Christ, according to St Paul, is both the head of the body of the Church, which includes only his members, and, extending beyond this central whole, the head of all creation. The totality of creation united to Christ as its head constitutes the 'Pleroma'.

Element is ultimately Christ, in as much as everything is integrated to it and consummated in it. It is the living *Form* of the incarnate Word, universally attainable and perfectible.[6]

With ever the same brilliance in all, Christ shines as a light at the heart, to which none can ever penetrate, of every life, at the ideal term of *every* growth. Everywhere he draws us to him and brings us closer to himself, in a universal movement of convergence towards Spirit. It is he *alone* whom we seek and in whom we move. But if we are to hold him we must take *all things* to, and even beyond, the utmost limit of their nature and their capacity for progress.

Of the cosmic Christ, we may say both that he is and that he is entering into fuller being.

He has already appeared in the world; but a long process of growth awaits him in this world, either in isolated individuals—or still more, perhaps, in a *certain human spiritual unity*, of which our present society is no more than an adumbration.[7]

The whole function, and task, and drama of the universe—the whole economy of human progress, of grace, of the sacraments (*the Eucharist*) take on their ultimate significance in this individualization of the Universal Element in which the Incarnation consists.

---

[6] Perfectible not in itself, but in the sense that it can inform a greater or smaller number of souls (or inform souls to a greater or less degree) according to whether they submit to Christ or reject him.

[7] It is possible in fact that side by side with our *supernatural unification* in Christ a *natural unification* of Spirit may be taking place in the world (= the work of natural human effort, the natural term of progress), the latter providing the *foundation* for the former. On that hypothesis, Christ would act vitally upon the universe by means of (by taking the place of) what would almost be a 'Soul of the World'. (Note by Père Teilhard.)

III

The Properties of Christ,
the Universal Element

We can see, then, that what characterizes the Universal Element as we find it realized in Christ, is not that it is a quasi-matter, a plastic or informable element, an agent of absorption, but a quasi-soul, a plasmatic[8] or informing element, a force of determination.[9]

The unique, universal, *necessarium*, so defined, possesses the twofold power

(i) of dominating us, as a power that assimilates us.

(ii) and at the same of completing us individually to the degree that it fuses us into itself.

The transcendence of God, and the persistence of human personality—necessary conditions

of Christian orthodoxy

and of the complete satisfaction of our cosmic desire (cf. p. 289)

—are thus completely safeguarded.

Through the totality of its properties, the Christian Universal Element is seen to be capable of uniting upon itself the most diametrically opposed tendencies of both human thought and act.

(i) Fundamentally, it effects within itself the union *of God and the world*. The two supreme loves, the natural and the supernatural, that, seen from one angle, appear to draw our hearts in

---

[8] The manuscript reads *plastique*, where the sense calls for *plasmatique*, which we find, moreover, in the 'Note on the Universal Element' (p. 273).

[9] We should add, a force of union and therefore of consolidation. The consistence of being lies in spirit (the principle of union) and not in matter (the principle of disintegration). 'Everything hangs together from on high,'[*] through the soul and final purpose. The Universal Element (the total Christ) is thus, in one sense, *ultima substantia rerum*. (Note by Père Teilhard.)

[*] See above, *Operative Faith*, p. 240.

contrary directions—towards the kingdom of heaven or towards mastery of the earth—are reconciled in the impassioned quest for the cosmic Christ.

The two stars, whose attractive forces seem to conflict with one another, are seen to be in reality each an extension of the other: it is *through the fulfilment of the world* that we reach Christ.

(ii) In our own particular destiny, this conjunction manifests itself in the reconciliation (already pointed out) *of the One and the Multiple*. Through the extreme perfection of its action, the Form of Christ allows the determinations of the element it integrates in itself to subsist, and even accentuates them. It unites us to itself to the degree that each one of us, according to our vocation, is more fully differentiated.

(iii) We can thus, in our effort to enter into Christ, make *equal* use (according to circumstances) of either of the two extremes to which our will may be directed: we may both *surrender ourselves and resist, accept and fight*. On the one hand, *if we have faith*, the irresistible forces of life and matter become *for us*, in very reality, the organizing activity of Christ assimilating us to himself.[10] On the other hand, since all well-ordered activity here below is directed *towards Spirit*, and Spirit *towards Christ*, our *total* human effort (*the more* it is undertaken with *good intention*) collaborates in the plenitude of the Incarnation. All Christian imperturbability in the face of earthly vicissitudes, and all human enthusiasm in the face of a world to be conquered, are reconciled in those who have built their lives in the 'mystical milieu' constituted by the Universal Element.

(iv) The more, following every human line of development, we seek to win the unique *necessarium* in the fulfilment of our own personality and of the world, the more it leads us, through its universal embrace, to reject our self-centred interests for ever more immense ends. Moreover, *as a result of its tendency to isolate itself* (in the pure state) from the particular forms in which we apprehend it (cf. p. 290), it gradually causes us to enter into a close and direct relationship with itself: when we contemplate it, when we make it the object of our prayer, we are transported to

[10] See above, *Operative Faith* and *Forma Christi*; also *Le Milieu Divin*, pp. 135–6.

the vital point to which all things flow together and become open to influence in the depth of their spiritual being. The effort we make within that element to realize ourselves according to the fulness of our powers, thus ends *in making us renounce ourselves*, and become stabilized in an inflexible tension—and that is the most effective form of action.

= The Universal Element makes *the transcendent immediate; it unifies, by differentiating, the Multiple;* it allows us *to complete what already exists and to win full possession of what we already hold; it detaches us from the world by attaching us to it.*

In that element, the apparently most incompatible attitudes of monism and pluralism—of (moral) pragmatism and self-surrender —of contempt for the world and the cult of the earth—are effortlessly combined.

Through that element, it becomes possible to use *all life's forces to produce one and the same real thing.*

If, in conclusion, I had to sum up in one word the 'spirit' and course of life of the man who has seen the smile of the universal Christ at the term of all things, I would choose the word that narrow usage has made offensive: *Integrism.*[11]

Integrism in purity—that goes without saying; and it means, *in the first place*, the authentic Christ, Christ in his truth and super-naturality. Simply in that form, without further qualification, Christ has the power to conquer the world and incorporate it in himself.

But *integrism*, too, *in universality*—not a single element of created energy, not one iota of the redeemable world, must be lacking to the plenitude of Christ.

Around every distinct truth there spreads a *penumbra*, and at the root of every disciplined energy there lies a *disorder*, which absolute-minded men fear and wish to suppress, in their anxiety to include in their inflexible systems nothing that is not *certain* and *crystal clear*. They forget that the area of uncertain illumination and ill-defined aspirations that they reject from *their* universe is not a by-product or waste product, but the *living surface* of the

[11] Offensive, because of its association with ultra-conservatism in the Church.

Spirit of man: they are trying to cut away the sap-wood and yet keep alive the heart of the oak.

Not only so that no chosen particle may be omitted from the Pleroma (nothing is so small as to be inessential to its totality) but so that the universe *may be given its* true *form under the influence* of Christ, *we must* bring about the reign of Christ even—indeed, above all—*in the continually nascent fringe of the world.*

The first privilege of the incarnate Word—and the most powerful appeal he makes to our generation—is that he is the Principle in whom the universe develops.

Above all, then, we seek Christ *in his integrity.*

21 February 1919[12]

[12] Cf. p. 289.

Index

Index